INTERNATIONAL INTERIORS 5

International Interiors

Jeremy Myerson
Co-ordinating researcher:
Jennifer Hudson

Laurence King

Published 1995 by Laurence King Publishing
Copyright © 1995 Calmann & King Ltd

A catalogue record for this book is available
from the British Library.

ISBN 1 85669 017 7

Designed by Mikhail Anikst
Printed in Hong Kong

Acknowledgements. The author and the publishers would like to thank all the designers and architects involved and the photographers whose work is reproduced. The following photographic credits are given, with page numbers in brackets: Daniel Aubry (31); Courtesy Shigeru Ban (67-69); Ch. Bastin & J. Evrard (239); Reiner Blunck (Arcaid) (87 bottom, 89); Luc Boegly (Archipress) (100-103); Tom Bonner (46-49); David Brittain (71 bottom,105-107); Richard Bryant (Arcaid) (70 left, 81-83); Santi Caleca (2 centre, 109 centre, 151-153); Martin Charles (11 bottom, 27-29, 162 bottom, 213-215); Lucy Chen (98-99); David Churchill (Arcaid) (36-39); Peter Cook (43-45); Grey Crawford (131-133); Peter Ecer (162 centre left, 170-171); Klaus Frahm (108 top, 111-115); Dennis Gilbert (185); John Gollings (3 centre, 71 top, 86, 87 top); Yoshio Hata (181); Courtesy HKO (202-205); Timothy Hursley (3 second from left,162 far right, 186-187, 189, 217, 219-221); Reto Halme (10 second from top, 22-25); Shinwa Jitsugyo Inc. (117-119 right); Christian Kandzia (194-197); M. Karamatsu (119 left); Simon Kelly (Belle/Arcaid) (11 centre, 59 bottom, 61); Yutaka Kinumaki (6 right, 182-184); Toshiyuki Kobayashi (165 top, 168); John Edward Linden (79, 135-137, 163 left, 191-193, 223, 227, 234-237); Jannes Linders (199-201, 231-233); Antonio Martinelli (2 second from right, 173); Ian McKinnell (70 second from top, 95-97); Trevor Mein (10 second from bottom, 41); Nick Merrick/Hedrich Blessing (52-54); Michael Moran (147, 149); James Morris (226); Nacasa & Partners (3 second from right, 6 second from right, 33-35, 155-157, 162 top, 164, 165 bottom, 166-167, 169); John O'Brian (57); Tomio Ohashi (206-211); Courtesy Ove Arup (180); Keith Parry (141); Paul Rafferty (Arcaid) (162 left, 174, 176-177, 225); Marvin Rand (59 top, 60); Christian Richters (240-241, 243-245); Jordi Sarra (10 left, 63-65); Yoshio Shiratori (70 bottom right, 84-85, 108 right, 109 top left, 139); Christian Smith (10 top right, 51); Timothy Soar (2 second from left, 18-21, 228-229); Katsuhiko Togashi (125-129); Rafael Vargas (10 top, 72-77, 90-93); Deidi von Schaewen (159-161); Paul Warchol (2 left, 6 left, 12-17, 179); Jens Willebrand (109 bottom, 142-143, 145); Andrea Zani (2 right, 108 left, 121-123).

C O N T E N T S

INTRODUCTION

These are the best of times and the worst of times for interior architects and designers to be working in. The good news is that profound cultural and technological changes have brought with them a raft of new approaches to space, function, light and material. The ways in which we are choosing to redefine communication within our communities, reinvent our working and living patterns, and recycle the redundant quarters of our cities, provide a catalyst to the art of the interior. Less welcome is the evidence that economic recession continues to squeeze construction budgets and lead to the cut-price procurement of buildings. This threatens the credibility of a profession which has based its appeal on the idea that the interior designer is part-structural technician and part-spatial poet, engaged in higher ideals than the lowest common denominator and appealing as much to the user's psyche as the developer's pocket.

However, it says much for the skill, stamina and flexibility of the profession that this volume, now in its fifth edition, provides considerable grounds for optimism in the richness and variety of work undertaken. *International Interiors 5* represents a selection of nearly 60 leading interior design projects from around the world completed between December 1992 and December 1994. In cultural terms, it covers a period when public and civic values other than shopping and spending began to reassert themselves, when green scepticism began to cool the ardour of environmentalism, and when a more modest and austere mood in design kicked the last traces of conspicuous late-1980s interiors glamour into touch.

In economic terms, it covers a period when Britain and the USA began to emerge from deep recession, but continental Europe, especially Italy, France and Spain, dipped into the global downturn. Even those two great engines of post-war economic growth – Japan and Germany – showed signs of self-doubt, while Australia's financial bubble well and truly burst. Despite this, or perhaps because of it, all these countries have provided an abundance of projects which combine fresh thinking with time-honoured quality in interior architecture and design. None more so than Australia which is represented by some of the most unusual and compelling work in this volume, including the most user-friendly dentist's surgery you are likely to encounter and a Melbourne hotel which cantilevers a 25-metre roof-top swimming pool out over a busy street.

In summing up a distinct era of the early 1990s – a time of technological transition and social redefinition – any selection of interior schemes will necessarily be subjective, selected perhaps to shape a thesis. My selection, however, is based on a simple overriding motivation: the search for the genuinely innovative approach, often in response to the toughest of briefs (a Dutch bank to operate without staff), the tightest of budgets (a Manhattan fashion showroom creating style on a shoestring), the greatest of spatial constraints (a Santa Monica clothing store with a diameter of just 20 feet), the mightiest of spaces (the world's largest import trade centre in Osaka), or the heaviest burden of cultural expectation (the new Holocaust museum in Washington DC).

It is a selection which rejects the merely decorative, and ignores the suspect or the ersatz, no matter how superficially appealing. It is a selection which also reaffirms the special place of interior design in relation to its mother profession of architecture – not as an introspective, independent and essentially self-referential exercise in interior finishing, but as a substantial technological and artistic discipline which relates to the fabric of the building and also beyond to the bigger picture of the built structure within the cityscape or rural setting.

The interior projects in this volume are shown wherever possible with exterior façades and site plans to set them in the broader context. They are also accompanied by quotations from the architects and designers involved, which summarize the key challenges and aspirations of each scheme. These comments direct from the horse's mouth are revealing: some are highly practical, reflecting the primacy of marketing and technical considerations; others are more philosophical and aesthetic, discussing the depths of the soul, not just the width of the site. The language of the interior designer reflects the sheer diversity of the profession.

Many projects reflect what could be described as a Modernist perspective, with truth to materials, functionality and economy to the fore. But if that is the case, then it is a restless, progressive Modernism, which explores the changing design patterns and preoccupations of the age, not the static Modernism which simply salutes the historical white-walled International Style of the 1930s. Certainly the absence of swags and drapes, of opulence and decadence, in even the "richer" leisure and public interior schemes shows the concern to match the environment to the mood of the time. What price signature interiors when so many homeless people go without basic shelter? Even the two opera houses in this book – the Lyons Opera House, by Jean Nouvel, and Glyndebourne, by Michael Hopkins – supplant the sumptuous European opera-going traditions of plush red velvet with red light (Lyons) and rustic plainness (Sussex).

Projects do not pursue a kind of frozen monolithic perfection in architecture; instead they readily engage with the constantly evolving and often contradictory times which we are all experiencing. There is more emphasis on design as a process than design as a product – an approach epitomized in a scheme for a group of Californian building engineers by Morphosis which is a deliberately complex and challenging dialogue about the materials of construction designed to get the creative juices flowing.

Innovation and ingenuity take many different forms in this selection. There is material innovation of the kind which can see the walls of a rural Italian wax factory lined with filter mesh and folded aluminium to create an intriguing exhibition display showroom, or the floor of a chic low-budget New York showroom laid using recycled tyres. There is technical innovation of the kind which uses a vast oval diaphragm blind to filter sunlight through a conical void between floors in the British Council headquarters in Madrid, or audaciously inserts a giant steel scaffolding storage unit right up the spine of the Netherlands Design Institute. There is creative innovation of the kind which can fashion a soft, synthetic and decidedly surreal seafood restaurant in the high-tech heart of Amsterdam's Schiphol Airport, or bathe the merchandise of a Hamburg shoe shop in ethereal blue light.

Then there is the project which combines material, technical and creative innovation in one unique environment: Shigeru Ban's extraordinary paper-tube gallery for Issey Miyake in Tokyo integrates sculpture with science in a way which gloriously reaffirms the power of interior design at its very best to transcend existing thinking with an original solution.

Ban's work – graphic, structural and spiritual by turn – defies conventional categorization. But then so many schemes in this selection also have a hybrid nature, reflecting the myriad of new social influences upon them: the fashion-statement Zygo showroom in London which is also an administrative office; the Aigen church in Austria which doubles as a community centre; the Cable & Wireless College in Coventry where the traditional university campus meets new technology in a new built form; the Tai Pan restaurant in Cambridge, Massachusetts which curiously combines Chinese food with Japanese karaoke; or the fragrant Kashin emporium in Tokyo which cleverly sells flowers and incense from the same outlet.

Each of the four sections of the book – Work, Leisure, Retail and Public – is prefaced by its own introduction to the selection. Suffice it to say here that there has been an acceleration of a trend notable in the previous edition of *International Interiors*: public interiors increasingly command the lion's share of premier-league commissions and budgets. Local, regional and national governments are using landmark architecture and interior schemes in a conscious campaign to define the identity of cities and regions, win investment and jobs, and create wealth and prosperity. This volume reflects on a golden age for the public interior. If the private entrepreneur financed the more conspicuous design successes of the late 1980s, now it is the public authority's turn to play patron at the leading edge. From the Tate Gallery overlooking the waterfront at St Ives to Renzo Piano's Kansai International Airport Terminal right out on an artificial island in Osaka Bay, public sector commissions have enabled interior designers and architects to ride the storm of recession.

That is not to say that other sectors have provided less interest – just less grand projects. Workplace design remains an important discipline which has witnessed the transformation of the office over the past couple of years into gallery, club and hotel – a cognitive centre for collaboration and creative ideas, not simply a machine to turn the cogs of bureaucracy. Leisure too has caught the eye for the way in which the most unpromising settings – basements, garages, even disused Victorian swimming pools – have been turned into high-grade attractions, while retail environments have traded transient graphic appeal for more solid, properly engineered solutions and look all the better for that.

Ultimately, *International Interiors 5* demontrates that quality interior design and architecture can be achieved by gifted individuals (Kristian Gavoille, Torsten Neeland, Andreas Winkler, Soichi Mitzutani) just as well as multinational design firms (Fitch, Gensler) or the master architectural practices (Foster, Hopkins, Grimshaw, Calatrava, Piano). The only bar to entry is lack of talent and courage. The projects in this volume reveal verve and nerve in equal measure.

Jeremy Myerson

3

8

11

15

W O R K

AS THE MANAGERIAL QUEST FOR GREATER PRODUCTIVITY AND QUALITY AT WORK GATHERS PACE, THE CULTURAL VALUES OF THE TOWN SQUARE ARE REPLACING THE COLD RATIONALITY OF THE MACHINE AS THE DOMINANT MOTIF IN WORKSPACES.

The powerful Modernist idea of the office or studio as a machine for working in – the dominant design theme for a century – has run its course; the workplace is instead becoming a creative and social centre, a thinktank, a place for team collaboration, decision-making and even meditation, as advances in portable technology and management thinking redefine the nature of work itself.

This selection of projects demonstrates how the new

14

work environment is beginning to reflect corporate and individual priorities in far more expressive ways. The boundaries are blurring between work, study, social interaction and time out as the workplace becomes progressively the library, club, gallery or hotel. And to respond to more fluid and varied patterns of work, new configurations of space and furnishings reflect not the cold, linear rationality of the machine but the time-honoured community values of the village or town square. The San Francisco waterfront office of the Babcock & Brown investment bank, for example, has the topology of a medieval town, complete with gatehouse guarding executive offices and open space akin to the *parvis* in front of a cathedral. "Work villages" are evident in the new Manchester headquarters of the British Council, while the Salas Studio scheme for a firm in Barcelona making batteries and electric components also adopts a village-square metaphor.

A vibrant project for MTV Latino in Miami Beach by Arquitectonica introduces the idea of neighbourhoods, each defined by the different treatment of micro-architectural elements such as fences and rooflines. If it all sounds a lot more friendly than bland corporate International Style, then that is because managers have realized that real productivity gains are not achieved by sterile workhouse conditions.

Creating a sense of local place and culture is part of the equation. Geyer Design's reception area scheme for a Melbourne banker, for example, has a display of contemporary Australian art. There is also renewed emphasis on looser, less finished environments, which enhance the work process, rather than simply presenting a flashy corporate front. The Santa Monica offices of building engineers Ove Arup & Partners – a dynamic spatial dialogue on the materials of construction – captures this idea perfectly.

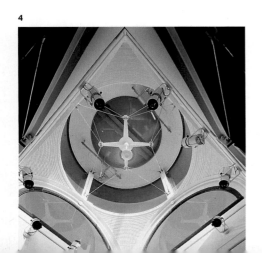

4

The growing belief that work is about creativity, not simply hard labour, is being matched by the appearance of more cultural and artistic schemes. Shigeru Ban's extraordinary paper-tube gallery for Issey Miyake's design studio in Tokyo is a shadow-crossed place of calm; Lorenzo Apicella's London design studio reception for Wickens Tutt Southgate has the composition of a Mondrian painting. Even Alfredo Arribas' sculptural, new-build office block for a broadcasting company in Japan has floors devoted to a Spanish art gallery, reflecting the fact that work architecture no longer means school rows and partitioned pens in the sky. Nicholas Grimshaw's Western Morning News building, which sits on a British hillside like a beached ocean liner, makes a similar point in the way the sum of its organic high-tech parts creates a community, not a machine.

STUDIOS
ARCHITECTURE

**BABCOCK &
BROWN**

SAN FRANCISCO,
USA

The Hills Brothers Building was built in 1926 on the San Francisco waterfront south of Market Street for a coffee trader who stored and roasted bulk coffee on the lower five floors and divided the top floor between a corporate office and a space for a team of special roasters who tested and blended new coffee. Today, this top floor with its 5.5-metre-high ceilings, large bay spacing and magnificent views of San Francisco Bay and Oakland Hills has an altogether different flavour. It provides the headquarters for Babcock & Brown Inc., an international investment bank, following a complete refurbishment of the entire concrete and masonry warehouse to create a first-class office building complete with new services and a central atrium.

Babcock & Brown's interior has been designed by STUDIOS Architecture to exploit the natural characteristics of the 3,085-square metre top-floor space in a way that reflects what the designers describe as "the typology of a medieval town". The light and the views, not an artificial grid, dictate the siting of key elements, with circulation between a hierarchy of public and private spaces a matter of natural evolution. "The medieval town typology was overlaid on the traditional concept of exterior perimeter offices and interior support space," explains STUDIOS principal Darryl Roberson. "As a result, six different neighbourhoods, each with its own public space, were created. Four were formed by corner cluster, two by raised platform."

The best views are given over to the East Conference Room and a number of executive offices in a private cul-de-sac, guarded by a symbolic "gatehouse" occupied by the office manager. Open space in front of conference rooms allows people to gather in a way "similar to a *parvis* in front of a cathedral," according to the STUDIOS design team. To complete the medieval town analogy, two raised "neighbourhoods" are described as "hilltop" work areas: one is accessed by a meandering ramp, the other by a more formal stair.

But there is a further twist to this convincing interior scheme, which was achieved in the face of scheduling constraints caused by the previous tenant being unable to move until the last moment. Babcock & Brown's expertise in transport leasing finance led the designers to allude to the evolution of modes of transport, with airplane wings, ship's handrails and other elements detailed within the environment. The original concrete structure, stripped back by the previous tenant, was left unfinished. This is counterpointed by the insertion of new materials – stone, concrete, plaster, glass, steel, and bent and curved aluminium – to give a young and aggressive bank the type of lofty, commanding headquarters it required. Not unlike, one might conclude, a medieval ruler surveying all before him.

THE TOP FLOOR OF A FORMER COFFEE WAREHOUSE ON THE SAN FRANCISCO WATERFRONT HAS BEEN ORGANIZED LIKE A MEDIEVAL TOWN TO BECOME THE COMMANDING HEADQUARTERS OF A MODERN BANK.

The Babcock & Brown banking headquarters occupy the top floor of the Hills Brothers Building in San Francisco (opposite). Inside, the traditional office planning concept of interior support space surrounded by perimeter offices is overlaid by the typology of a medieval town.
This page: A raised platform area within the space signifies a particular "neighbourhood".

Left: A high ceiling and a commanding view of the San Francisco waterfront give this perimeter conference room powerful appeal. The exposed concrete and brick structure retains the flavour of the industrial setting, but coloured plaster, glass and steel reflect the intervention of new design and materials. The custom conference table was designed by STUDIOS, as was the reception desk (below) and the low-voltage lighting system, developed in conjunction with Neidhardt Lighting.

"THROUGHOUT THE
PROJECT, NEW AND OLD
MATERIALS AND
VOCABULARIES ARE
JUXTAPOSED, ALLUDING TO
AN EVOLUTION OF MAN'S
HABITAT AND MODES
OF TRANSPORTATION.
AIRPLANE WINGS, SHIP'S
HANDRAILS, BIRDS, CLOUDS
AND OTHER ELEMENTS
OF MOTION, FLIGHT AND
TRANSPORT RESONATE
THROUGHOUT THE SPACE....
HUTS, VILLAS AND
TRIUMPHAL ARCHES EVOKE
MAN'S HABITAT."
STUDIOS ARCHITECTURE

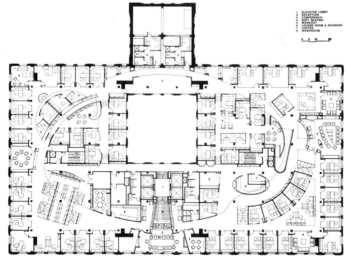

Opposite: A ramped walkway leads to a distinct office "neighbourhood" on a raised platform. Ship's handrails and curved interior detailing (above) allude to the evolution of transport – a Babcock & Brown business speciality.
Right: Office floor plan showing the medieval hilltown transposed to late twentieth-century space planning.
Above right: A workstation area using Steelcase's Context range, beneath early-industrial-chic light fittings.

APICELLA ASSOCIATES

WICKENS TUTT SOUTHGATE

LONDON, UK

Wickens Tutt Southgate is a London-based graphic design consultancy specializing in brand packaging and identity. Clients range from Tango soft drinks to Anglepoise Lighting. The group has developed a reputation for being dynamic and professional, and for introducing many advertising agency techniques to design practice. It has grown rapidly in recent years to 36 staff, in the process outgrowing the premises in which it started business.

THE RECEPTION AREA FOR THE STUDIO OF A LEADING LONDON DESIGN CONSULTANCY HAS THE COMPOSITION OF A MODERNIST PAINTING IN ITS SOPHISTICATED USE OF COLOUR AND SPACE.

Architect Apicella Associates was commissioned to design a new headquarters to unify Wickens Tutt Southgate in one space and present a coherent image of brand design expertise. The chosen site for the consultancy's new base was a 725 square-metre unit comprising two light industrial workshops with an abundance of north-facing rooflights at their centre, but with restricted access off a small London mews. The brief called for a single open studio plus meeting rooms, private offices, storage and ancillary accommodation. Central to designer Lorenzo Apicella's approach was the creation of a new reception area using splayed and curved walls to create alcoves and niches for displays of creative work and to frame restricted glimpses into the main light and airy studio behind, through coloured and etched glass.

The achievement of this scheme has been the sensitive creation of a sophisticated design language for visitors to the studio – a style which is not, in Lorenzo Apicella's words, "antithetical to the raw and robust aesthetic of the original workshops". Some of the views through reception have the clarity of a Mondrian painting, yet the project itself was low-budget given the extensive floor area. Another key consideration was to allow for a seamless transition from the excellent natural light streaming in through the rooflights during the day to artificial lighting in the studio at night. The solution here has been the predominant use of metal halide uplighting, although tungsten is a flexible supplement in presentation and meeting rooms.

Overall, the scheme is a conscious statement of contemporary design values which shapes the space and uses colour with great purpose and restraint. It subtly delineates the boundaries between areas for different uses without shutting off too many rooms and losing the generous proportions and volumes of the original industrial space.

Opposite: The reception area subtly communicates contemporary design values.

Above: A column detail juxtaposed with the curved white plaster wall reflects

the purposeful and colourful shaping of the space.

"A KEY CHALLENGE WAS TO CONSCIOUSLY CREATE A MORE SOPHISTICATED DESIGN LANGUAGE FOR VISITORS TO THE STUDIO THAT WOULD NOT BE INTERPRETED BY THEM AS ANTITHETICAL TO THE RAW AND ROBUST AESTHETIC OF THE ORIGINAL WORKSHOPS."

LORENZO APICELLA

Opposite, top: View from the
studio to the reception,
a demonstration of designer
Lorenzo Apicella's ability to
artfully frame tantilizing
glimpses from one space to
another.

Opposite, below: Architectural
and desk details form
elements in a composition
akin to a Modernist painting.

Right: The reception desk
in spray-painted medium-
density fibreboard bisects
a beechwood floor.

The raw aesthetic of the
industrial workshop is given
a sophisticated treatment in
this scheme.

LAIRD LIBRARY
Glasgow College of Building & Printing

AN ELEGANT MODERNIST VOCABULARY IS BROUGHT TO THE RESTORATION OF A CLASSICAL FERRERA BUILDING IN MADRID TO CREATE NEW OFFICES FOR THE BRITISH COUNCIL.

JESTICO & WHILES

THE BRITISH COUNCIL

MADRID, SPAIN

The British Council is the UK's cultural ambassador over-seas. In recent years this government institution has placed growing emphasis on creating a high-quality architectural presence wherever in the world it is based. The British Council's activities in Spain have been consolidated in a classical three-storey building in Madrid, originally designed and built by Ferrera in 1907, and now imaginatively restored by London-based architects Jestico & Whiles. Over the years Ferrera's handsome building, listed by design historians as having special merit, suffered from wear and tear as a school – and from unsympathetic alterations and extensions. Lean-tos and additions profilerated around the original structure. But today all those unsightly add-ons have been swept away. The Calle General Martinez Campos 31, a building comprising basement and three upper floors with rendered and stucco external walls and slate roof, has been totally refurbished. Its 1,800 square metres of space now houses administrative offices for the Director, Deputy Director and staff of the British Council, plus library, information, education, science and arts facilities. This follows a series of bold structural and spatial interventions by the architects to reorganize all interior spaces to suit new uses, as well as to restore the exterior and landscape the site.

Public facilities have been organized on the ground floor, with key administrative staff on the first level and support staff on the second floor. To brighten a rather dark and oppressive attic storey, and link it to the rest of the building, Jestico & Whiles has punched an elliptical, conical void through the roof and down through the first- and second-floor slabs. Its axis tilts slightly to north and east to ensure that early morning sun penetrates deep into the building, even to the ground-floor reception through an oval etched-glass panel at first-floor level.

A new lightweight perforated metal stair fills the void, linking the first and second floors. The main granite staircase linking ground and first floor remains as one of the surviving period features, together with ground-floor cornices and ceilings. Elsewhere, new partitions, fittings and furniture in lightweight steel, glass and fabric reflect the aim of the architects to create good quality, well-serviced office accommodation using a calm, elegant Modernist vocabulary which enhances rather than detracts from the historical setting of a period building.

Externally the only clue to this dramatic interior transformation is a curved segment of an oval diaphragm blind made of stretched fabric on a metal frame which peeps over the ridge of the roof in its role as sunlight filter. This blind filters out excessive solar glare in summer when rotated to a position so that it deflects a heat build-up of warm air at the top of the building to the outside. But during Madrid's cold, bright winters it can be adjusted to utilize solar gain, directing warm air down through the building to the public areas at ground-floor level.

Bold structural interventions in a 1907 building by Ferrera express the spirit of the modern while maintaining the dignity of a classical structure.
Left: The glazed linkway between the main building and the arts block.
Opposite: The oval diaphragm blind is an imaginative environmental filter that dominates the roofline.

"ONLY THE SEGMENT OF A CURVED ROOFLIGHT, ANGLED TO
INCREASE THE PENETRATION OF EARLY MORNING SUN INTO
THE BUILDING, GIVES AN EXTERIOR CLUE TO THE INTERIOR
TRANSFORMATION. OVAL IN SHAPE AND CONSTRUCTED OF FABRIC
STRETCHED ON A METAL FRAME, THIS BLIND FILTERS OUT
EXCESSIVE SOLAR GLARE IN SUMMER WHILE UTILIZING SOLAR
GAIN TO WARM THE AIR IN PUBLIC ROOMS AT GROUND-FLOOR
LEVEL DURING THE WINTER."

JESTICO & WHILES

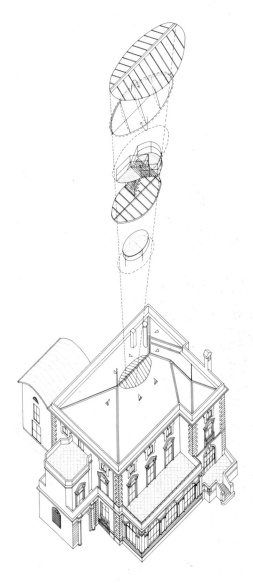

Left: A new lightweight staircase takes over
from the original main granite staircase at first-
floor level, spiralling upwards in an elliptical,
conical void punched through the building
towards the roof. This intervention ensures that
natural light penetrates deep into the building.
Above: Axiometric diagram showing the textile
blind in position to influence the building's
climate control.

EDWARD CULLINAN ARCHITECTS

ST JOHN'S COLLEGE LIBRARY

CAMBRIDGE, UK

Commercial organizations around the world have been turning redundant industrial warehouse space into quality office accommodation in response to changing economic times. But the need to recycle historical buildings to create new places of work and study has also become a feature of higher education in Britain in response to growing student numbers. Nowhere does this type of remodelling work demand more sensitivity than in the hallowed halls and courts of Cambridge University, where any new design intervention disturbs centuries of tradition. Edward Cullinan's masterful creation of a new library for St John's College, Cambridge – by cleverly extending rather than demolishing a Victorian building by Francis Cranmer Penrose – is a textbook study of how major transformations can be gently and effectively managed.

Over the past 100 years Scott and Maufe as well as Penrose were commissioned to design for St John's College's fine sequence of early courts. But by the late 1980s, its library facilities were hopelessly outdated and urgently needed attention. The College's Upper Library, completed in 1628, had expanded over the centuries into adjoining residential accommodation. Even 30 years ago the library occupied buildings in no less than three of the College's courts. New pressures in the shape of additional students, lack of storage and study places, and the requirement to improve services through automation in the 1980s finally brought things to a head.

The 1885 Penrose building in Chapel Court, much altered internally over the years, was chosen as the site for a new high-tech, purpose-built library. But Cullinan believed it should be saved and converted, not demolished. In the original structure's arrangement of ground-floor lecture rooms with upper floors the architects saw "the bones of a new library". Cullinan's scheme penetrates the Penrose building with a new axis to add more accommodation and provide a formal entrance from Chapel Court through one wing extension. The other wing extension emerges in the Master's garden as the axis crosses through the other side of the original structure.

The historical character of the setting is respected by the use of specially matched loadbearing brickwork with thin cylindrical stone columns for the extensions, and by the form of the library entrance, which addresses the Gilbert Scott Chapel across Chapel Court. Internally, however, the new configuration achieves study areas of unprecedented space and light. The formal porch entrance from Chapel Court takes you into the old double-height volume of the Penrose building lecture rooms where you are greeted with a curved librarian's desk adjacent to the red drum of a stairwell. Above, a mezzanine with reading desks projects over the void. Behind, the portion of the building extending into the Master's garden links a glazed area to a book-lined apse. Exposed materials, either wood, white plaster, polished or black steel, give the interior a calm, informal aesthetic. Maple panelling within oak frames is intended to contrast with white-painted walls and green carpeted floors, say the architects.

These themes recur on the upper floors as standard bookstacks – custom-made within an oak enclosure, with integral lighting – are organized in regular patterns. On the top floor beneath the Victorian building's lantern, the roof space bathed in natural light has been organized to accommodate a computer room. Add an ingenious system of environmental control, using a central duct to enable natural ventilation and avoid sealed air-conditioning, and the skilful conversion of a Penrose pile into a library for the new millennium is complete. Cullinan's reputation for reconciling old and new without compromising either is enhanced by this scheme.

Penrose's Victorian library in Chapel Court has been sensitively
restored and extended by Edward Cullinan's scheme,
which penetrates the original building with a new axis.

Above left: The new formal entrance in Chapel Court.
Above: The new wing emerges at the rear to form a vaulted
semi-circle in the Master's garden.
Opposite, right: The entrance hall features exposed materials,
mainly maple panelling. The snake-like librarian's desk and a red
drum enclosing the lift shaft pick up the curvilinear lines of a
calmly expressive interior.
Opposite, left: Top-floor view up into the Victorian building's
lantern, the original structure adorned by new lighting technology.
The top-floor landing is bathed in natural light. The roof space was
reorganized to accommodate a computer room.
Opposite, below: First-floor plan.
Previous page: Tradition and modernity reconciled in a
Cambridge University courtyard: view from a reader's desk in an
extension to St John's College Library frames the Master's Lodge
opposite between thin, cylindrical stone columns.

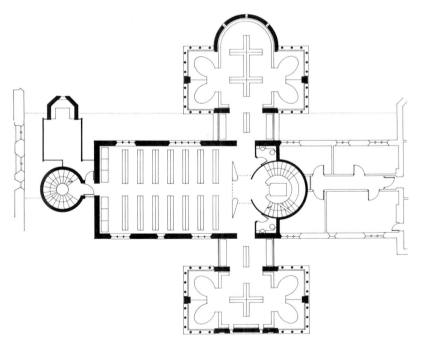

"THE THEME OF THE
NEW LIBRARY IS IN THE
ENJOYMENT OF THE
CONTRAST BETWEEN
THE DENSE STORAGE
OF BOOKS AND AIRY
PLACES FOR STUDY."
EDWARD CULLINAN
ARCHITECTS

ARQUITECTONICA

MTV LATINO

MIAMI BEACH, USA

Regular readers of *International Interiors* will be well-acquainted with the Florida-based design practice Arquitectonica through its powerfully sculptural work on the Lima headquarters of the Banco de Credito, Peru's largest private bank, in the late 1980s. The scheme recommended Arquitectonica for its ability to find an architectural vocabulary for international business that embraces local cultural forms.

Now Arquitectonica has returned to the theme of finding an appropriate cultural response to a global phenomenon at a local level, albeit in a very different context, with new offices for MTV Latino in Miami Beach. MTV stands for Music Television. It is a powerful media influence in many parts of the world. Cynics may argue that MTV has developed some of the characteristics of the large corporations and establishment institutions that its punchy, offbeat and anarchic "youth culture" style lampoons. Nevertheless, despite such criticism, MTV retains a distinctly individualistic and "counter-cultural" identity. This is reflected in its working practices. The staff at MTV Latino, for example required a workspace that would be down-to-earth and accessible, not luxurious and expensive, and one that would enable employees to personalize their own spaces.

Arquitectonica was briefed to create an "intimate" working environment for 86 individuals in 20,000 square feet of space in a building on Lincoln Road in Miami's South Beach area, the location for many advertising and film companies. The provision of four conference rooms, a dining room and a reception area where music videos could be viewed by visitors was also part of the brief. The result is a vibrant office with a tropical theme that relates to both Miami and Latin America. It is planned on a small urban scale as a micro-city, complete with such architectural elements as fences, rooflines, streets and walls. The marriage of a modern, functioning, high-tech office with the natural spirit of tropicana was clearly difficult to achieve. At times the scheme borders on the banal, but raw imaginative zest carries it through, with much colourful and unpredictable detailing to enjoy. The main workspace is divided into three different areas or neighbourhoods, each defined by differently coloured vinyl tiles on the floor and by different space barrier treatments: one area has stretched canvas shower curtains that can be personalized, another has black wrought-iron grids into which personal items can be inset, and a third comprises low-tech angled bamboo lashed together. The four corners of the space are given over to egg-shaped conference rooms and the president's office with its own specially designed conference table. The interior features much custom design work by Arquitectonica, from tropical fabric wall panels in the main conference room and an abstract Italian mosaic tile mural in reception to the desking, built by Desk Concepts. Even a mundane area such as the elevator lobby is uplifted with a patchwork vinyl floor and vertically striped walls to match.

MTV Latino is design with the volume turned up loud. It will not be to everyone's taste but it captures the irreverent flavour of its occupants with the instant hook of a three-minute pop song.

THE RHYTHM OF THE TROPICAL JUNGLE MEETS THE HIGH-TECH DEMANDS OF THE MODERN MUSIC BUSINESS IN MTV LATINO'S VIBRANT AND DECORATIVE MIAMI BEACH HEADQUARTERS.

Opposite, top left: Zestful architectural elements, suggesting fences and rooflines, convey the idea of a neighbourhood within the micro-city of the office.
Opposite, top right: An Italian mosaic wall forms the backdrop to the reception area as MTV Latino mixes and matches its styles.
Opposite, below: Floor plan showing how the scheme is divided into three main workspace neighbourhoods.

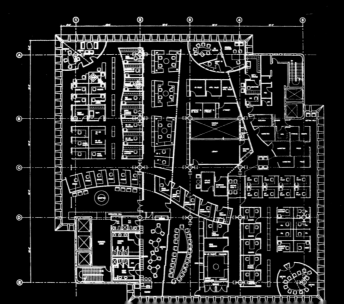

**A BUILDING WITH A SCULPTURE GARDEN,
OR A GARDEN WITH A SCULPTURAL
BUILDING? ALFREDO ARRIBAS' NEW OFFICE
BLOCK FOR A JAPANESE BROADCASTING
COMPANY TAKES THE ART INDOORS.**

ALFREDO ARRIBAS/
FRANCISCO
DE PATERARROYO

**MARUGAME
OFFICE BUILDING**

MARUGAME, JAPAN

The Japanese city of Marugame has been twinned with the Spanish city of San Sebastian for some years. As a reflection of the Japanese love of Spanish expressionism, one of Spain's best known building designers, Alfredo Arribas, was commissioned by the Nishinipon broadcasting company to design a new office building in Marugame to sit in a sculpture garden. Widely renowned for his carefully crafted and idiosyncratic interiors, Arribas approached the project with the practised eye of stage director and set designer.

The rectangular site is studded around its perimeter with head-on parking bays hidden by a row of trees. Within this, an oval-shaped metal screen marks out the location of the garden, a semi-circular paved patio, and the building itself, which is also oval in plan. Front and rear façades are sliced in at the base, and then rise gradually to a slightly wider seventh floor. Cut-outs on the ground floor are mirrored on the roofline, which dips on both sides to a dramatic V. The roof itself fills in the dip of the V.

Almost inevitably Arribas' obsession with tactile elements, materials and surfaces, serves him well. The roof is clad in green oxidized copper, while the blocks used for the exterior walls are pre-cast concrete coloured a rich dull bronze. The main façade has a six-storey steel mesh screen structure standing in front of a same-size glass curtain wall, the idea being to provide an element of privacy for those within while giving tantalizing glimpses of activity to those outside. The rear façade has a free-standing prism holding the services and two lift and staircase shafts. Covered in dot-punched metal, it also lights up at night to reveal movement inside. This structure frees the interior, allowing its unusual geometry to be enjoyed. At the far side of the patio, a row of one-storey pavilions house a showroom and cafeteria with interiors by Arribas, and a newspaper production office.

The main building was originally planned to be used for offices only by the broadcasting company. But as the project developed, it was decided to turn the lower floors into an exhibition area for the work of young Spanish artists; this space has been designed with engaging clarity by Francisco de Paterarroyo. The unexpected development of the scheme into a cultural centre means that the office building now contains art rather than sitting amid art in a sculpture garden. Meanwhile, as Arribas points out, the sculptural building itself performs the landmark role in the absence of any artworks on the site – although a large sculpture by a San Sebastian artist will be placed in the garden at some stage.

This is a large-scale project, designed in collaboration with architects and engineers Shimizu and involving more than 3.5 million square metres of space. The main building has seven storeys and a basement level; even the single-storey pavilions have two basement levels. As a design scheme, it is essentially a quixotic exercise in architectural form-giving by Arribas which produces as a by-product some good interior spaces which have provided offices and, under de Paterarroyo's skilful tutelage, a Spanish art gallery. It is in the very ambiguity of the project – the building has a schizophrenic brief to be both a backdrop to the sculpture park and a landmark in its own right – that Arribas has found the freedom to organize the plan and detail the Marugame office environment in a way which is dynamic and expressive.

Opposite, top: Ground-floor office space skilfully converted into a gallery for young Spanish artists by interior designer Francisco Paterarroyo.
Opposite, left: The front façade of Arribas' landmark building is the main artwork in an empty sculpture park.
Opposite, right: Interior configurations, including a ground-floor Spanish art gallery, viewed at night through the six-storey steel mesh screen structure that fronts Alfredo Arribas' Marugame building for the Nishinipon broadcasting company.

"THE BUILDING HAS A DOUBLE AND CONTRADICTORY
ROLE, BOTH AS AN OBJECT WITH A SILHOUETTE
RECOGNIZABLE FROM A DISTANCE AND AS
A BACKGROUND OR NEUTRAL SUPPORT FOR THE ONE
OR MORE THREE-DIMENSIONAL ARTWORKS TO BE
INSTALLED IN THE FUTURE."
ALFREDO ARRIBAS

Above: Art gallery interior, designed by Francisco de Paterarroyo.

Right: Arribas dissolves the divide between internal and external space, through the use of gliding glass partitions beneath the steel mesh screen.

Above left: The elegant cafeteria designed by Arribas sits in single-storey alongside the main building.

AN INNOVATIVE SHIP-LIKE BUILDING BY NICHOLAS GRIMSHAW CREATES A SPACIOUS AND UNIFIED WORKING ENVIRONMENT FOR ONE OF THE MORE PROGRESSIVE MEMBERS OF THE UK PRESS.

NICHOLAS
GRIMSHAW &
PARTNERS

**WESTERN
MORNING NEWS**

PLYMOUTH, UK

While most of Fleet Street's famous national newspapers have been scattered to London Docklands and points beyond, borne on a wind of technological change, the British regional press has also been on the move. The Western Morning News has relocated from city-centre premises in Plymouth to a green field site on the Plymouth to Tavistock Road from where Nicholas Grimshaw's innovative building can be seen glowing at night like a luminous ocean liner beached on the steeply sloping hillside.

This expressive nautical structure houses editorial, administrative, production and printing facilities in some 15,000 square metres of space. At the eastern "bow" end, private and open-plan office accommodation runs over three floors and wraps around a full-height central triangular atrium, occupying one-third of the total space. At the "stern", the presses, set on a rock foundation, occupy all three storeys. There is even a "captain's bridge", 22 metres high, complete with concrete mast from which is cantilevered an aluminium and glass-clad boardroom – the inevitable setting for editorial conferences. For those whose minds wander from the day's news agenda, there are good views of the sea.

Grimshaw's familiar high-tech vocabulary is evident in the interior, yet with a difference. Corrugated ceiling panels, exposed ducts, metal ribs or "tusks" bearing the weight of the glass curtain walling, and tens on wires linked into the foundations convey the idea of the office as a machine for working in The concave glass façade is designed to minimize reflections and enhance the building's transparency, and is independent of the internal concrete structure. However, the organic curvature of the glass façade softens the building as Grimshaw's work moves in a new direction, one less absorbed in linear logic and more concerned to find accommodation with natural forms. Indeed, the building's relationship with its surroundings is one of the most successful aspects of the project, especially for those editorial and production staff sitting at radiating workstations close to the glass façade.

In its delicate and innovative configuration, the Western Morning News building is in many ways an unBritish building. While the Mirror and Telegraph newspaper groups have relocated to Cesar Pelli's corporate US-Modern skyscraper at Canary Wharf, while Express Newspapers has chosen developer Deco at Blackfriars, and the Observer briefly picked the post-Modern pastiche of the Marco Polo building at Battersea, this regional publisher has opted for the kind of progressive work architecture more commonly seen on mainland Europe.

The concave glass façade of the Western Morning News building minimizes reflections and affords countryside views from window-side work stations on the upper deck (above). It also enhances the building's transparency when lit at night (opposite).

Above: A full-height central triangular atrium provides an anchor for office accommodation on three floors, giving circulatory access to both private and open-plan spaces.

Opposite: Classic Arne Jacobsen chairs in the staff restaurant. The organic curvature of the glass curtain walling, linked by tension wires into the foundations, is sympathetic to the natural landscape in which the building is set.

"THE CLIENT WAS VERY GOOD AT GETTING HIS SENSE OF
EXCITEMENT ACROSS TO US.... TWO HUNDRED AND FIFTY PEOPLE
ALL WORKING TOGETHER: PRINTERS, ACCOUNTANTS, JOURNALISTS,
EDITORS, COOKS, CLEANERS, SECRETARIES, ADVERTISING PEOPLE,
GRAPHIC DESIGNERS AND SO ON, ALL WORKING IN AN INTENSE
ATMOSPHERE WITH A GREAT BELIEF IN THEIR OWN NEWSPAPER.
WE TRIED TO EXPRESS ALL THIS IN THE BUILDING."
NICHOLAS GRIMSHAW

GEYER DESIGN

BANKERS TRUST

MELBOURNE,
AUSTRALIA

Many manufacturers this century have had an instinctively powerful capacity for making monuments of their work architecture, from the General Motors Building in Detroit to the Hoover Building in London. Their products, after all, are tangible things. But financial service companies, the new Goliaths of world markets, have a tougher task to make their mark simply because what they are selling is impossible to see and often impossible to understand.

A HIGH-QUALITY SHOWCASE FOR AUSTRALIAN ART OCCUPYING A MODERN, LIGHT-FILLED RECEPTION SETS A MELBOURNE FINANCIAL SERVICE COMPANY APART FROM ITS PEERS.

The problem is compounded when financial organizations take space within speculative, nondescript office buildings. How can they project their corporate culture when their product is so hard to define and their surroundings so potentially bland? There are, however, solutions for the brave and the imaginative, as this resourceful reception area for a Melbourne financial service company demonstrates.

When Bankers Trust Australia took 1,760 square metres of space on the 23rd and 24th floors of a Melbourne high-rise, the company wanted to suggest to visitors from the money markets that it was individualistic and innovative, with a strong technological bias. Geyer Design's solution combines classic virtues of the Modernist interior in terms of space, light and materials with some individual touches of creativity. Level 23 comprises general office areas and meeting rooms. This is linked by an internal staircase of stainless steel and brushbox timber with glass balustrade to level 24 which incorporates a reception area with client meeting and dining facilities providing excellent panoramic views of the city. There are also dealing and computer rooms, and kitchen facilities on this floor.

The internal reception space forms the heart of the scheme, the place where favourable first impressions of Bankers Trust Australia are encouraged. A flame mahogany "wave wall" extends through to the meeting and dining rooms, creating a sense of continuous movement for visitors as they pass through the space. A dynamic display of artworks by John Davis, John Firth-Smith and Guiseppe Romero reflects the aim of the designers to showcase high-quality Australian art throughout the scheme. These contemporary artworks counterpoint the timeless values of Mies van der Rohe's Barcelona chairs in a setting described by the designers as "a modern, light-filled oasis" in a standard office building.

Overall, the scheme creates a strong visual identity and a pleasingly local sense of place at a time when the electronic financial information of the global village is usually manipulated in environments betraying the most impoverished applications of less-is-less international corporate style.

Above: A flame mahogany wave wall (made by Parkview Joinery of Victoria) extends from the Bankers Trust reception area – a showcase for contemporary Australian art – to meeting rooms with a panoramic view of Melbourne.
Left: Artworks enliven a Modernist, light-filled space within a speculative office building.

MACCORMAC
JAMIESON PRICHARD

THE CABLE &
WIRELESS COLLEGE

COVENTRY, UK

In the battle royal between the Classicists and the Modernists in British architecture, MacCormac Jamieson Prichard has been cast in the role of peace-maker. Its work shares with that of Edward Cullinan the ability to combine a Palladian organization with a progressive Modernism in the use of materials and forms. In a series of commissions for Worcester, Wadham and St John's Colleges at Oxford, and Fitzwilliam and Trinity Colleges at Cambridge, the practice has created a body of work that successfully blends old and new.

This track record in academic buildings probably influenced Cable & Wireless when the telecommunications giant commissioned MacCormac Jamieson Prichard to design a new £14 million training headquarters on a green field site close to Coventry. But the resulting building, which sits on a self-contained 10-acre campus, is no university clone: it combines academic and social functions in a 12,000 square-metre flagship facility in a way that says as much about the future of telecommunications as it does about the spires of academe. True, a traditional central courtyard lies at the heart of the scheme. However, the thoughtful integration of different building types within a pleasing overall composition reflects a more unorthodox approach to the business of learning.

Around the elliptical courtyard are located a refectory, common rooms, library and museum. A south-facing cloister links these facilities with the residential wings, providing accommodation for more than 160 people. Opposite are the teaching and administration wings. There is also a free-standing three-floor leisure pavilion with bar, sports facilities and swimming pool. The plan was conceived as a series of layers traversed by the diagonal axis of the entrance.

The rippling, wave-like roof-forms of the new complex recall the model of a Palladian villa with curved, colonnaded wings stretching out to embrace the landscape. Yet the covering materials – turquoise ceramic tiles set in stainless steel framing – are used in an inescapably contemporary way. The effect is Oriental, unconsciously drawing attention to the Cable & Wireless heritage in Hong Kong. Beneath this dramatic roofline, the interiors are carefully composed to extend the main architectural themes of landscape, layering and light. The double-height refectory looks on to open countryside. The single-storey teaching wings are naturally ventilated due to the innovative wave-like roof structure – an important factor given the heat generated by the use of telecommunications equipment by students. The teaching wings also have rooflights that permit deep penetration of natural light into teaching corridors. Metal stud partitions permit modular rearrangement of classrooms within the flexible teaching space. The accommodation wings arrange hotel-standard rooms, all with *en suite* facilities, in college style around nine staircases.

Within a structure of concrete columns, banded blockwork walls, glass, steel and copper, the interior spaces of the complex are developed with close attention to detail and the diagonal axis of the plan. There is much custom design work to admire, from artist-engraved glass screens in the leisure pavilion to maple furniture in the residential accommodation. Maple was chosen because it is sustainable and the grain matches the striations of the college buildings. Throughout the scheme, the determination shown by MacCormac Jamieson Prichard to successfully resolve complexity in plan, materials and detail reflects Cable & Wireless's own determination to invest properly in training its employees.

A NEW TELECOMMUNICATIONS CAMPUS ON A GREEN FIELD SITE BRINGS PALLADIAN ORGANIZATION AND LOW-TECH VENTILATION TO THE BUSINESS OF TECHNOLOGY TRAINING.

Above: A common room overlooking the elliptical courtyard. This calm double-height space reflects the key themes of landscape, layering and light.

Left: View at dusk of the elliptical courtyard, the social hub of the college around which refectory, common rooms and other facilities are located.

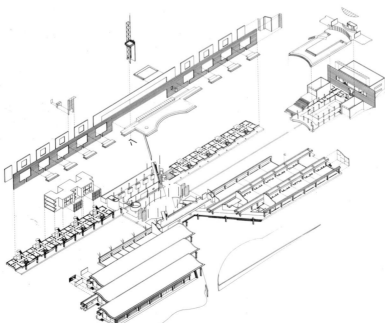

Above: The double-height
refectory, penetrated by the
drum of a conference room,
looks on to open countryside.
Left: Exploded isonometric
showing the successful
resolution of a complex
scheme.
Opposite: A brim-full
swimming pool on the main
axis of the college.

"ITS FORMAL IDEAS ARE THOSE OF AN ENGLISH COUNTRY HOUSE.
THEY ORIGINATE FROM A LANDSCAPE APPROACH TO THE SITE.
THE BUILDING'S WINGS ASPIRE TO POSSESS THE LAND ON THE OTHER
SIDE OF THE ROAD. THE DESIGN CHALLENGE WAS TO GENERATE
AN ARCHITECTURAL COMPOSITION THAT WOULD UNITE FOUR
DIFFERENT BUILDING TYPES – RESIDENTIAL, TEACHING,
ADMINISTRATION AND LEISURE – INTO A VISUALLY COHERENT CAMPUS."
DAVID PRICHARD, MAcCORMAC JAMIESON PRICHARD

MORPHOSIS

OVE ARUP & PARTNERS

SANTA MONICA, USA

This low-budget but highly resourceful remodelling of a large old warehouse in Santa Monica, California, to provide a studio for multi-disciplinary engineering practice Ove Arup & Partners creates a dynamic environment uniquely tailored to its function in terms of spatial and material organization.

A NEW STUDIO FOR A GROUP OF SANTA MONICA BUILDING ENGINEERS PROVIDES AN EXPANSIVE BUT INEXPENSIVE SOLUTION TO THE PROBLEMS OF MULTI-DISCIPLINARY WORK.

At a cost of just $41 per square foot, Thom Mayne led a Morphosis design team in creating an expansive 14,250 square-foot single-floor office that only a building engineer could fully appreciate. Ove Arup provides services in structural, mechanical, electrical, plumbing and acoustical engineering. But in keeping with its multi-disciplinary ethos, it wanted no separate departments within the space. Accordingly, desks and reference tables are laid out within L-shaped configurations so that seven people representing the different disciplines can gather together to discuss a project and lay out engineering drawings. This desking arrangement with adjoining low walls to enable eye and ear contact takes up half the studio space, where the engineers noisily confer. A quieter entrance and reception area, library and space for support staff is divided from the engineers by a grouping of conference rooms, offices and a kitchen, which comprise a largely transparent bar running through the interior.

Throughout, materials project on dynamic planes, reflecting the idea of a total environment dedicated to the way buildings are constructed. Glass walls, perforated aluminium panels and stained natural plywood elements add to the visual complexity of the space without adding to the cost.

Above: The informal studio
environment with desk
configurations designed
to encourage inter-disciplinary
team working.
Opposite: Perforated aluminium
detail. The low-budget
remodelling of a warehouse
space creates an office that
is itself a dialogue about the
materials of construction.

Above: Conference rooms and offices
are grouped together to form a bar which
separates the quieter entrance and reception
(see opposite, left) space from the noisier areas
where the engineers confer.

Opposite: Illustration of how materials
project on dynamic planes, bringing spatial
complexity to an open warehouse environment.

"IT IS A SPACE THAT TALKS ABOUT MATERIALS
OF CONSTRUCTION – THE BUILDING OF BUILDINGS.
EXPOSED STEEL COLUMNS, NATURAL PLYWOOD,
PERFORATED ALUMINIUM, FRAMELESS GLASS AND
A POLISHED, LIGHTWEIGHT, CONCRETE-PANEL RAISED
FLOOR ARE THE FINISHES MAKING REDUNDANT THE
NEED FOR DRYWALL, PAINT AND CARPET."
MORPHOSIS

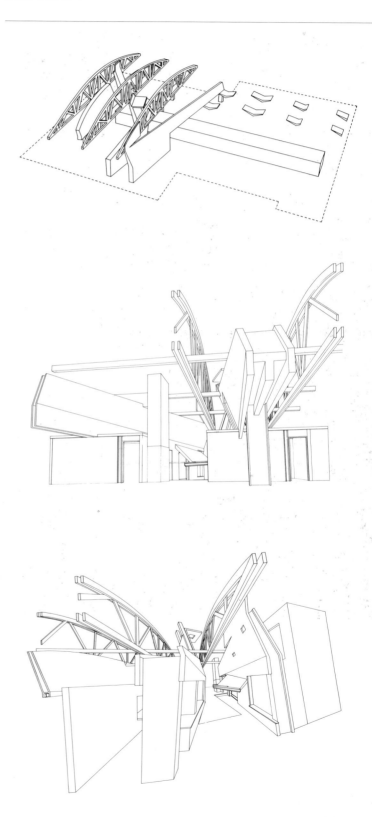

BDG/McCOLL

THE BRITISH COUNCIL

MANCHESTER, UK

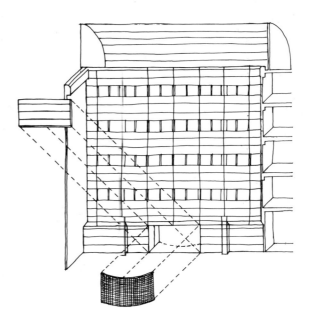

Left: Perspective drawing shows relationship of atrium to the building. Opposite: View of the main atrium space, a creative centrepiece to the building with two specially commissioned artworks: a carpet by Patrick Caulfield, and a clock by Bill Woodrow.

Stand in the centre of the atrium of the British Council offices in Manchester and you get a totally erroneous impression of the way UK government agencies view design. This spectacular artistic centrepiece says far more about growing management interest in creating humane work environments that raise productivity than it does about how official state-run bureaucracies normally go about their business. Part of the reason why the British Council

FROM UPLIFTING ARTWORKS IN A SOARING ATRIUM TO WORK VILLAGES CLUSTERED IN OPEN PLAN, THE UK HEADQUARTERS OF THE BRITISH COUNCIL MOVES BEYOND BUREAUCRATIC CONVENTION.

stands outside the norm is due to its remit: to promote British culture and language, and to encourage cultural, scientific, technological and educational co-operation between the UK and other countries. In this context, the British Council sees itself as a patron of British art and design as well as an employer committed to best work practice.

These themes combine to startling effect amid the artworks in the atrium – the main space that unifies the 116,000 square-foot building and around which all its facilities are grouped. The atrium features a specially commissioned Patrick Caulfield carpet, designed to be "uplifting, warm and generous" according to BDG/McColl, the firm responsible for planning, designing and constructing the building's interior. On the south wall of the atrium is a clock designed by Bill Woodrow, which is composed of two semi-circles: the upper one moves through 360 degrees to create a golden sun at midday and a black half-circle at midnight.

The building itself was originally designed by the multi-disciplinary architectural practice Building Design Partnership as a speculative office block for developer British Gas. In fitting out the interior, BDG/McColl created new entrances to the atrium at ground-floor level to encourage people to use the space as they move through the building, and inserted a new staircase to link the first three floors and improve circulation. This was in direct response to a design brief that emphasized that the environment should be innovative and stimulating, promoting informal interaction between people of different departments as much as possible. Therefore the interior was conceived in terms of every employee's day being a "journey" through the building.

The atrium showcase for two major pieces of art naturally holds the eye, but it would be a mistake to think all the interest in this unusual office scheme starts and ends there. When the British Council relocated 650 jobs to Manchester in 1992, it decided to rethink its approach to organizing the work environment. The result is a series of "work villages". These cluster desks within the largely open-plan space, giving a sense of identity to working groups but at the same time achieving a desired sense of openness. Cellular offices, storage, library and kitchenette facilities are located to suit the operation of each "village". In addition, such progressive areas as a well-designed creche for 30 children, a gym, club room, coffee shop and restaurant reflect the transfer of more and more of the office footprint from traditional workspace to public space. This shift brings a new and refreshing dimension to the working day.

GENSLER &
ASSOCIATES

SOCIETY NATIONAL BANK

CLEVELAND, OHIO,
USA

What happens when you outgrow the landmark building with which you have been traditionally associated, but do not want to vacate the space because of its valuable historical associa-
tions? The Society National Bank of Cleveland found itself in precisely that dilemma. Since
1890 it had proudly occupied a handsome ten-storey building designed by Burnham & Root in
the city's downtown. But by the mid-1980s its operations were fragmented over a number of
scattered outposts as the main accommodation proved inadequate for its needs. The bank
badly wanted to consolidate its corporate offices and seriously considered leaving the classic
Burnham & Root building for a new purpose-built headquarters. But that would have meant
the loss of an historic presence in Cleveland.

Lateral thinking eventually solved this knotty problem: a developer made an alternative proposal to erect a giant new 56-floor, 1.2 million square-foot tower designed by Cesar Pelli directly adjoining the old Burnham & Root bank building. Original floor slabs above the splendid
double-height banking hall were gutted and replaced with new ones which matched floors
three to ten of the Pelli tower. The Society National Bank was therefore able to maintain its
presence in its old banking headquarters while extending its space into the new development.
It also took new executive penthouse offices right at the top of the new tower on the 55th and
56th floors: these are reached by high-speed elevators rising at 1,200 feet per second.

A total of 450,000 square feet was involved in a multi-faceted interior architecture and
design scheme handled by the Houston office of Gensler & Associates. The project embraces a
series of spectacular contrasting interiors. The grand main banking hall has been expertly
restored, with damaged surface patterns, faded colours and handpainted wall fabrics all
repaired using old photographs and newspaper accounts for documentary guidance.
Meanwhile, upper floors of the original Burnham & Root building have been given a different
traditional treatment: offices, conference rooms and lobby spaces are marked by cool, conser-
vative good taste with fine fabrics and discreet woodwork an integral part of the environment.

**A BANKING HALL OF CLASSIC GRANDEUR
IS ADJOINED TO A NEW OFFICE TOWER TO
GIVE A CLEVELAND BANK A MUCH LARGER
HEADQUARTERS WITHOUT IT HAVING
TO ABANDON ITS HISTORIC ROOTS.**

There is a further change of accent in the lavish executive
penthouse suites of the new Pelli tower where sweeping
staircases and stone floors convey a sense of corporate
power. But the real capping act by Gensler is a new 350-seat
employee cafeteria on the top floor of the Burnham & Root
building: beneath a giant skylight, a swaggered canopy and
palm trees lend a lighter touch to a very serious business.

Contrasting interiors in a multi-faceted scheme. Opposite: A break area outside a ninth-floor conference room in the refurbished Burnham & Root building. The seating is from the Bright Chair Co. with a Knoll fabric; the arch frames the wooden partition of a presentation theatre. This page: The ground-floor banking hall, with patterns and fabrics expertly restored using old photographs and newspaper accounts for documentary guidance. The lighting consultant was Steven Bliss of Theo Kondos Associates.

"THIS SITE OFFERS PRESTIGE AND HIGH VISIBILITY
IN DOWNTOWN CLEVELAND AND CAPITALIZES ON THE
BANK'S IDENTIFICATION WITH AN HISTORIC BUILDING....
SOCIETY NATIONAL BANK'S MISSION WAS TO MAKE THIS
PROJECT ONE OF THE 10 BEST URBAN DEVELOPMENTS
IN THE COUNTRY."
GENSLER & ASSOCIATES

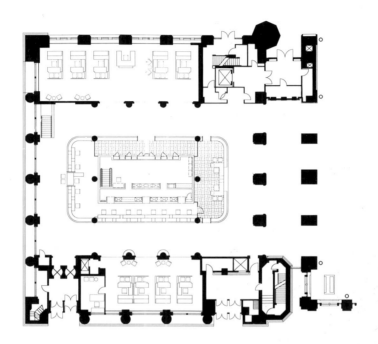

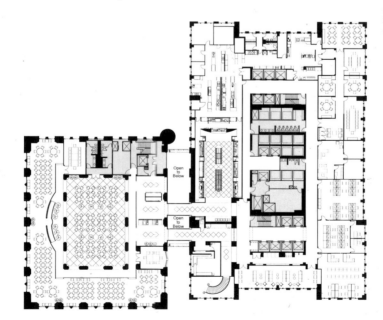

Opposite: The top-floor
cafeteria in the Burnham &
Root building rises to 50 feet
at the skylight's apex.
Custom tables were made
by Steelworks, and a custom
carpet by Harbinger.
Above right: Floor plan of the
banking hall.
Right: Floor plan of the tenth
floor, including cafeteria.

"THE BUILDING AND THE CLIENT WERE BOTH COMPLEX AND CONFUSING, AND OUR AIM WAS TO CHANGE THE IMAGE INTO ONE OF CLARITY AND CONFIDENCE."
RASSHIED DIN

DIN ASSOCIATES

ZYGO

LONDON, UK

Zygo is a young and fast-developing London fashion company. When it moved into a speculative office building on five floors in an industrial area close to Battersea railway station, it wanted to create a distinctive environment that combined office and showroom space – and presented a contemporary image to fashion retail buyers.

The problem was the building. In the words of interior designer Rasshied Din, "it had little or no distinguishing features or character". The most interesting spaces were the ground floor, which had a generous ceiling height, and the top floor, a completely glass-walled rooftop addition that provided panoramic 360-degree views of the local cityscape but was virtually useless as office space because of blinding sunlight. Din decided to create a series of "deliberately inward-looking" interiors because of the industrial locality, and space-planned the building to reflect Zygo's new thinking on combining promotional and administrative functions within one headquarters.

At ground-floor level, the reception area, café area and main meeting room have been designed to open up into a single space to host presentations and parties, with the use of a large pivoting panel door. The first floor contains cellular management offices, open-plan sales offices and the first of three showrooms. The open-plan second floor is occupied by design, PR and marketing teams; the third floor by administration, accounts and computing staff. The problematic glazed top floor has been turned into two Zygo brand showrooms, using full-height fabric screens to diffuse the light and also act as a backdrop to the merchandise and displays.

Throughout the interiors, decorative plaster walls, stripped floorboards, low-voltage and concealed fluorescent lighting, and tables and fixtures custom-designed by Din Associates complement the fashion merchandise in a very natural and relaxing way. The new Zygo headquarters makes a very simple and compelling statement about this fashion company, but does so in a way that is undogmatic and welcoming.

PROMOTIONAL AND ADMINISTRATIVE FUNCTIONS ARE COMBINED IN A STYLISH, RELAXED OFFICE-CUM-SHOWROOM FOR FASHION COMPANY ZYGO, WHICH SCREENS OUT INDUSTRIAL LONDON.

Promotion, display and administration combined in one informal fashion head-quarters.
Right: A large pivoting panel door divides the multi-functional ground-floor space, with stripped floor-boards, concealed lighting and simple plaster walls.
Below: Zygo showrooms. Full-height fabric screens diffuse the light in the glazed top-floor showroom on the left.

MICHELE SAEE

DENTAL SURGERY

BEVERLY HILLS, USA

PERUMAL BOGATAI KENDA & FREEMAN

DENTAL SURGERY

SYDNEY, AUSTRALIA

FROM DYNAMIC USE OF CONTEMPORARY MATERIALS IN CALIFORNIA TO ARTFUL PLAY ON COLOUR AND FORM IN SYDNEY, A VISIT TO THE DENTIST WILL NEVER BE THE SAME AGAIN.

They are on opposite sides of the world but both of these projects have the same objective: to make a visit to the dental surgery less of a stressful, sterile and unsympathetic experience. What is interesting is the totally different design strategies deployed to achieve equally successful results.

The American scheme by designer Michele Saee converts 372 square metres of office space into a cosmetic dental clinic for two Beverly Hills dentists. Within a primary concrete and steel structure, its use of glass, plywood and Gypsum board partitioning, granite tiles and surfacing, and stained oakwood flooring presents a strong-minded work environment that is contemporary, uncompromised but ultimately very human.

The Australian scheme by Sydney interior design firm Perumal Bogatai Kenda & Freeman creates a 2,000 square-metre dental and optical centre at Parramatta, Sydney, for the Government Employees Health Fund, a large private health insurance fund, by refurbishing two lower floors of an early 1980s speculative general-use building. Its exuberant use of colour and form is designed to provide psychological comfort to patients. Modern art, pleasing textural details and patterns of natural light are there to take your mind off the drilling.

Both projects are the result of detailed research into how dental surgeries work. Saee's Beverly Hills concept focused on the need for "dentist and patient to be at peace in their own time and space, but not be completely isolated". Professor Desmond Freeman, who led the Sydney refurbishment scheme, developed the surgery areas as "self-contained 'pods' each containing all necessary technical functions but given individual character by the use of colour. The patient is the driving force behind the quality of the space – its proportions, its form, its ergonomic relationships". Freeman was concerned not only to de-institutionalize the dentist-patient relationship, but also to give the Government Employees Health Fund a more professional and confident image. Visiting the dentist will never exactly be a pleasant experience, but these two projects help to dispel the old image of white tiles, harsh lights, cold linoleum – and cold comfort.

A dynamic and uncompromising use of
contemporary materials – granite tiles,
plywood, Gypsum board – in Michele
Saee's Beverly Hills dental surgery (above)
contrasts with the softer approach (right)
of Perumal Bogatai Kenda & Freeman,
which accentuates vibrant colour and
pleasing form.

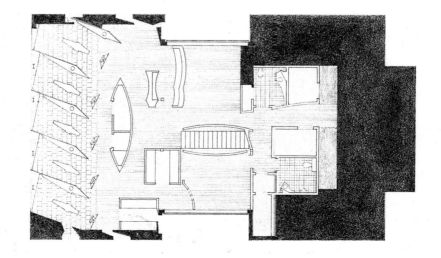

Both surgeries are based
on detailed study of the
dentist-patient relationship.
Michele Saee's spare,
clinical approach with its
formal row of work stations
(opposite, above and floor
plan below) contrasts with
the use of light, shape, detail
and modern art in the Sydney
surgery (below), which
distracts the eye and soothes
the mind while the dentist
goes to work.

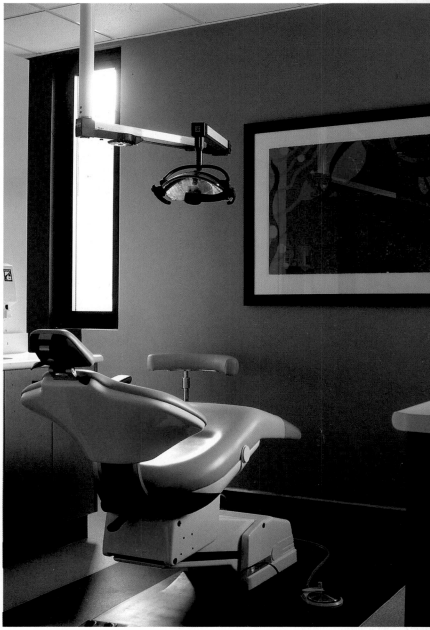

1|15

FERNANDO SALAS STUDIO

SILVER SANZ

BARCELONA, SPAIN

Communication is the electric current of the functioning office. When it is cut off, the organization cannot spark. Spanish designer Fernando Salas was swift to see the spatial problems when appointed to design the offices of Silver Sanz, a distributor of batteries and electronic components. The existing plan had unnecessarily long corridors leading to a series of small rooms, which caused communication problems and resulted in alienation.

The Salas Studio concept was to create space and improve communications by abolishing partitions wherever possible and using plate glass to allow vistas throughout the building. The main entrance hall passes through a patio within the building line. A block of stainless steel, seemingly suspended in space, forms the reception desk situated on the ground floor. White silestone flooring exaggerates the feeling of spaciousness, and is continued up a totally open stairway without rails – a major and dramatic architectural feature. The upper floor was planned according to relationships between the various departments of the company with administration, as the common denominator, taking the central position beneath exposed roof girders in open space. Space planning on this level also reflected the idea of the town square, through which everyone would pass; a key element was the total elimination of passageways, and the incorporation of all spaces into a unified scheme.

Offices along two of the outer walls make use of natural light; the other sides are taken up by the archive, a store room, and a meeting room. All use either plate glass or partial partitions with large geometric glazed apertures, or no partitions at all, to underline the flow of space. Services are located within a false ceiling, which gives way to full ceiling height in the central area. This is clad in wood, to accentuate the pitched roof shape above.

The building is subtly lit with directional halogen lighting, which increases the sense of space. All tables, storage and shelving, much of which is in cedarwood with steel frame or black silestone, were designed by Fernando Salas Studio. Chairs are by Antonio Citterio and Philippe Starck. Salas remarks: "When faced with a project I subordinate myself to the problem; I never attempt to project my own personality. From this approach, an aesthetic emerges, though it is important not to accentuate this unnecessarily." This well-resolved interior results from Salas' belief that "the rationality of the planning process" should drive the scheme. Yet the fact that the Silver Sanz offices are not a sterile glass machine for working in, demonstrates that there is room for aestheticism as well as functionality in Salas' work.

THE CONCEPT OF THE TOWN SQUARE WAS APPLIED TO SPACE PLANNING IN THIS BEAUTIFULLY UNDERSTATED CATALAN OFFICE INTERIOR WHERE OPEN VISTAS HAVE REPLACED CLOSED CORRIDORS.

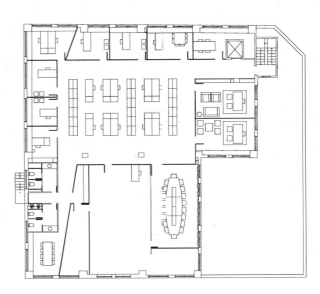

Above: Upper-floor offices are housed around
a glazed central administrative space, which functions
like a village square. The main purpose of the scheme
was to improve internal communication.
Opposite, left: Upper-floor plan.
Opposite right: Reception floor plan.

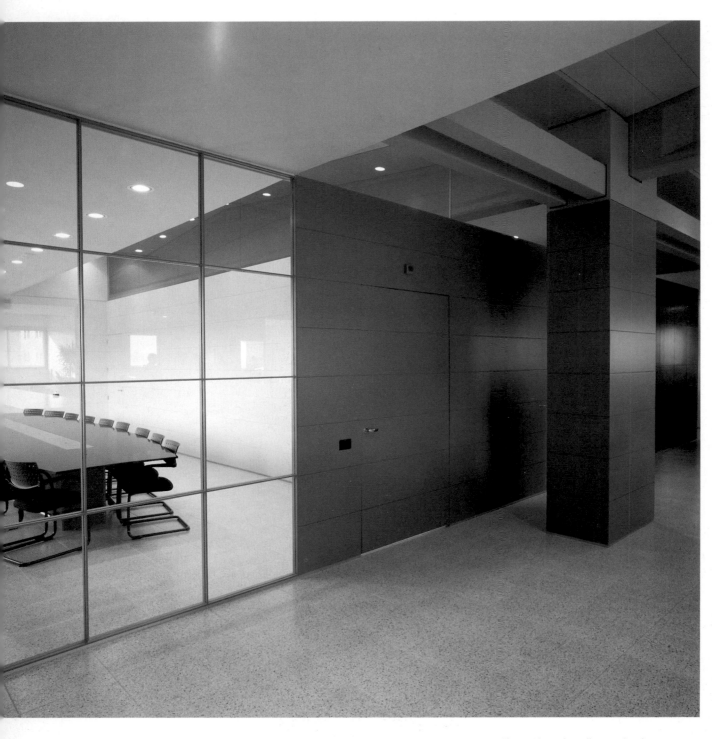

Above: Plate glass allows a view into an
upper-floor conference room.
Opposite, top: The open staircase to the
upper floor is a focal architectural feature,
which accentuates the sense of spaciousness.
Opposite, below: Silestone flooring and
cedarwood panels bring warmth
to a rational approach to space planning.

"CONCERN ABOUT
COMMUNICATION WAS
DECISIVE WHEN WE SET OUT
ON THE PROJECT PLAN.
AN URBANIST RATHER THAN
DECORATIVE SOLUTION
WAS DECIDED ON.
WE QUICKLY CAME UPON
THE TRADITIONAL LAYOUT
OF THE VILLAGE SQUARE,
THE BASIC CORE WHERE
EVERYTHING CONVERGES."
FERNANDO SALAS

**A NEW OFFICE GALLERY FOR LEGENDARY
FASHION DESIGNER ISSEY MIYAKE
TRANSFORMS THE HUMBLE RECYCLED
PAPER TUBE INTO A STRUCTURAL MATERIAL
OF GREAT SCULPTURAL POTENTIAL.**

SHIGERU BAN

MDS
GALLERY

TOKYO, JAPAN

Material invention and ecological awareness have been two key features of the career of fashion designer Issey Miyake, a living legend in Japan. So there is a certain aptness in the use of recycled paper tubes to create a stunning new gallery within Miyake's design studio complex. The MDS Gallery, known as Paper Tube Structure 06, is the work of Shigeru Ban, a Tokyo architect who has been experimenting with this structural form since 1986. Ban collaborated with structural engineers Gengo Matsui and Shuichi Hoshino to give the Miyake fashion business a work environment that is a watchword for minimalist purity and environmental consciousness.

In a floor area of 86.9 square metres, giant compressed paper tubes comprise a curved back wall facing a floor-to-ceiling glass façade lined with a row of paper tubes. Shafts of sunlight break through the space, casting angular lines of shadow in rhythmical patterns. At night an artificial indirect lighting scheme is similarly dramatic as the tubes create their own shadow patterns. Stylish chairs and glass-topped tables are also made from compressed, specially treated paper tubing.

Ban discovered the beauty and structural potential of paper tubes in the mid-1980s when, during a project to design an installation for an Alvar Aalto exhibition, a limited budget forced him to replace wooden walls and ceilings with the paper material. He then plunged energetically into a period of development, experimenting with elasticity, and with various diameters, thicknesses and lengths. He discovered how to make the tubes waterproof and fire retardant.

At the 1989 Nagoya Design Expo, Ban built a small temporary outdoor Paper Arbor from recycled tubing. It successfully survived six months of rain and wind. He then used the material to create the temporary Odawara Pavilion, using paper tubes as non-structural walls and introducing a post-tensioned paper tube truss. Neither project needed a building permit. However, Ban was finally given a building permit for a paper-tube Weekend House at Lake Yamanaka. It was because of the Weekend House that the MDS Gallery project was able to proceed. Its successful execution creates a place of spatial and material integrity and spiritual calm. These are precisely the qualities that Miyake's clothing design is said to uphold.

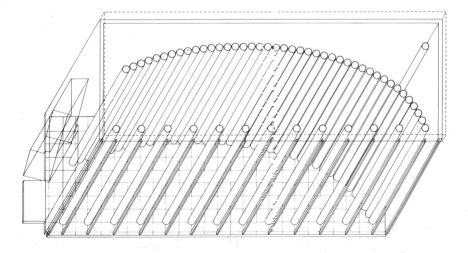

Left: Axonometric view of the MDS Gallery's construction. Opposite: Giant compressed paper tubes form a curved back wall in the glass-fronted MDS Gallery of legendary Japanese fashion designer Issey Miyake: the innovative use of an ecological material creates a place of simplicity and calm.

Stylish chairs and glass-topped tables, also made from specially treated paper tubing, enhance a uniquely sculptural space.

Natural light penetrates a row of paper tubes fronting the gallery, creating rhythmical lines of shadow.

2

1

3

7

4

L E I S U R E

FROM RECYCLED WAREHOUSES, BATHHOUSES AND GARAGES TO NEW PURPOSE-BUILT CENTRES, THE EMERGING GENERATION OF LEISURE ENVIRONMENTS IS PLAYING TRICKS WITH PHYSICAL SPACE AND HUMAN PERCEPTION.

In a burgeoning age of leisure, the skills of interior designers and architects are being deployed in a growing number of contexts. Old spaces and structures are being imaginatively recycled to accommodate new uses just as new leisure facilities are being purpose-built.

The type of lateral thinking required to turn a Victorian stone swimming baths in the West End of London into a stylish student café – as architects Sheppard Robson have done for the University of Westminster – is, on the surface at least, different from the dynamic vision needed to create the Pacha "macro-discothèque" with seven themed bars totally from scratch at a Spanish coastal resort. But, despite the different contexts, in their use of space, light, detail and material relationships both schemes share a determination to engage the human senses. It is a determination demonstrated, in fact, by all the schemes in this selection. The boundaries of leisure interior design are beginning to form a proscenium arch within which many tricks with physical space and human perception are being played on paying audiences.

5

At Terence Conran's popular Quaglino's Restaurant in London, the basement setting is countered by a giant, seasonally adjusted, artificially illuminated skylight, which spans the ceiling. Nigel Coates' exotic new eaterie in Schiphol Airport's second terminal surreally inserts soft-edged playground fantasies of forest and coral reef within the high-tech skin of the building. Lawrence Man's Tai Pan Restaurant in Cambridge, Massachussetts, seeks to reconcile Chinese food with Japanese karaoke via a spatial exploration of the ancient philosophy of Yin and Yang.

It is in the total transformation of seemingly incongruous and inappropriate sites that many leisure schemes draw their creative *frisson*. Thus a grotty Barcelona garage becomes a premier disco-club in Alfredo Arribas' scheme for the Estandard Bar, and a 1930s concrete warehouse in the centre of Melbourne is miraculously metamorphosed into an arty "boutique" hotel by Denton Corker Marshall, complete with swimming pool audaciously cantilevered out over the roof above the street. Sometimes the transition between old and new requires sensitive management. Nowhere is this better demonstrated than in the Royal National Theatre complex on London's South Bank where Virgile & Stone's new Mezzanine restaurant is a deft intervention in the architectural fabric of Sir Denys Lasdun's controversial Modernist masterwork.

Of course, the process will continue. Redundant warehouses, garages and office buildings will increasingly be turned over to house the leisure facilities for the new millennium. Ageing cultural facilities built in the first wave of post-war leisure development will need to be restored. It is to interior designers and architects – with their acute reading of space and structure, and understanding of people – that leisure operators will increasingly look for solutions.

10

CAPELLA LARREA CASTELLVI

PACHA LEISURE CENTRE

VILA-SECA, SPAIN

A taste of post-Francoist freedom can no longer be an excuse for the extravagant way in which the Spanish enjoy their nightlife. Local architects and designers have been spectacularly upping the ante in club, bar and restaurant interiors for more than a decade now. The Pacha Leisure Centre, designed by Juli Capella, Quim Larrea and Jaume Castellvi at the Pineda Beach, Vila-Seca, near Tarragona, marks the latest stage in developing the "ballroom of the twenty-first century", say its architects.

This self-styled "macro discothèque" covers a total area of 5,677 square metres, and encompasses seven bars, an external terrace, viewing tower, garden, restaurant, swimming pool with changing facilities, and parking for 1,000 cars. The latest leisure technology, however, lives within a mythical framework: the lower floor of the main structure is inspired by the four classical elements – earth, water, air and fire. The main dance floor is a luminous transparent structure suspended over a water-filled pool and flanked by three bars: the Earth Bar, entirely made of rocks and stone slabs; the Air Bar, which features 10,000 fibre-optic points of light constantly changing colour across two large elements; and the Fire Bar, which is fronted by the undulating metal scales of a mythical serpent and topped with decorative flames.

Above the dance floor, a grand balcony or "firmament" provides the perfect vantage point to view the action below. This area has the Satellites Bar, which is crowned by 100 luminous Perspex spheres and encloses an elliptical internal service area like the funnel of a large ship; at one end, on a circular platform supported by a steel mast, revellers can gather to observe the entire environment. Between the upper floor and the discothèque floor, a lounge area reserved as *Prive* sits behind a continuous panoramic window, which is 20 metres wide and 3 metres high; this feature area visually links the interior of the building to a large external terrace, which is arranged around an irregularly shaped 300 square-metre lake. Here another bar masquerades as a pseudo-Roman ruin. There is also a circular pool 12 metres in diameter, and the viewing tower that crowns the whole scheme from a height of 40 metres.

Pacha is not for the faint-hearted. It is a full-blooded design response to the new leisure age, full of alienating high-tech wizardry in the form of lasers, video-walls, sound and light, but seasoned with a dash of humanism in the material definition of the spaces.

THE PACHA LEISURE CENTRE AT PINEDA BEACH NEAR TARRAGONA COMBINES HUMANISM AND HIGH TECHNOLOGY IN A RICH AND EXPANSIVE MONUMENT TO HAVING A GOOD TIME.

Above and left: In the Spanish ballroom of the twenty-first century, disco dancers at the Pacha Leisure Centre gyrate across a luminous transparent floor suspended above a water-filled pool.
Opposite, top: Exterior view of the Pacha building and grounds at night.

Below: Ground plan of the
leisure centre with a total
area of 5,677 square metres.
Right and opposite: Sequence
of upper-floor spaces, which
enclose an elliptical internal
service area like the funnel
of a ship.

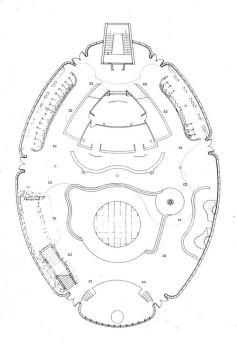

"PACHA SETS OUT TO BE A TEMPLE
OF MODERN LEISURE IN THE NEW
SPAIN OF THE TURN OF THE CENTURY,
A BOX FULL OF SURPRISES WHERE THE
ARCHITECTURE, INTERIOR DESIGN AND
SPATIAL TECHNOLOGY INVITE PARTYING
AND STIMULATE THE SENSES."
CAPELLA LARREA CASTELLVI

Three themed bars at the
Pacha Leisure Centre.
Left: The Air Bar, which
features 10,000 constantly
changing fibre-optic points
of light on two large displays.
Opposite, top: The Fire Bar,
fronted with serpent scales
and crowned with decorative
flames.
Opposite, below: The Earth
Bar, redolent of stone-slab
primitivism.

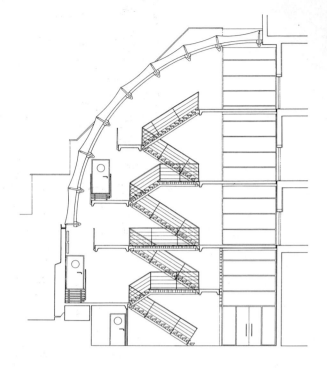

SHEPPARD ROBSON

DEEP END CAFÉ

LONDON, UK

The Deep End Café in the flagship headquarters of the University of Westminster on Regent Street in London has been created within the shell of a disused stone swimming pool by architects Sheppard Robson. The practice was responsible for leading a major refurbishment of the building to provide new teaching, catering, social and circulation facilities.

The project is an excellent example of the kind of stylish, space-efficient and cost-effective student facility that higher education institutions in the UK have been struggling to develop amid rapidly growing student numbers. It is also an imaginative reworking of a derelict space to carve out a new 392 square-metre café right in the heart of the building.

The project had to overcome considerable technical difficulties: damp posed problems, as did a phased schedule to fit construction work into student vacations. Nevertheless, the result is highly satisfactory. The main space on the floor of the former swimming pool has been given a new maple floor. Existing pilasters and cast ironwork have been restored and retained, together with the stone swimming pool surround and exposed steel beams above. Existing concrete soffits in the ceilings have been restored and painted. A new mezzanine floor has been inserted to link the existing levels of the pool floor, pool surround and an adjacent gymnasium gallery. The scheme is tied to existing accommodation (a marble entrance hall under construction) via a new 32-metre-wide stair tower covered with a fabric roof. A glass block wall divides the Deep End Café from this staircase.

Subtle colours, lightweight aluminium furniture and fittings supplied by Astro Designs, and a sensitive artificial lighting scheme using fittings supplied by Concord and Erco, add to a sense of contemporary expression that is new and fresh but does not wash away all traces of the original ornate qualities of the disused pool.

A DISUSED SWIMMING POOL HAS BEEN IMAGINATIVELY CONVERTED INTO A STYLISH CAFETERIA FOR STUDENTS IN THE NEWLY RESTORED FLAGSHIP BUILDING OF THE UNIVERSITY OF WESTMINSTER.

Opposite: Section through the staircase and fabric roof.

Left: A new mezzanine floor coexists with the ornate cast ironwork of the original swimming baths. The former swimming-pool floor is now covered in maple. Lightweight cafeteria furniture is made of aluminium.

Below: Imposing vertical lines of the colourful Deep End Café.

"CAREFUL INSERTIONS OF THE NEW ELEMENTS INTO THE EXISTING SPACE USING LIGHTWEIGHT STRUCTURES, NEW ROOFLIGHTING AND COLOUR AIM TO RETAIN THE INTEGRITY OF THE ORIGINAL WHILE AT THE SAME TIME ADDING A NEW DRAMATIC HEART TO THE BUILDING."

SHEPPARD ROBSON

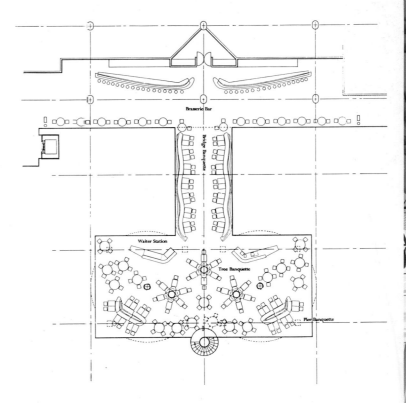

BRANSON COATES ARCHITECTURE

SCHIPHOL AIRPORT RESTAURANTS

AMSTERDAM, THE NETHERLANDS

Modern airport terminals are symbols of the advanced technology of jet flight. Within a glass and steel skin, these cavernous spaces combine a hard-edged functionalism with the glinting promise of supersonic travel. Little concession is usually made to the softer human dimension of experiencing these environments, as if a sense of awe can substitute entirely for a feeling of comfort. But within the new Terminal Two at Amsterdam's Schiphol Airport – designed with high-tech finesse by Dutch architects Bentheim Crowe – an exotic and arresting exception can be found in the shape of two new restaurants designed by Nigel Coates.

NIGEL COATES HAS CREATED TWO NEW RESTAURANTS WITHIN THE HIGH-TECH SKIN OF SCHIPHOL AIRPORT'S SECOND TERMINAL, USING SYNTHETIC MATERIALS TO PLAYFULLY EVOKE NATURAL FORMS.

Coates is the self-styled British master of "narrative architecture". His storytelling approach to buildings and interiors has produced some highly imaginative work in Europe and Japan. He describes the project to design La Fôret and Nautilus – the two new restaurants at Schiphol – as the "fountainhead" of a long-time concern within his practice Branson Coates Architecture, to explore the idea of the airport of an analogue of the city. "Our Caffè Bongo in Tokyo," he explains, "has an aircraft wing strapped above the window. Our Taxim club complex in Istanbul lays out the main dance floor as if it were a runway, with drinkers in an upstairs bar peering down towards it as if from the airport control tower."

La Fôret and Nautilus, however, take the thinking a stage further. "We've gone on to quote the sort of exotic coasts that we would like planes to bring us to," says Coates. Accordingly, these restaurant spaces for 500 people reflect the idea of land meeting sea, and of intermediate space between the runway and the city. On an upper balcony in the terminal, La Fôret is a 650 square-metre brasserie that groups tables beneath giant organic playground trees made of spun resin and adorned with fibre-optic lights. On the main floor below, Nautilus is a 400 square-metre seafood and landfood bar conceived as an underwater world with sculptural space-defining coral reef furniture and shoals of exotic multi-coloured fish moulded from resin-coated aluminium mesh and suspended above the heads of diners.

These two surreal stage sets use synthetic materials, suspended surfaces and light in an overtly artistic way to create a natural oasis in the heart of a busy commercial airport. Their combined effect is to alleviate the often jarring experience of air travel. Yet diners are not entirely distracted into a fantasyland – the restaurants afford excellent views of jets taking off and landing. Perhaps the idea of hundreds of people shooting into the sky in a metal tube is the most surreal element of all.

Above: View of La Fôret brasserie on the upper balcony from the seabed of the Nautilus bar. The bar is surrealistically styled as an underwater experience complete with aluminium-mesh fish, coated with resin and suspended above the heads of diners (left).

Opposite: Floor plan showing the relationship of the two restaurants.

"LA FÔRET AND NAUTILUS SET OUT TO MAKE THE
AIRPORT A PLACE TO ENJOY, A PLACE YOU'D GLADLY
COME BACK TO. BEFORE REACHING YOUR GATE,
YOU'LL HAVE DINED IN AN EXOTIC PLACE WHERE
FOREST MEETS CORAL."

BRANSON COATES ARCHITECTURE

Left: A stage set at the edge of the
runway. Long banquettes emulate
coral reefs, but between the shoals of
artificial fish, the hard-edged, high-tech
reality of jet travel is glimpsed.
Opposite: With La Fôret's giant organic
trees in spun resin, adorned with
fibre-optic lighting by Absolute Action,
Branson Coates Architecture brings
a playful, festive spirit to Schiphol
Airport.

4

SOICHI MIZUTANI

**SETSUGEKKA
RESTAURANT**

TOKYO, JAPAN

This tiny jewel of a restaurant in the Shibuya-ku district of Tokyo powerfully expresses the distinctive talent of Kyoto-born designer Soichi Mizutani in a manner that confined spaces rarely achieve. Restaurant Setsugekka (it means literally snow, moon, flowers) seats just 23 people in a space measuring 83 square metres. It follows on from another small leisure facility – the Hana bar in Kyoto, designed by Mizutani for the same client – in developing a rich and pure dialogue between ancient Japanese design tradition and western Modernism.

This dialogue has been refined to high art in post-war Japanese interior architecture and design by such notable practitioners as Arata Isozaki, Shiro Kuramata and Ikko Tanaka. But for the younger generation of Japanese designers, recently given unprecedented opportunities by Japan's consumerist society, reconciling old and new has become a burden. Some young Japanese designers have been tempted to complexity and baroque, according to the English architect David Chipperfield, an admirer of Soichi Mizutani who has done more than most to bring his considerable body of work to Europe's attention. But, says Chipperfield, "Mizutani has shown the power of restraint and the poetic of simplicity."

This is true of the Setsugekka project. Light, space, geometry and material form the dominant themes, reflecting a Modernist's clarity. Yet the use of glowing *washi* walls (made of traditional Japanese paper pasted on to acrylic boards) creates a softer atmosphere and locates the restaurant in a particular cultural continuum. As planes and volumes interlock, boundaries become ambiguous. Yet perimeter routes are highlighted by the use of recessed lamps and washed pebbles to fill the gaps between floors and walls.

Fourteen of the 23 restaurant covers are accommodated along a single wooden bar with a clear urethane finish. Two private rooms accommodate the other diners. The flooring is in white ash. In this restaurant stripped of all novelty and decoration, Mizutani shows a spatial understanding that confirms his rare ability.

SOICHI MIZUTANI'S TINY TOKYO RESTAURANT RECONCILES THE GEOMETRY OF WESTERN MODERNISM WITH THE SPIRITUAL TRADITIONS OF ANCIENT JAPAN IN A SOFT AND GLOWING ENVIRONMENT.

The simple poetry and spatial understanding of Soichi Mizutani in a small restaurant seating just 23 people, 14 of them along a single wooden bar with a clear urethane finish (opposite, top). A *washi* wall (opposite, below), made of traditional Japanese paper, enhances the softness and ambiguity of an environment composed of light, space and geometry (right).

"THE USE OF SPECIALLY LIT WALLS COVERED WITH JAPANESE *WASHI* PAPER CREATES A REALLY GOOD, SOFT ATMOSPHERE AND IS SOMETHING I FAVOUR."

SOICHI MIZUTANI

DENTON CORKER
MARSHALL

ADELPHI HOTEL

MELBOURNE,
AUSTRALIA

While Sydney flaunts its architectural gems over its spectacular harbour, Melbourne has a habit of hiding them away in its urban hinterland. The Adelphi Hotel is a case in point: located right in the gritty high-rise heart of Melbourne on Flinders Lane, this imaginative conversion by architects Denton Corker Marshall of an eight-storey concrete warehouse repays close inspection. But you need to know where to look amid an intense and largely undistinguished cityscape.

**A SMALL "BOUTIQUE" HOTEL FASHIONED
FROM A 1930s CONCRETE WAREHOUSE
IN THE HEART OF MELBOURNE CANTILEVERS
AN AUDACIOUS ROOFTOP POOL OUT OVER
THE URBAN STREET.**

Only the long, narrow overhang of an audacious rooftop swimming pool cantilevered above the street gives any real clue to the skill with which the simple grid-structure warehouse – 7 metres in width, 48 metres in length, and built in 1938 – has been transformed into the very antithesis of the bland international hotel clone. The Adelphi is rich in contemporary design character, yet the fabric and structure of the original building has been carefully retained – partly on grounds of cost, partly to clarify the juxtaposition of old and new elements. The exterior has been repainted but remains essentially the same, with damaged original ceramic tiles replaced by aluminium ones at ground level. Where new components have been added – signs, rooftop structures and the 25-metre glass-bottomed, salt-water pool, for example – they have been brightly coloured to signal their newness.

The Adelphi Hotel is a five-star "boutique" hotel, with 34 rooms, two restaurants, a private members club, bar, recreation and pool facilities arranged on 11 floors. The total space is 3,217.5 square metres. Diagonal lines punctuate the interior imagery with single-minded purpose. A neutral framework – achieved with black granite floor tiles, stainless steel and natural maple wall panels, and perforated metal ceilings – is enlivened with architect-designed furniture pieces treated as sculptural elements.

Denton Corker Marshall's design work is all-encompassing: public area sofas, coffee tables, rugs, bar stools, restaurant tables and chairs, standard lamps, and bedroom and bathroom fittings. The aim, according to designer Barrie Marshall, "is to reinforce the Adelphi's image as more friendly and casual than other small hotels". Designer hotels can sometimes be uncomfortable places in their restless urge to make an overt creative statement. But not this one. Strong colours, challenging art, spacious rooms and large windows remind you constantly that you are not incarcerated in a predictable multi-national chain hotel, but the Adelphi is not off-putting in its artistic pretensions. Quite the reverse, in fact.

Above: The Adelphi Hotel
is an imaginative warehouse
conversion in the high-rise
centre of Melbourne which
flaunts its contemporary style
in unpromising surroundings.
Left: Dynamic angular
furniture on black granite
floor tiles, custom-designed
by the architects to suit the
uncompromisingly Modernist
mood of the place.

"THE AIM WAS NOT TO TRANSFORM THE BUILDING THROUGH EXTENSIVE RESHAPING AND REMODELLING, BUT VIA THE ADDITION OF NEW ELEMENTS AND COMPONENTS. THESE ARE BRIGHTLY COLOURED TO REINFORCE THEIR 'NEW' PRESENCE."

DENTON CORKER MARSHALL

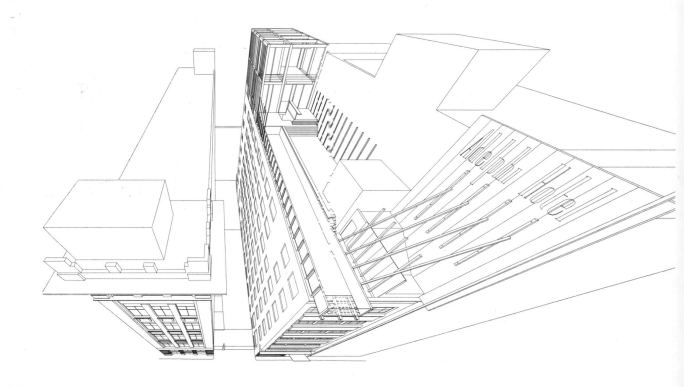

Opposite: A glass-bottomed rooftop swimming pool 25 metres in length is cantilevered out over the street. The exploded perspective of the Adelphi Hotel illustrates the audacity of the scheme.

Right: Distinctive bedroom design, with the austere style of black floor, white blinds, brushed steel writing desk and futon-style bed contrasting with the brightly coloured two-seater sofa back.

ALFREDO ARRIBAS

ESTANDARD BAR

BARCELONA, SPAIN

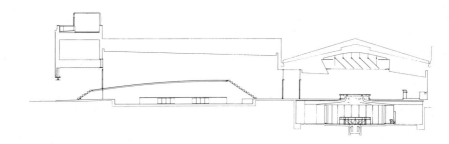

The playfulness of architect Alfredo Arribas, designer of some of the most popular clubs and bars in Barcelona, is only temporarily curtailed in his Estandard project. In his previous projects, all strongly stamped with his personality and obsessions, his trademark has been to surprise and disconcert. But the first impression of Estandard is of sophistication. A low concrete ceiling over a polished wooden floor creates an intimacy that is symbolized by a row of large semi-circular white leather banquettes – most inviting for the foot-weary. To one side and behind a glass partition, a slope rises from street level, along the former garage ramp, to the restaurant, which again has wooden floors, polished concrete walls and a row of orange trees planted in the floor to add a touch of the surreal.

To the rear of the cocktail bar, subdued lighting and a resounding thud signal the location of the discothèque, a vast room with a stage at one end for live bands. Snaking around the perimeter of the room is a wood and steel continuous bar, which provides more space for waving vainly at bar staff as well as creating areas for social interaction. Rough concrete walls and a stainless steel bar counter provide a sparse aesthetic, which is livened up by the treatment of ceiling and floor. The ceiling has an unlikely array of suspended acoustic screens intersecting at dangerous angles, like an exploded bottle crate.

Arribas' favourite play area, the gents and ladies toilets, has not been forgotten. A circular lantern pushing up through the centre of the dance floor is the transparent ceiling of the unisex washroom area, where a series of doors forming a large circle comprise entrances, exits, routes to offices, and a series of WCs. Which is which is left to the imagination. The group handwashing area, a marble circle with steel basins, can be spied on from the dance floor above.

The chief materials of Arribas' interiors are, in order of importance, his imagination, lighting and texture. His lighting often comprises a clever combination of uplighting, downlighting, warm and cold, blue, purple and red to create complex moods and atmospheres. His juxtaposition of hard and soft textures – such as, in this project, golden wood, polished concrete and steel – reveals a less frenetic and more composed side of the designer not seen in many of his earlier projects. Some have suggested that Arribas has shown a move to personal maturity in this 1,500 square-metre project on three floors. But he rejects this idea with affable cynicism: "In this project I am appealing to the more mature sector of the market".

ALFREDO ARRIBAS TRANSFORMS A FORMER GARAGE INTO A PREMIER BAR, RESTAURANT AND DISCOTHÈQUE, SHOWING A MORE MATURE SIDE TO HIS NATURE IN SPARSE USE OF CONTRASTING MATERIALS.

Above: Longitudinal section from the entrance to the discothèque.

Opposite, top: The vast discothèque floor is bordered by a snaking glass-and-steel counter and crowned by intersecting acoustic panels suspended threateningly above the action. The glazed platform in the centre of the floor is the lantern above the washrooms.

Opposite, below: The circular unisex washroom area in marble and steel, playfully overlooked from the dance floor above.

"ESTANDARD BAR IS A POST-
1992 PROJECT – A SIMPLE,
ASYMMETRICAL COMPOSITION,
WITH INDISPENSABLE ELEMENTS,
A CONCENTRATION OF GESTURES,
AND A SEVERITY OF RHYTHMS
AND MODULATIONS."

ALFREDO ARRIBAS

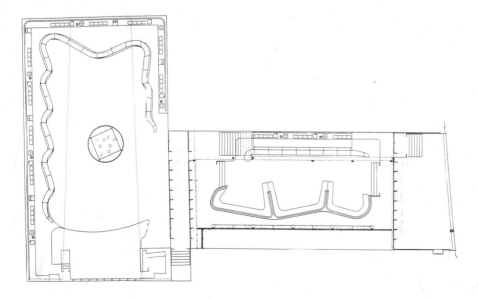

Above: The sinuous
bar, which stretches around
the dance floor.
Left: Floor plan for the
former garage given a
surprisingly sophisticated
treatment.
Opposite: On the upper
level close to the entrance,
Arribas plays with contrasts
in materials, textures and
light to create an engaging
atmosphere.

VIRGILE & STONE
ASSOCIATES

ROYAL
NATIONAL THEATRE
RESTAURANT

LONDON, UK

THE NEW MEZZANINE RESTAURANT AT THE ROYAL NATIONAL THEATRE BREATHES FRESH LIFE INTO A MODERNIST MONUMENT WHILE RESPECTING THE INTEGRITY OF THE ARCHITECTURE.

Sir Denys Lasdun's National Theatre on London's South Bank is one of Britain's most controversial buildings. Since opening in 1976, it has succeeded in polarizing opinion – an undeniable cultural monument, the masterwork of an uncompromising Modernist genius to some, but also widely condemned as a concrete bunker. Respect for Lasdun's complex geometric vocabulary of concrete platforms, terraces, stepped sections and towers is abundant. But this is a building hard to love – and even harder to find your way around. Its vast, awe-inspiring interior spaces retain a kind of grandeur. But the honeycomb grid ceilings, purple carpeting, patchy lighting, confusing layout and invisible silver signing system on stretches of exposed banded grey concrete imprison the National within a 1970s time warp.

The National's management, aware of the need to create more user-friendly public spaces and amenities, has been trying to modernize the place in piecemeal fashion for years. Recently it commissioned a new architectural masterplan from Stanton Williams, a practice with impeccable Modernist credentials, but this has met Lasdun's fierce resistance to change. One proposal, to remove a tier of the building to simplify its confusing double-entrance, was likened by Lasdun to "removing a pediment from St Paul's".

Amid the furore surrounding attempts to update Lasdun's architecture at the National, a single interior design intervention has successfully punctured the time capsule and, in the words of one leading commentator, allowed some of the stale air of the 1970s to escape. Virgile & Stone has redesigned the National's existing restaurant, Ovations, on its mezzanine level, replacing an under-used facility with a smart new 230 square-metre brasserie, which boosted trade by 30 per cent within six months of opening.

Legend has it that the long, narrow space for the eaterie had been earmarked by Lasdun in the original design as a ticket office before a last-minute change of use. It does, however, have the advantage of providing views of the Thames at one end and the bustling foyer at the other. The new informal and cosmopolitan brasserie, branded as Mezzanine, was designed to compete directly with the best West End and Soho restaurants. It respects the integrity of the architectural fabric but very much does its own thing. Walls, for instance, are clad in timber-ribbed panelling, set in front of the concrete to create a double skin, with upper areas leaving the original texture exposed. A gently curved glass front opens up the restaurant to public view, drawing visitors in, with the curve echoed in the polished stainless steel top of the restaurant bar. A dark hardwood floor of recycled Panga Panga wood extends from the restaurant into the lobby to allow for overspill from the bar and to integrate this new facility into the main theatre building. The familiar honeycomb grid above is hidden by a suspended plaster ceiling.

Mezzanine provides covers for 130 people, changing mood from sunny tranquillity during the day for lunch and tea, to a more vibrant atmosphere after dark. Uplighting from the ribbed timber wall sceening creates a feeling of space and height, while low-voltage downlighters accentuate specific features. Table lamps by Ecart add to the ambience, as do mirrors at both ends of the restaurant, which catch the light, river views, and reflect the abstract classic theatrical figures in a 12-metre-long mural that runs the length of the restaurant behind the Finnish-made banquettes. The mural was specially designed by Jon Turner and painted by the Royal National Theatre's scenic design department.

In contrast to Sir Denys Lasdun, who is reportedly less than enthusiastic about the impact of Mezzanine, diners in ever growing numbers have voted with their wallets. In a setting which could have been an excuse for dramatic overstatement, the framing context of the Lasdun architecture has drawn an understated, relaxed and respectful response from Virgile & Stone.

Above: A gently curved glass
front subtly opens up the
Mezzanine brasserie to
visitors without interfering
with the familiar geometries
of Sir Denys Lasdun's
National Theatre building.

Left: Lasdun's famous concrete panels are respectfully half-concealed behind timber-ribbed panelling, which creates a double skin in Virgile & Stone's informal restaurant, lit by Ecart table lamps.
Opposite, top: A long, narrow space is enlivened by Jon Turner's abstract mural and by the arrangement of Finnish-made banquettes.
Opposite, below: How the restaurant floor plan fits into the grid of a masterful Modernist building.

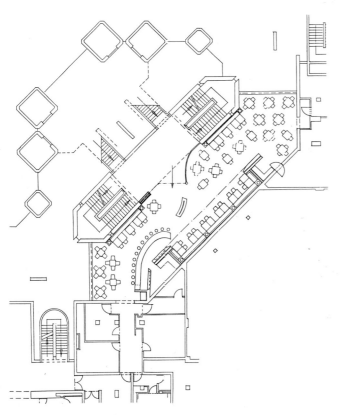

"HARMONY WITH THE EXISTING ARCHITECTURE WAS AN IMPORTANT CONSIDERATION. VIEWED FROM THE MAIN LOBBY, THE RESTAURANT IS AN INTEGRAL PART OF THE IMPRESSIVE CONCRETE WALLS AND GRIDDED CEILING OF LASDUN'S DESIGN SCHEME. THE INTENTION WAS TO CREATE A MORE APPROPRIATE AMBIENCE AND IDENTITY FOR A RESTAURANT WITHOUT DESTROYING THE ESSENCE OF THE ORIGINAL."

VIRGILE & STONE

LAWRENCE MAN

TAI PAN RESTAURANT

CAMBRIDGE, MASSACHUSETTS, USA

Hybrid food and entertainment concepts are a growing feature of 1990s America as restaurateurs cross cultural and culinary pursuits in a bid to find new formats to win customers. A striking example of this trend can be found in an urban mall in Cambridge, Massachusetts, where the owners of Tai Pan brokered a marriage between a traditional Chinese restaurant and a Japanese karaoke lounge and bar.

THE MODERN URBAN STREET MEETS THE ANCIENT CONCEPT OF YIN AND YANG IN LAWRENCE MAN'S AMBITIOUS INTERIOR FOR A RESTAURANT COMBINING CHINESE FOOD WITH JAPANESE KARAOKE.

Architect Lawrence Man has divided the space between open dining area, karaoke lounge and bar, and kitchen and support facilities, by introducing a free-standing curved wall as a zoning device and main focal point of the design. The concept is deliberately urbanistic: to strengthen the idea of an interior "street" with individual buildings, a series of abstracted façades, small-scaled fenestration and trellis roof overhangs punctuate the wall. Shelves along its length enable patrons to stand and have a drink. "The street serves as a place of activity," explains Man, "where patrons and staff alike can mingle and interact." Above, black ceiling tiles inset with spotlights evoke a night sky.

Each zone has its own distinct ambience, but the transparency of the curved wall allows the different spaces totalling 4,300 square feet on one floor to achieve a spatial cohesion. A dining area on the outside of the wall is open and airy, facing a real city street and park beyond the mall. An intimate area enveloped by the gold leaf-painted wall looks into the mall: this is the karaoke bar and lounge, with dramatic low-voltage recessed lighting and atmosphere to enhance its function.

The idea of openness and intimacy counterpointed within Tai Pan reflects the broader conceptual theme of Man's design: the notion of Yin and Yang, the two opposing principles of Chinese religion and philosophy, which influence destiny. His interior can thus be seen as an ambitious essay in reconciling opposites, an ironic commentary perhaps on the uneasy cultural hybrid being served up to customers.

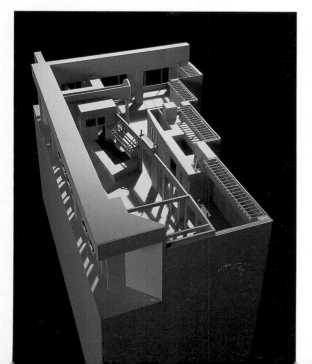

Tai Pan is a spatial study in reconciling opposites. An eaterie that serves up Chinese food and Japanese karaoke, it creates a curved interior street to divide its different functions and play on the counterpointing of openness and intimacy (above and left). Even the elegant entrance to the restaurant from the street (opposite) is mirrored by another from inside the mall.

KRISTIAN GAVOILLE

CAFÉ GAVOILLE

AMIENS, FRANCE

Former Philippe Starck collaborator Kristian Gavoille has emerged as one of the most imaginative and influential young French designers of the 1990s through a series of projects that combine an idiosyncratic personal vision with a highly detailed practical approach. The Café Gavoille is typical of Gavoille's unusual, slightly quirky style: this new street-level cafeteria in the centre of the town of Amiens, designed as part of a more general renovation of the main cultural centre to which it belongs, is at once both mysterious and oddly familiar.

The Government-run Maison de la Culture in Amiens contains two theatres and one cinema, and is 30 years old. When it was renovated by architect Gilles Dubez, a 200 square-metre space was set aside for a café, and Gavoille was invited to give the facility his individual stamp. Gavoille describes the brief he was given: "It's incredible but the client said only '150 persons and a kitchen'." In circumstances of such artistic freedom, Gavoille made the radical decision that the glass-fronted café should turn its back on the main town square because of the indifferent views and the inclement weather most of the year. Instead customers face an immense, luminous, orange screen of sand-blasted glass with walnut frame, which draws on the vocabulary of theatre and cinema. In summer, however, the large glass frontage opens and the back of the seating unfolds into flap-seats which swing the action round to the open space outside. All the furniture was custom-designed by Gavoille in common with the marble-and-walnut bar 11 metres in length, and even door handles, aluminium coat-pegs and washbasins.

The designer plays games of ambiguity and intrigue with the interior of the café that bears his name: the space has a ceiling half in raw concrete (to remind people of the Maison de la Culture in its earlier guise, says Gavoille) and half covered in white plaster. Crystal chandeliers do not light up themselves but are lit by spotlights. Smoking and non-smoking areas are conspicuously marked by giant totems bearing the signs Oui and Non. A wine bottle rack in polished stainless steel protrudes from the screen. A red leather bench 22 metres in length enables customers to move about, says Gavoille, "as in the rooms of theatres at the beginning of the century".

Gavoille wanted his customers to look into their own imagination, not into the street outside. This is an ambitious and beguiling scheme, redolent with cultural messages and inescapably French in its graphic style and slightly whimsical spatial and material relationships.

The glass-fronted Café Gavoille turns its back on the main Amiens town square in winter, but opens out in summer. All of the furniture items, including the distinctive door handles (opposite), were custom-designed by Kristian Gavoille.

KRISTIAN GAVOILLE'S QUIRKY CULTURAL-CENTRE CAFÉ IN THE TOWN OF AMIENS DRAWS ON THE VOCABULARY OF THEATRE AND CINEMA, INVITING CUSTOMERS TO LOOK INTO THEIR OWN IMAGINATION, NOT OUTSIDE.

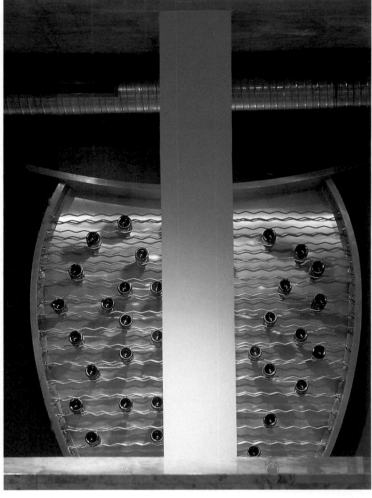

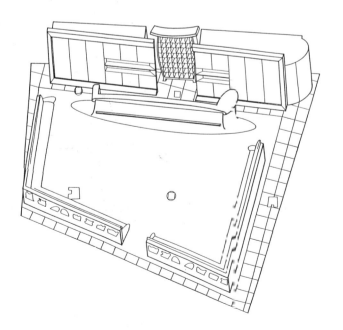

Above: Customers at the Café Gavoille are players in a game of material and spatial intrigue, reflecting the idea of the passage of a century of French culture. Classic crystal chandeliers do not light up themselves but are lit by modern spotlights. A stainless-steel wine bottle rack protrudes from a giant walnut-frame screen of sand-blasted glass which confronts customers.

Left: Perspective.

Opposite: Giant totems bearing the signs "Oui" and "Non" signify smoking and non-smoking areas in typically idiosyncratic fashion.

"IN THE IMAGE OF A COCTEAU FILM,
YOU CROSS THE SCREEN TO GO
TOWARDS THE SET OF PIGEONHOLES
FOR WINE BOTTLES. AND AS IN THE
THEATRE, THE UNLIT CRYSTAL
CHANDELIERS ARE EQUIPPED WITH
SPOTLIGHTS, FORMING A LINK
BETWEEN THE PAST AND PRESENT."
KRISTIAN GAVOILLE

TERENCE CONRAN, KEITH HOBBS, LINZI COPPICK

QUAGLINO'S RESTAURANT

LONDON, UK

Quaglino's, the faded London St James's nightspot now miraculously restyled as the hottest restaurant ticket in town, occupies a special place in the resurrected career of its creator, Sir Terence Conran. The man who worked as a young designer on the 1951 Festival of Britain, defined the King's Road image of swinging London in the 1960s, created the burnt orange beanbag look of the 1970s and owned half the pastel-coloured high street as a retail magnate in the 1980s, is not finished yet. And the design triumph of Quaglino's proves it. Conran's comeback as the restaurateur of the 1990s has been confirmed by the skilful conversion of a cavernous basement venue for lesser known variety acts into a colourful and glamorous Parisian brasserie frequented by the famous. Since it opened on Valentine's Day 1993, Quaglino's has had the glitterati queuing round the block for supper from four in the afternoon.

Conran describes running a restaurant as the complete design challenge. The product is both manufactured and served on the premises, and the logistics involved are many. On the Quaglino's project, he was client, proprietor, manager and designer all at the same time. A key early consideration was to banish all notions of diners being in a basement space. An illuminated skylight was installed, running the length of the restaurant: this not only provides artificial lighting which emulates natural lighting, and is seasonally adjusted, but also houses the main vents and ducts for the restaurant's air-conditioning.

A mezzanine level was inserted to increase the overall floor space to 15,000 square feet. The mezzanine contains a bar and private dining room, which overlook the main bustling restaurant space below. The entrance to Quaglino's on Bury Street is deceptively small and seductive, leaving diners quite unprepared for the sheer scale and volume of the restaurant as they descend from the bar down a wide, glamorous staircase on to the main floor.

Working with Keith Hobbs and Linzi Coppick, Conran's achievement is not simply in the grand plan with its large element of surprise. Every decorative detail, from the sinuous curves of counters and balustrades to the Q-shaped ashtrays, is superbly resolved. Conran's continuing love affair with France's culinary culture is reflected in much of Quaglino's ornamentalism. But practical problems such as providing extraction from the basement to the roof eight floors above and not disturbing neighbouring residents during the eight-month building programme have also been skilfully managed. Oh, and the food isn't bad either.

THE STARTLING TRANSFORMATION OF A FADED BASEMENT NIGHTSPOT INTO ONE OF LONDON'S SMARTEST RESTAURANTS REFLECTS SIR TERENCE CONRAN'S LOVE OF FRENCH BRASSERIE CULTURE.

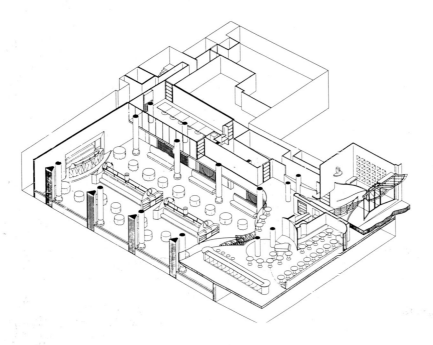

A deceptively small and seductive entrance (oposite, top) leads diners down to a cavernous restaurant (opposite, below) of unexpectedly generous proportions and exceptional creative flair, modelled on the finest Parisian brasseries. Artist-painted columns, a mural by Ned Conran, bas-relief plasterwork by Dhruva Mistry, and a wealth of individual design detailing enhance this artistic showpiece.
Left: Diagrammatic exposition of the entire basement-sited scheme.

"QUAGLINO'S CREATES
A SENSE OF OCCASION
IN AN ENTIRELY MODERN
RESTAURANT OF GLAMOUR
AND ENTERTAINMENT,
SO REFLECTING THE
ACHIEVEMENT OF LONDON
WHICH HAS BECOME
THE GASTRONOMIC CENTRE
OF THE WORLD."
TERENCE CONRAN

Above: A wide and glamorous staircase incorporating the Q-mark of Quaglino's leads on to the restaurant floor. Right: Vista through a restaurant interior which has confirmed the resurrection of Sir Terence Conran's career. Opposite: A giant artificially illuminated skylight by Marlin Lighting, seasonally adjusted to emulate patterns of natural light, cleverly dispels the notion of dining in a basement.

1

7

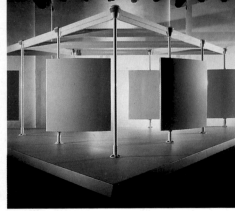

3

6

R E T A I L

**STRUCTURAL INTEGRITY, FLEXIBLE FORMATS
AND MODEST MATERIALS ARE BACK IN
VOGUE AS RETAIL ENVIRONMENTS LEAVE
THE TRANSIENT TWO-DIMENSIONAL
GLAMOUR OF PAST SCHEMES FAR BEHIND.**

Retail interior design shows signs of emerging leaner and fitter as a discipline after the physical and psychological battering it received during worldwide recession. To judge by this selection of projects, designers are now placing more emphasis on the solid virtues of retail engineering and on architectural place-making, leaving behind the kind of flimsy graphic two-dimensionality that characterized so many schemes before the consumer downturn. A focus on improving the *fabric* of environments, not just on delivering transient if beguiling surface treatments, is leading to a new type of design innovation in retailing. This is epitomized by Sottsass Associati's scheme in Italy which uses a flexible aluminium cladding system to turn buildings and structures on Erg petrol forecourts into a chain of attractive convenience stores.

In the drive to boost retail earnings using less store space and fewer staff, designers are developing some enterprising solutions. Andreas Winkler's music centre in Karlsruhe for a firm of violin makers shows what can be achieved in a secluded space away from the main shopping thoroughfare. O'Herlihy & Warner's tiny jewel of a clothing store for Harriet Dorn in California has a vertical plan which dramatically suspends the merchandise in space beneath a fabric layered skylight. Fitch's scheme for the Ing Bank in Holland creates the world's first totally unstaffed bank branches, relying on the quality of the interior to deter vandalism.

After an era of glamour and glitz, retail design is now turning towards more modest materials. The Go Silk fashion showroom in Manhattan, for example, has maroon-stained plywood doors and floor tiles made from recycled tyres. King Miranda's showroom scheme for an Italian manufacturer of exhibition systems exposes the beams of a rural wax factory. Lighting is becoming less a show business turn in retailing and more of an integrated architectural element. In the case of Torsten Neeland's stunning Go Shoe shop in Hamburg, the lighting *is* the architecture.

Merchandising, too, is becoming less precious and more tactile – a key focus of the revamp of the Habitat chain in the UK by Din Associates. Perhaps this is a reflection of the growing trend for shoppers to want to acquire experiences, not simply possessions. A visit to the Kashin emporium in Tokyo – which ingeniously sells incense and flowers within a single space – will entail participation in an incense ceremony on the upper level. A visit to the Amlux "Toyota town" in Osaka will add a new dimension to the experience of choosing a car.

All over the world, retail design has climbed off its pedestal to utilize humbler materials, smaller spaces, and new and more flexible formats in a bid to bring the customers flooding back. The projects shown here reflect a new mood of freshness, vitality – and structural integrity.

11

9

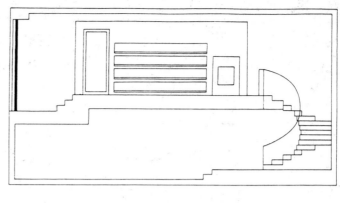

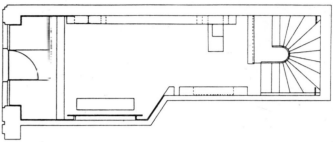

TORSTEN NEELAND

GO SHOE SHOP

HAMBURG, GERMANY

This pure exercise in using planes of light to display merchandise has been created by German designer Torsten Neeland for the Go shoe store in a turn-of-the-century Hamburg building. The historic setting melts into transparency as a subtle indirect lighting scheme is executed with cream-smooth precision.

Neeland uses general lighting for orientation and a higher intensity of light around the shelving to draw attention to the goods on sale. In keeping with the client's wishes, all the shoes are evenly illuminated. The use of a brilliant blue light is part of Neeland's strategy to create glowing focal points. Viewed through a frame, the blue lighting suggests spacious depth. Guzzini spots in the entrance area set the tone for what lies within.

The store is laid out over two floors, occupying 35 square metres of retail space. "Next to the lighting, only colour and space should exist," says Neeland. That is certainly the case. Material connections, such as steel elements or rods in the interior, are well hidden behind simply lit planes. The counter, made from the synthetic kitchen material Corean, is a seamless block. The ceiling is flat. Nothing is allowed to disturb the floating effect of the lighting.

Neeland has been fascinated with lighting since he began designing light fittings as a student at Hamburg College of Art. Since then he has designed lighting professionally, finding inventive new ways to use porcelain and medium-density fibreboard in fittings, and exploring the potential of fibre optics and light conductor systems. Rarely will he have been given such a pure, smooth canvas on which to paint a total interior with light as the Go shoe shop. One is reminded of Le Corbusier's comment: "Architecture is the masterly, correct and magnificent play of masses brought together in light."

A LIGHTING SCHEME FOR A HAMBURG SHOE STORE IN A TURN-OF-THE-CENTURY BUILDING DISSOLVES THE MATERIAL ENVIRONMENT UNTIL ONLY LIGHT, COLOUR, SPACE – AND SHOES – EXIST.

Above: Floor plans for lower and upper levels show the progression from one space to another.
Opposite: The spotlit entrance to the Go shoe shop sets the tone for the "light-as-architecture" theme inside.

Opposite: All the merchandise is evenly lit as indirect light dissolves the physical planes of the store, leaving only space and colour. Above: Lighting creates focal points and intriguing depths within the space.

Above and opposite: Steel, plaster and carpentry are reduced to a pure smooth canvas on which the designer
paints with light, turning the merchandise on show into exhibits in an art gallery.

STUDIOS
ARCHITECTURE

ASIA AND PACIFIC TRADE CENTER

OSAKA, JAPAN

Osaka is one of the mightiest industrial cities in the world, a place where business is taken very seriously and the colloquial greeting on the street is *Mokarimakka* ("are you making money ?"). As part of its development of the Osaka Bay area, the city has funded a giant new $1.4 billion building complex, the Asia and Pacific Trade Center, which is devoted entirely to promoting international trade. The Center is vast. Designed by architect Nikken Sekkei Ltd on a scale which makes it the world's largest showcase for foreign products, the facility comprises an enormous international trade mart in one building with 2.1 million square feet of space, and an eight-level leisure/convention centre next door. The international trade mart is a wholesale centre inspired by the Japanese cultural practice of *Omiai* (arranged marriage). It aims to bring potential business partners together who would not otherwise meet, and enable foreign companies to by-pass Japan's multi-tiered distribution system and sell direct to retailers.

San Francisco interior design firm STUDIOS was chosen by Nikken Sekkei Ltd to design key interiors in the trade mart following a worldwide trawl of suitable consultants. Apparently, the practice's ability to provide "unique design on restrictive budgets" determined the selection. STUDIOS' task was to humanize the vast space and create an environment in which buyers could see as much foreign merchandise and meet as many foreign companies as possible. It has given some 75,000 square feet of sky lobbies and atria a bright, energizing treatment to promote the idea of openness and playfulness and encourage buyers to make circular trips around what might otherwise be a building of daunting scale.

Colourfully painted walkways, lift shafts and other elements dynamically span horizontal and vertical spaces far greater in dimension than those normally encountered by interior designers. Japan has been criticized by its international trading partners for operating too closed a market. This is Osaka's typically big and bold response.

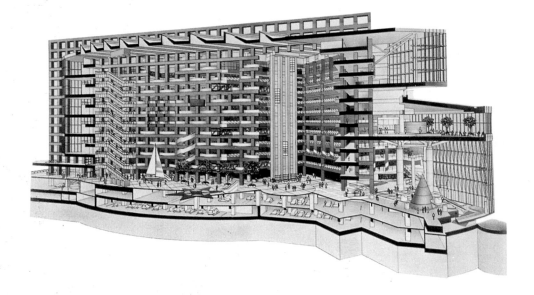

Left: Situated on the waterfront at Osaka Bay, the Asia and Pacific Trade Center is a vast complex combining an international mart with a leisure and convention centre next door. Opposite: Inside the trade mart, a giant atrium is given a playful and colourful interior treatment on a restricted budget.

THE SKY LOBBIES AND GIANT ATRIA OF A NEW INTERNATIONAL TRADE MART IN OSAKA – THE WORLD'S LARGEST SHOWCASE FOR FOREIGN GOODS – HAVE BEEN HUMANIZED BY BOLD USE OF COLOUR.

The purpose of the design scheme was to encourage buyers to circulate in a building of daunting scale. The atrium shown is 50 metres high and 100 metres in length. Painted metal walkways, lift shafts and other elements span the space vertically and horizontally. Lighting is by Matsushita. There is polished terrazzo on the central atrium floor and jet-printed carpet by Tori on the corridor floors.

"THE MAIN CHALLENGE WAS TO MAKE
A SUPERHUMAN-SCALE SPACE ACTIVE AND
ATTRACTIVE FOR PEOPLE."

ERIK SUEBERKROP,
PRINCIPAL, STUDIOS ARCHITECTURE

3

KING-MIRANDA

LA CASA ROSSA

TREVISO, ITALY

In the Italian countryside just outside Treviso, La Casa Rossa (The Red House) is a former ink and sealing wax factory now imaginatively converted into the trade showroom for a maker of exhibition systems. Applicazioni's new headquarters is intended as a place where architects and specifiers can see the Palo Alto exhibition system displayed in an unusual and enticing setting. The industrial designers of the Palo Alto system itself – the Milan-based partnership of Perry King and Santiago Miranda – were commissioned to design the conversion of La Casa Rossa. Malcolm S. Inglis collaborated.

The result is a resonant interior scheme with an apparent simplicity which belies a rich and complex approach to material and surface treatment. In this respect, the King Miranda design practice is developing a line of enquiry which emerged in its work on a series of showrooms for the Italian furniture company Marcatré during the late 1980s. La Casa Rossa is a two-storey building constructed at the turn of the century, with two open-plan areas linked by a wooden staircase. Another two-storey block at the side brings the total floor area to about 1,200 square metres. Despite minimal maintenance during its years as a factory then busy warehouse, the designers discovered that the building had stood the test of time well – in particular its original wooden roof.

Storage and services functions, including the heating, have been located on the ground floor; the upper level is devoted to the showroom to display the Palo Alto system, which is manufactured on another site and offices. Visitors pass from the car park into a large cantilevered-roof lobby area directly below executive office suites on the upper level. In this space, a giant sculptural totem with brass sun-like disc projecting from a rusted steel wall has more than merely decorative purpose: it cleverly disguises an ungainly steel column in the entrance hall which is part of the structure of the building. Walls are lined with painted wood panels and smooth sheet aluminium.

The stairs leading to the upper level feature textured aluminium and the wall of the stairwell is lined with Granitall. The varied surface treatments continue in the offices and showroom: lacquered and varnished wood panels and yellow-painted wall tiles with bronze-covered filter mesh and expanded and folded aluminium give a sense of material intrigue. Carpeting was custom-designed by King Miranda and made by Interface. General offices are located on the upper level of the two-storey addition to the main building.

Wooden roof beams have been expertly restored and façades cleaned to enhance a feeling of light and space in the showroom which is large enough to display several configurations of the Palo Alto exhibition system. Applicazioni wanted to achieve two objectives with the renovation: to make people talk about its new showroom; and to demonstrate its own credibility in the art of exhibiting products. La Casa Rossa succeeds on both counts, and the company is currently in a phase of further expansion.

MILAN-BASED INDUSTRIAL DESIGNERS KING MIRANDA HAVE MADE AN EXHIBITION OF A WOODEN-ROOFED WAX FACTORY IN THE ITALIAN COUNTRYSIDE FOR A MANUFACTURER OF DISPLAY SYSTEMS.

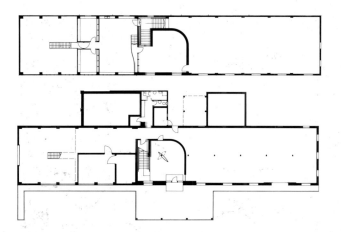

Above: The entrance for visitors under a cantilevered roof offers a glimpse of the sculptural steel totem in the lobby area which cleverly disguises an ungainly steel column.

Left: The exterior of La Casa Rossa: the original wax factory supplemented by a two-storey block at its side.

Opposite: Ground- and first-floor plans.

La Casa Rossa is a rich study in material and surface detail. Original wooden roof beams are exposed in the upper floor gallery which displays the Palo Alto exhibition system. The walls of the simply expressed staircase leading up to this display space are lined with textured aluminium. Other treatments include bronze-coloured filter mesh and painted wooden panels and wall tiles. Opposite: A rusted steel wall dominates the lobby area.

"TO MAXIMIZE THE EMPHASIS ON HOW THE
EXHIBITION SYSTEM WORKS WITHIN
ARCHITECTURAL SPACE, WE WANTED TO KEEP
THE SURFACES AS SIMPLE AS POSSIBLE. THE
MORE TAUT AND CLEAN THEY ARE, THE MORE
AN INHERENT RICHNESS GIVES THEM STRENGTH.
BUT THE PROCESS TO ACHIEVE THIS
SIMPLICITY IS ACTUALLY VERY COMPLEX."
PERRY KING, KING MIRANDA ASSOCIATI

TOGASHI
DESIGN STUDIO

KASHIN STORE

TOKYO, JAPAN

In a tiny neighbourhood of embassies and foreign residences close to Roppongi, one of Toyko's liveliest nightlife districts, the Kashin emporium sells flowers and incense from a single outlet. The word Kashin literally means "Heart of the Flower"; the store combines two synergistic commodities which are close to nature in an old two-storey wooden residence converted with finesse by Togashi Design Studio.

KASHIN IS TWO SHOPS IN ONE: A SUBTLE BLEND OF COLOURS, SHAPES AND MATERIALS BASED ON TRADITIONAL FORMS OF JAPANESE ARCHITECTURE WHICH SELLS BOTH FLOWERS AND INCENSE.

The client had been in the floral business for years but wished to supplement that trade with a business developing new kinds of incense. The aim was to cater for a growing interest in incense among urban Japanese youth. Instead of creating two separate shops within a space just 5.4 metres in width, Togashi designed a single glazed entrance framed in green zinc sheet which leads into a 70 square-metre ground floor combining flower shop on the left and incense shop on the right beneath two curved ceilings.

The incense shop is the narrower of the two, measuring 9 metres in length by 1.8 metres in width. Its atmosphere is dim and mildly humid to preserve the aromas of the incense. Furnishings throughout are minimal. The reason, says designer Katsuhiko Togashi, is not to follow contemporary minimalist design fashion but to reflect *Sukiya*, the Japanese architectural style based on proportional harmony which was developed during the sixteenth century.

Simplistic modern design can often be flat and prosaic, says Togashi. *Sukiya*, on the other hand, freely mixes a rich and complex variety of materials but achieves a spirit of calm and tranquillity as a result. Copper sheet, cherrywood floors and fitments, coloured concrete, and painted and textured mortar-coated plasterboard achieve a harmony within Kashin's interior spaces.

At the rear of the ground floor, a seasonal flower-adorned stairwell draws on the idea of *Tokonoma*, a decorative alcove which evolved from the traditional Buddhist altar. The staircase linking the two floors is itself a delicate visual play on the Japanese paper-folding art of *origami*. The 60 square-metre upper level is devoted to a classroom where visitors can learn flower arranging or participate in an incense ceremony; cherrywood desking, flooring and cabinets enhance a quality environment.

Kashin is an unusual achievement. It combines the sale of flowers and incense in a way which respects their different merchandising needs but presents a natural and holistic vision for the store as a whole. And despite its restricted dimensions – total floor area is just under 130 square metres – Kashin has an expansive interior feel, reflecting the wide streets of the mid-town Tokyo district in which it is situated.

Above: The Kashin flower and incense shops have distinct identities but are combined in one outlet and share a single glazed façade 5.4 metres in width and topped with green zinc sheet. The flower shop is on the left, the incense store on the right. Both sit beneath curved ceilings. Left: Front façade at night.

Above: The ground-floor
incense shop is long and
narrow, 9 metres in length
and 1.8 metres wide.
It is dimly lit and mildly humid
to preserve the aromas of the
incense which is displayed
in custom-designed cabinets
and drawers.
Opposite: View from the back
of the ground-floor flower
shop. Here the ambience is
lighter and more spacious.

"THE CONCEPT FOLLOWS THE TRADITIONAL
JAPANESE ARCHITECTURAL STYLE OF *SUKIYA*:
THIS COMBINES MANY DIFFERENT MATERIALS
TO CREATE A HIGH-DENSITY VISUAL IMAGE
WHICH AT THE SAME TIME REMAINS TRANQUIL."
KATSUHIKO TOGASHI

Left: The stairwell linking the two floors of the Kashin emporium is a delicate visual play on origami, the Japanese art of paper-folding.

Opposite: The upper-floor classroom where visitors can learn flower arranging or participate in incense ceremonies. The warm cherrywood cabinets, flooring and table sit beneath a ceiling of smooth cloth-coated and painted plasterboard.

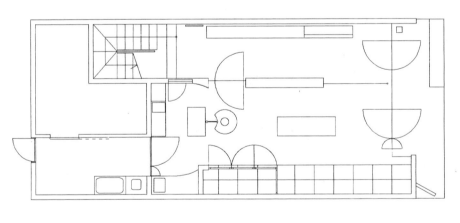

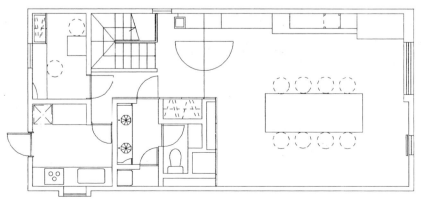

Below: Plan showing the vertical and circular nature
of the scheme to mitigate the constrained space.
1 Display shelves 2 Changing room 3 Hanging display
4 Steel rods.

35

O'HERLIHY & WARNER ARCHITECTS

HARRIET DORN CLOTHING STORE

SANTA MONICA, USA

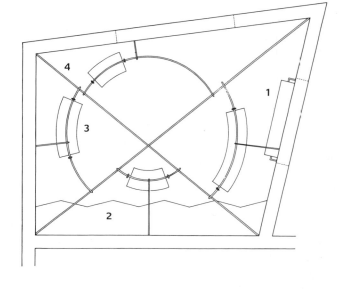

Located in Frank Gehry's Edgemar development in Santa Monica, the Harriet Dorn women's clothing store shows just what can be done in tailoring a small space which is suffused with sunlight. Architects Lorcan O'Herlihy and Richard Warner have created an appealing retail interior in a 290 square-foot trapezoidal space,

FASHION IS PLACED IN SUSPENDED ANIMATION BENEATH A FABRIC-FILTERED SKYLIGHT IN THIS UPWARDLY MOBILE CALIFORNIAN CLOTHING STORE WHICH MAKES A VIRTUE OF A SMALL SPACE.

with a diameter of just 20 feet and a height of 52 feet. Due to the compression of space, they developed a vertical plan which "led to the section as the primary generator of the architecture". Instead of a progression of rooms leading one to another, the architects established a series of stacked spaces reaching up to a skylight which floods the room with sunlight. To filter this light, a nylon parachute hangs above the void. This solution lowers the ceiling to more manageable proportions but still suggests the vertical scale of the space. As many components as possible are suspended from above to leave the small concrete floor area clear. Adjustable plywood and metal clothes racks, for example, are hung from curved rods attached to the cross bracing – hot-rolled steel rods, five-eighths of an inch thick.

Along the back of the store, a folding wall of light birch plywood made by cabinetmaker Steve Shelley provides exhibition and storage space as well as a changing room. Display shelves are also made of birch. Lighting is indirect: uplighters mounted high on the walls reflect light off the nylon parachute; incandescent fixtures over the storage unit wash the back wall with light.

The overall effect is pleasingly distinctive, the combination of light birch, metal rods and translucent fabric in the store providing a sense of enclosure without inducing claustrophobia. The slimness of the budget – just $8,000 – matched the smallness of the space. But O'Herlihy & Warner have shown that breadth of vision can be turned on its side and sent skywards.

Opposite: A series of stacked spaces reach up towards a sun-filled skylight spanned by a nylon parachute in this tiny Santa Monica clothing store.

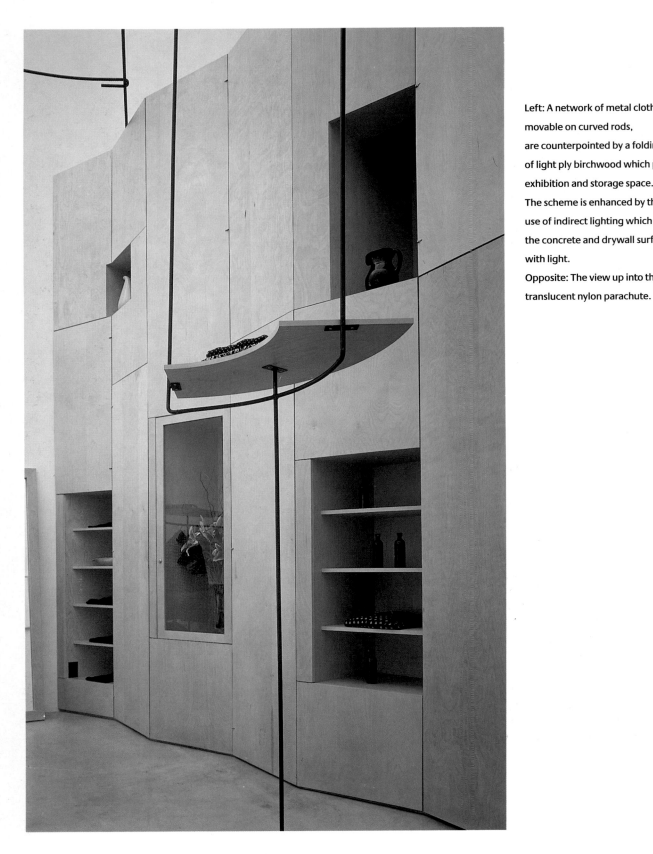

Left: A network of metal clothes racks,
movable on curved rods,
are counterpointed by a folding wall
of light ply birchwood which provides
exhibition and storage space.
The scheme is enhanced by the clever
use of indirect lighting which washes
the concrete and drywall surfaces
with light.
Opposite: The view up into the
translucent nylon parachute.

6

**THE WORLD'S FIRST COMPLETELY
AUTOMATED BANK BRANCHES HAVE OPENED
IN HOLLAND WITH NATURAL, ORGANIC
ENVIRONMENTS AIMING TO DETER
VANDALISM THROUGH GOOD DESIGN.**

It is a problem facing retail banks all over the world: how can they serve dispersed communities with a local branch network, but not run up crippling staff overheads? Holland's third largest banking group, the Internationale Nederlanden (ING) Bank, believes it has found an answer. In a radical and far-sighted experiment, it has opened two fully automated bank branches at Rijkswijk and Amersfoort, which offer a wide range of services yet are completely unmanned.

British design consultancy Fitch, which already enjoyed a close relationship with ING Bank, was chosen to design prototype environments identified in the brief as a new banking cross-breed between a normal, staffed branch and an automated lobby. The project began with an analysis of customer needs: the length of time to conduct any transaction was plotted on a graph and the design took shape from there. Speedy functions such as cash withdrawal from an ATM (Automatic Teller Machine) were placed at the front of the branch. Slower, more inter-active tasks, such as conducting an information search on loans or mortgage rates, were situated in a more private area at the back of the branch. A cheque printing facility – the Dutch, uniquely, do not use cheque books – was placed in the centre of the branch. This front-to-back, fast-to-slow time agenda was underpinned by an interior design scheme with a colour palette which progresses from a sense of immediacy and efficiency at the front (red for fast and functional transactions) to a more mellow and comfortable ambience at the back (terra-cotta hues for slower and more in-depth activities).

In the approximately 60 square-metre space of each branch, some 50 per cent of the floor area was set aside for non-public space in order to accommodate the large automated bank-ing machines. A second space division concerned the distinction between banking technolo-gy (represented by a wall of machines on the left as you enter) and banking information (by a series of framed posters on the right). The solid blockwork technology wall, faced with painted panels, is modular in design with linear grooves so that sections can be replaced with new machines without disturbing the overall visual effect.

The two branches open automatically at 6am and stay open seven days a week until 10pm. They are visited three times a day by security teams but are otherwise completely unstaffed. Entry is by magnetic card – any card, it does not have to be an ING Bank card. This precaution deters young children and vagrants, but not potential customers who may be visiting the bank for the first time.

Dutch customers have a strong cultural aversion to the use of security cameras. So a key pri-ority was to develop a language of design and materials which would deter vandalism through the intrinsic quality of the environment. The floor plan was kept simple so that there would be no dark corners to hide in. Lighting was set at a high level, especially in the entrance area. Use of linear halogen fittings, tungsten wall-washers and white sodium downlights with good colour rendering help to give the interior a comfortable ambience. At the back of the branch, the plan is rounded so that the interior "hugs" the customer. The curved wall visually and archi-tecturally shortens the space and makes it more relaxed. So far the design strategy has been successful: not a single incident of vandalism has been reported, proving that the futuristic vision of a totally unmanned bank is more than just a Dutch pipedream.

Above left: The inviting exterior of the automated, unstaffed ING Bank reveals
an open, brightly lit interior with a language of design and materials aimed at
reassuring the visitor. Entry is achieved via a magnetic card swipe.

Above right: The view from the more private carpeted area at the back of the
branch to the front door. The plan is simple and clearly delineated with no dark
corners for people to hide in – a new banking cross-breed between a traditional
staffed branch and an automated lobby.

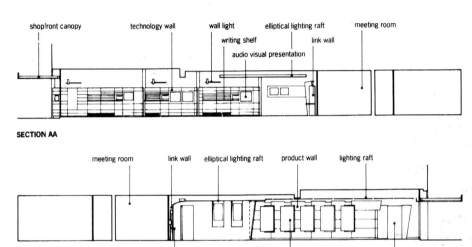

SECTION AA

shopfront canopy · technology wall · wall light · elliptical lighting raft · meeting room · writing shelf · link wall · audio visual presentation

SECTION BB

meeting room · link wall · elliptical lighting raft · product wall · lighting raft · writing shelf · product panel · automated poster display

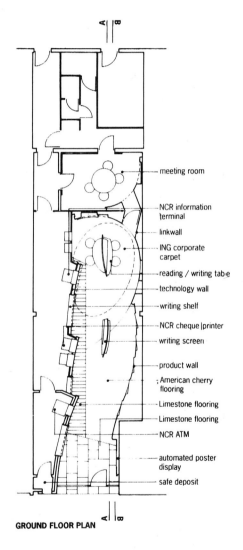

meeting room
NCR information terminal
linkwall
ING corporate carpet
reading / writing table
technology wall
writing shelf
NCR cheque printer
writing screen
product wall
American cherry flooring
Limestone flooring
Limestone flooring
NCR ATM
automated poster display
safe deposit

GROUND FLOOR PLAN

Opposite: Inside the main entrance, Automatic Teller machines are placed closest to the front of the branch for immediate customer needs. Next in line are cheque-printing machines. The blockwork technology wall on the left is modular in design so that sections can be replaced without disturbing the visual balance of the interior. The colour scheme reflects the transition from swift transactions at the front to more in-depth, contemplative activities at the rear.

Above: Sections through the built interior.

Far left: Ground-floor plan showing the organization of elements.

Left: A curved American cherry timber wall encases the intriguing poster communication of ING Bank. Lighting and finishes aim to deter vandalism.

Retail **137**

SOICHI MIZUTANI

IMAGINE
SHOWROOM

FUKUODA,
JAPAN

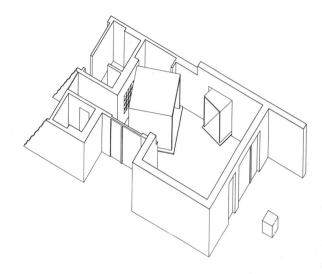

On a hill site in Fukuoda, this two-floor information technology showroom reflects Japanese designer Soichi Mizutani's fascination with manipulating scale and space by inserting cube-form elements into the interior. These cubes or boxes are a recurrent theme in Mizutani's work, providing a mechanism to create intrinsic richness without resorting to surface ornament. In some schemes, such as the Restaurant Setsugekka (see page 84), they are delineated in space with almost invisible subtlety. But in Mizutani's showrooms, such as this one for the Imagine company, they are much more overtly placed in an interior landscape of the designer's own composition which both arrests and suggests space.

Both floors of the Imagine showroom are designed to receive visitors. At the ground-floor level, measuring 103.9 square metres, you enter the environment through a glass box, then discover an aluminium cube and glimpse a red-lacquered box out on a terrace. The upper level contains boxes of light, yellow-lacquered cubic shelves and square skylights in 96.4 square metres of space.

It is in the playful but restrained interrelationship of light, space, material and cubic volume that Mizutani, who runs a design office of growing reputation in Tokyo, avoids sterility and makes a geometry of emptiness so appealing.

THIS JAPANESE SHOWROOM DESIGNED BY SOICHI MIZUTANI IS AN INTERIOR EXERCISE IN LIGHT, SPACE AND CUBIC FORM WHICH PLAYS ON THE IDEA OF THE BOX IN INFORMATION TECHNOLOGY.

Above: Perspective diagram showing the angled cube in the ground-floor plan.
Opposite: The cube form repeats throughout the two floors of the Imagine showroom in overt elements (top) and in shelves, skylights and entrances (below).

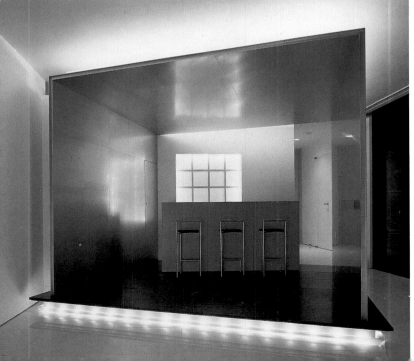

HABITAT'S WAREHOUSE-BASIC AESTHETIC INFLUENCED A GENERATION BEFORE BECOMING LOCKED IN A TIME-WARP. NOW A SOFTER, MORE DOMESTIC APPROACH HAS BREATHED NEW LIFE INTO ITS STORES.

DIN ASSOCIATES

HABITAT STORES

LONDON
(KING'S ROAD)
AND BROMLEY,
UK

Habitat, established in 1964 by Terence Conran, has a special place in post-war British design history as the chain store which played a key role in revolutionizing the lifestyles of an entire generation with affordable, well-designed household basics and furnishings. Today, after a period in the doldrums, Habitat is back in the vanguard of taste-making following its acquisition by retail giant IKEA and the introduction of a new retail design concept by Din Associates – the first environmental design firm to be appointed by Habitat since Conran's original blueprint 30 years ago.

Rasshied Din describes the project as "one of the most difficult design challenges we have faced". Habitat was regarded with great affection by many people but by the start of the 1990s the stores were looking tired and trapped in a time-warp. Conran was no longer in charge, new management was in place, and the product lines had been largely redeveloped. Yet the Habitat retail environment still bore the old, austere industrial-warehouse stamp for want of a new direction. The potential conflict between tradition and innovation was crystallized in Habitat's flagship store on the King's Road in London. This is where it had all begun. This is where it all needed to change. Din took an evolutionary approach which he describes as "non-design". He introduced a softer, more domestic feel to the store while respecting the architectural character of the building and retaining trademark Habitat elements such as the complex configuration of the central metal staircase and the brick merchandise bays.

The exterior of the store was completely refurbished, with a bronze canopy and limestone cladding added to give presence and help to locate the entrance. Internally, the 18,000 square-feet of space organized on three floors was enhanced with warm tones, upgraded materials, and the use of curves to soften the environment. A long curving wall was introduced to create circulation from left to right along the rear of the store. Sandstone and American white oak floors add to the sense of quality and freshness. Merchandising was rethought, too, with layout and displays more dense and less precious to create a more tactile experience for shoppers. Significantly, Conran has given the new look for Habitat King's Road his blessing.

Din Associates has since gone on to introduce the new, more relaxed format in other Habitat stores. At Bromley in Kent, Habitat's move into a new shopping centre development as anchor tenant gave Din the opportunity to work straight from concrete shell on a two-level, 11,000 square-foot city concept store. Habitat city concept stores are aimed at the urban shopper and have an emphasis on accessories. Din Associates developed a design strategy at Bromley to exploit the store's unusually large windows, introducing a dramatic staircase into the void to enable light and vision from many angles and to encourage circulation to all parts of the store.

The King's Road and Bromley stores show that Terence Conran's original mission for Habitat – to give everyone a decent salad bowl – lives on in the 1990s. Skilful contemporary retouching by Rasshied Din has opened a new chapter for a legendary design name many feared might be consigned to the scrapbook of retailing history.

Left: A dramatic staircase penetrates the light-filled void of the new Habitat city-concept store in Bromley, Kent, uniting the two levels of the development and enhancing circulation. Below: Exterior of the Bromley Habitat. Bottom: Habitat's King's Road flagship store has been given a subtle update by Din Associates to create a more tactile experience for shoppers.

"THE ASSOCIATION BETWEEN TERENCE CONRAN AND HABITAT IS PART OF DESIGN HISTORY. WE ARE THE FIRST DESIGN CONSULTANCY IN 30 YEARS TO BE APPOINTED. OUR CHALLENGE WAS TO DEVELOP AND UPDATE HABITAT INTO A MODERN AND EFFICIENT RETAILER, WHILST RETAINING ITS CHARACTER AND STYLE."

DIN ASSOCIATES

WHEN A FAMILY FIRM OF VIOLIN MAKERS
IN KARLSRUHE WITHDREW FROM A SITE
FACING A BUSY SHOPPING PRECINCT TO
OCCUPY A MORE SECLUDED SPACE,
A NEW INTERIOR SCHEME GUARANTEED
CONTINUED INTEREST.

ANDREAS WINKLER

PADEWET
MUSIC HOUSE

KARLSRUHE,
GERMANY

Andreas Winkler's scheme for a Karlsruhe music centre makes a virtue out of necessity. The client, an old family firm of violin makers, decided to withdraw from premises looking directly on to the Kaiserstrasse, Karlsruhe's busiest pedestrian shopping precinct, and occupy a rear space which looks on to a courtyard. The specialist business of making, repairing and selling musical instruments was not really dependent on passing trade, so the firm let out the front of the store to a fashion business more suited to a frontline position and withdrew to a more secluded space parallel to the pedestrian shopping zone.

Winkler's interior compensates for the loss of a shopfront on to a busy thoroughfare with a thoughtful approach which makes the most of the new arrangement. The new facility has three main areas: a music shop, selling sheet music, literature and concert tickets; an instruments department, specializing in stringed and plucked wooden instruments; and a small workshop for repairing instruments. A covered passageway links music shop and instruments department.

In the music shop, beechwood fitments holding sheet music and literature for sale stand on a black granite floor. A special folding glass wall held by handmade steel elements displays further merchandise. Above, a wave-like element in five shades of coloured laminated plastic (blue, turquoise, lilac, yellow and green) is suspended from the ceiling, cleverly concealing fluorescent lighting and loudspeakers. This colour scheme is reflected throughout the music centre and in its new graphic identity. In the instruments department, the display of five coloured glass cases indicates that each suspended instrument has its own colour. The room is elongated and narrow. To avoid a tube-like effect, Winkler explains that he angled instrument cupboards and glass cases "so that they project like saw-teeth into the room". This area is carpeted for acoustic reasons, and punctuated with square desks which can be converted to tables for instruments by raising the leather-clad sides. The instrument department is separated from a small, functional workshop by a sand-blasted glass door with visible steel frame.

In colour and tone, the Padewet music centre is a calm and effective place in which to discuss and sell products associated with music. The details and lines of the interior do not detract from the beauty of the instruments themselves. The old violin makers are unlikely to miss the bustle of the Kaiserstrasse.

Above: Cupboards and glass cases in the long, narrow instrument department continue
the colour-coding evident in the music shop and are angled into the room to avoid
a tube-like effect.

Opposite: The music shop selling sheet music, literature and concert tickets uses a wave-
like ceiling element in five shades of coloured laminate to conceal fluorescent lighting and
loudspeakers. Merchandise is stored on beech fitments and there is a black granite floor.

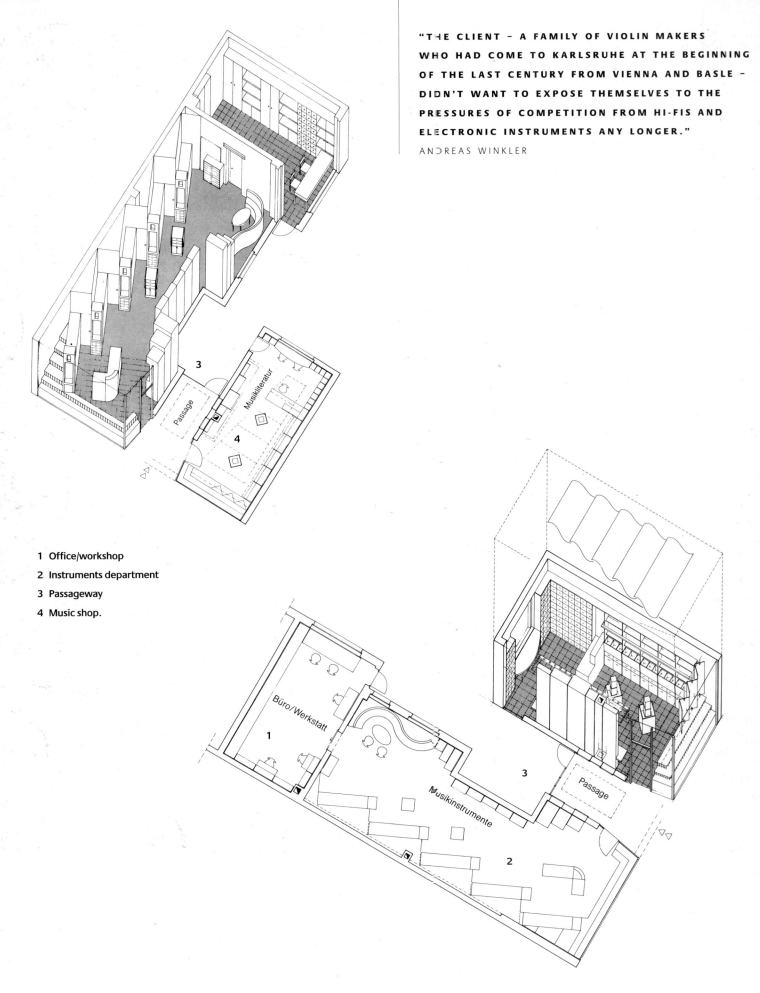

"THE CLIENT – A FAMILY OF VIOLIN MAKERS WHO HAD COME TO KARLSRUHE AT THE BEGINNING OF THE LAST CENTURY FROM VIENNA AND BASLE – DIDN'T WANT TO EXPOSE THEMSELVES TO THE PRESSURES OF COMPETITION FROM HI-FIS AND ELECTRONIC INSTRUMENTS ANY LONGER."
ANDREAS WINKLER

1 Office/workshop
2 Instruments department
3 Passageway
4 Music shop.

Above: The carpeted
instruments department,
which is separated from the
repair workshop by
a sand-blasted glass door.

Opposite: The flowing, ethereal quality of Go Silk's fashion is reflected in the silk ribbons hanging from the ceiling, and the gently curving wooden walls in the central passageway of the showroom (top and below left). These walls are attached to the standard drywall structure by steel angles and screws and are lit by recessed fluorescent lighting to give the impression of floating architectural elements. They have a hand-applied silver-leaf on the side facing the passageway and a deep maroon stain on the side facing the modestly-finished showrooms (below right).

TOD WILLIAMS, BILLIE TSIEN AND ASSOCIATES

GO SILK SHOWROOM

NEW YORK, USA

Right in the frantic metropolitan heart of Manhattan, there is a soothing sanctuary for harrassed fashion buyers. The new showrooms of the Go Silk fashion company have been calmly designed by architect Tod Williams Bille Tsien and Associates using modest materials in a spare, subdued style to create an environment which gently beckons rather than bombards the visitor. Architect and client, Go Silk president Jerry Hirsch, have a working relationship which dates back 12 years: Williams and Tsien designed Hirsch's first showroom in New York, his Greenwich Village townhouse, and a Go Silk store in San Francisco before tacking this latest project. "Since we know each other so well," says project architect Martin Finio, "there was really no brief – just confidence and friendship."

THE FLOWING SERENITY OF GO SILK'S FASHION MERCHANDISE IS REFLECTED IN THE CALM LINES AND SUBDUED COLOURS OF THE COMPANY'S NEW MANHATTAN SHOWROOM WHICH USES MODEST MATERIALS IN A RICH WAY.

This is reflected in the experimental quality of the 7,500 square-foot space. Sloping wooden walls in a curving central space create a passageway from a small reception area to a series of five individual showrooms. This central avenue has a flowing, ethereal simplicity which captures the essence of Go Silk's merchandise in silk ribbons draped from the ceiling and running the length of the room, and in recessed fluorescent lighting behind the tops and bottoms of the projecting walls which give the impression of floating architectural elements.

Inside the showrooms, there is a sense of humility in the way the interior displays the clothing, with brushed aluminium bars, multi-panelled wooden screens and aluminium-tube furniture designed by Jonas Milder reflecting a depth of interest in materials and finishes. Throughout the Go Silk showrooms, the architects have tried to stretch the aesthetic boundaries of humble, environment-friendly materials. The layered plywood doors, for example, which tie the environment together visually, have been given a simple, rich maroon stain: closed, they enable each showroom to function independently; open, they create a large show space with a central runway. Floor tiles in the passageway are made of coir (derived from coconut husks), and in the showroom are made of recycled tyres. The reception desk and conference room table are made of flakeboard and particle board; tack boards are newsprint-reconstituted fibreboard.

A sense of emptiness and quietness was an essential objective, say the architects, to make buyers feel more relaxed. Jerry Hirsch describes the space as "the decompression chamber". As the *Architectural Record* pointed out, in reviewing the interior: "In the razzle-dazzle go-go world of fashion, sometimes the best way to get people's attention is to whisper."

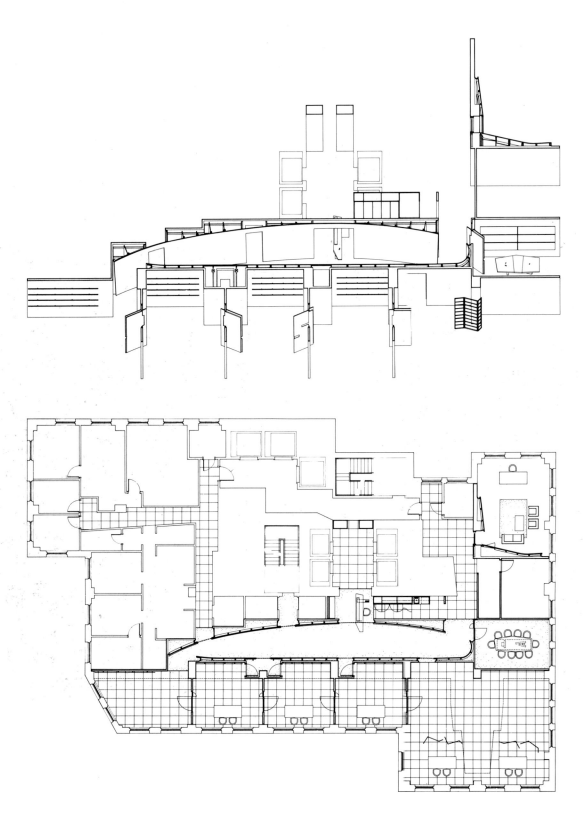

Left: Exploded axonometric showing the key elements – such as free-standing screens, wall-hung bars and tack boards – to be found in the five show-rooms off the central passage-way.

Below: Floor plan describing the entire layout of the showroom.

Opposite, left: A vista through the showrooms captures the sense of emptiness achieved by the use of simple, environment-friendly materials.

Opposite, right: Wooden screens and aluminium elements provide a calm backdrop to the merchandise in one of the showrooms.

"THE WHOLE IDEA WAS TO MAKE A SERENE SPACE,
TO MAKE AN EMPTY SPACE, TO STAY QUIET."
TOD WILLIAMS BILLE TSIEN AND ASSOCIATES

SOTTSASS ASSOCIATI

ERG CONVENIENCE STORE

BERGAMO, ITALY

In the 1980s, the Memphis design movement founded by Ettore Sottsass took many of its visual cues from the 1950s Italian *cappuccino* bar. In the 1990s, this project by Sottsass Associati – a highly visible prototype for a chain of forecourt convenience stores for the Erg petrol company – draws its inspiration from the 1950s American diner.

The name of the aluminium-clad store is La Bottega. Its upper parapet is reserved for oversized icons, also made of aluminium: these are back-lit to promote the services inside. The exterior system of flexible, modular aluminium cladding panels enables existing gas station buildings and structures in the Erg network to be converted into new convenience stores to suit new demands. This kind of flexibility is being increasingly prized by the petrol giants who must now maximize earnings from their gas station sites in addition to petrol sales. To improve on the cluttered and confused image common to roadside convenience stores, Sottsass Associati developed a new plan for the forecourt using colours, signs and materials to suggest order and cleanliness.

The same search for clarity is evident inside. The store interior has been designed as "an accessorized box" so that one individual can control the gas sales on the forecourt plus a small market and bar inside from a single cash desk. Sightlines have been carefully devised to enable this lone cashier to remain in control. Walls display merchandise, divided into different categories and topped by a continuous strip of colour photographs promoting the products on sale. Large niches house such facilities as restrooms, telephones and other services. You can stop off and send a fax at La Bottega.

Green acid colours and patterned motifs suggest the Memphis heritage of the design team. But more than a decade on from the avant-garde outrage of the Milan Furniture Fair, the style is muted and practical, bringing a decorative clarity and order to the greasy forecourt of the Italian gas station. And in the use of giant roadside symbols which require no words of explanation, the design also suggests a bold way forward for multinational petrol chains trying to communicate across national boundaries.

THE ITALIAN PETROL STATION FORECOURT HAS BEEN SMARTENED UP IN FINE STYLE BY THE INTRODUCTION OF A NEW ALUMINIUM-CLAD CONVENIENCE STORE WITH OUTSIZED ICONS SHOUTING ITS WARES.

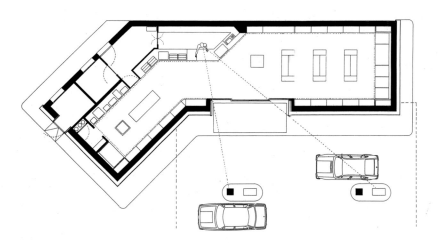

Left: Plan showing the retail engineering of the environment – one sales attendant has the sightlines to control sales on the forecourt as well as run the store inside from the cash desk.
Opposite, top: A view of the Erg convenience store through the petrol station forecourt shows the eye-catching appeal of its back-lit, over-sized icons made of aluminium.
Opposite, below: The Sottsass exterior combines familiar post-Memphis decorative patterning within a clever system of modular aluminium panels.

"THE EXTERIOR IS A FLEXIBLE MODULAR CLADDING
SYSTEM OF ALUMINIUM PANELS WITH AN INTEGRATED,
ILLUMINATED GRAPHIC STRIP PRESENTING OVERSIZED
SYMBOLS OF THE VARIOUS PRODUCTS AND SERVICES
AVAILABLE WITHIN. IT WAS INSPIRED BY THE
AMERICAN DINERS OF THE 1950S."

SOTTSASS ASSOCIATI

Inside the Erg convenience store, order and
clarity mark an improvement on the usual
standard of roadside Italian stores.
A continuous strip of colour photographs
runs round the perimeter (opposite),
highlighting the products on sale below
and playing with reality and illusion.
The bold graphic clarity of the exterior
is extended to interior fax facilities (above).

YASUO KONDO

TOYOTA CAR
SHOWROOM

OSAKA, JAPAN

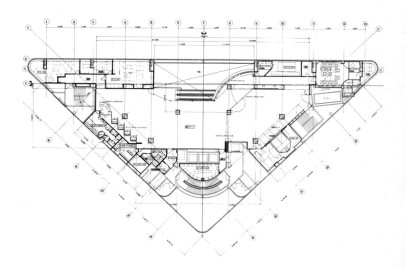

The automobile showroom sits uneasily between oil-splattered garage forecourt and conventional retail environment. Cars have arguably been the single most important artefact in our lives this century, but they have very rarely been displayed and sold in settings to reflect their true power and influence. Amlux in Osaka, however, is seeking to change all that: it is an entire "Toyota town" on three levels where, according to classic Japanese over-statement, car lovers can gather "to dream about a wonderful life enriched with cars, and deepen a love for cars".

THE THIRD LEVEL OF AN ADVANCED TOYOTA CAR SHOW-ROOM IN OSAKA - MODELLED ON THE IDEA OF VISITING A TOWN - IS A PLACE WHERE FIELD MEETS SKY AND FLUORESCENT LOUVRES FORM THE CLOUDS.

In architectural terms alone, Amlux Osaka is a stunning if somewhat bizarre achievement. On each of its three floors, a different designer has been commissioned to project a distinct personality. The first level – the Gallery, designed by Fumio Enomoto – combines liquid-crystal displays with a terrarium garden. The second level – the Campo, designed by stage artist Kappah Senoh – is a complete reproduction of an ancient Italian village with the new Toyota models set amid stone pavements, towers, churches and cafés. The third level – the Field, shown here – is the work of Tokyo designer Yasuo Kondo, whose clients range from the Comme des Garçons fashion chain to the Hitachi computer group. Kondo's brief was complex: to create a coherent and interchangeable setting in a 1,192 square-metre space on one level for a range of display, information, amusement and event functions. The Field features new sports cars, an autodrome, a techno-theatre and an information bank.

Kondo's scheme interprets the idea of the Field as situated beneath a sky at the very top of the building. To frame the space, the direction of the walls is divided into vertical, horizontal and diagonal axes. Three different reflective materials – specially treated and sand-blasted sheet glass, aluminium panels and coated medium-density fibreboard – are used for each axis so that the environment appears deep and spacious. To enhance this spatial concept, the flooring is coated with urethane resin and the ceiling comprises waves of fluorescent lamp louvres to suggest cloud formations.

Working with the environmental design department of Daiko Advertising and with consultants Lighting Planners Associates, Kondo succeeded in filling the Field with flat, soft light, so creating a very natural and human ambience half a world away from the polluting industrial realities of motor car production.

Opposite: Plan showing Yasuo Kondo's scheme for the third level of the Amlux Toyota showroom in Osaka, known as The Field. Above: A view of the softly-lit main showroom. Overleaf: The main showroom in The Field sits beneath "clouds" formed by waves of fluorescent lamp louvres. Wall treatments use three different reflective materials and are divided into vertical, horizontal and diagonal axes. The floor is coated in urethane resin.

THE COLOGNE FLAGSHIP FOR A WORLDWIDE
REFIT OF THE BALLY SHOE AND CLOTHING
CHAIN HAS BEEN DESIGNED BY ANDRÉE
PUTMAN OF ECART WITH WARM TONES,
SMOOTH SURFACES AND SPIRAL FORMS.

313

ECART

BALLY STORE

COLOGNE,
GERMANY

This flagship Bally shoe and clothing store in Cologne is the
style-setter for a new worldwide look for the chain. Devised
by French designer Andrée Putman of Ecart with a characteristic blend of function and elegance, it aims to assert
Bally's image and quality in a way which uses architectural
form to raise the status of the objects on display. Shoes are
placed in the ground-floor space on a luminous sand-blasted
glass staircase, and on a walnut and metallic mesh spiral akin to a helical ramp.
Complementary spiral forms focus the product presentation in a way which is self-consciously
aesthetic but never ostentatious or austere.

Warm tones predominate. Shoppers enter the two-floor, 300 square-metre store through a
glass sheet façade framed by beige stone and featuring the square pattern of a copper-
coloured metallic portico with the white enamelled Bally logotype at its top. This emblem
reappears in painted letters on exterior and interior blinds made of off-white canvas cloth, and,
indirectly lit, on the stone façade frame. Inside, smooth, soft surfaces and contrasting
materials suggest a comfortable and intimate domestic environment. A thick wooden parquet floor is covered with a woollen rug with linen border. Display cases are made of horn-
beam wood. Chairs are made of walnut and cloth. Changing rooms are integrated into the
architecture, closed by cotton curtains on a copper-coloured metallic rail.

In this relaxed environment, direct and indirect lighting plays a fundamental role. A pinkish,
spiral-form ceiling fixture, made of resin and reflecting the form of the shoe display spiral
below, casts an indirect, opalescent glow over the store. Ecart plans to develop this spiral light
on walls and in display cases as well as on ceilings throughout the Bally chain. Low-voltage
halogen ceiling spots cast a direct, sparkling display light.

The Cologne store devotes its upper floor to women's clothing because, says Andrée
Putman, women are more motivated shoppers than men and climbing a staircase may be a
barrier to the male psyche. The staircase is a key architectural element – "an invitation for discovery" with access discreetly protected by a theatrical blue-green cotton curtain, held back
by a small luminous resin spiral.

As a flagship store, Cologne belongs to the premier league of Bally shops. Ecart is grading its
new worldwide retail image for Bally within three hierarchies: flagship stores, prestige stores
and national stores. Each will have different staircase and flooring treatments. In flagship
stores, for example, the luminous stairs will be part of the architecture, but in prestige stores
they will be free-standing and in national stores they will simply be monumental pieces of furniture. This is a most accomplished and sophisticated refit, reflecting Andrée Putman's proven
skill at teasing high style out of simple, accessible material forms without regressing into hard-
edged high-tech.

Top: The spiral is the uniting image in the new flagship Bally store in Cologne. A walnut and metallic mesh helical ramp to display shoes is complemented above by a spiral-form ceiling light made of resin. The floor is a thick wooden parquet.

Above: Contrasting materials on the exterior façade – glass, stone, canvas and copper-coloured metal – are a prelude

Above: Spiral forms for display unit and lighting symbolize a soft-edged and sophisticated approach.

Opposite: Shoes on parade at Bally in a luminous sand-blasted glass staircase which leads to the women's clothing department on the upper floor.

1

1

SHIN TAKAMATSU ARCHITECT AND ASSOCIATES

KUNIBIKI MESSE

MATSUE, JAPAN

2

VOLKER GIENCKE & COMPANY

CHURCH OF AIGEN IM ENNSTAL

AIGEN, AUSTRIA

3

JEAN NOUVEL ET ASSOCIÉS

OPERA HOUSE

LYONS, FRANCE

4

SMITH-MILLER & HAWKINSON

ROTUNDA GALLERY

NEW YORK, USA

5

RENZO PIANO BUILDING WORKSHOP

KANSAI INTERNATIONAL AIR TERMINAL

OSAKA BAY, JAPAN

6

ANTOINE PREDOCK

AMERICAN HERITAGE CENTER AND ART MUSEUM

WYOMING, USA

7

NICHOLAS GRIMSHAW & PARTNERS

WATERLOO INTERNATIONAL TERMINAL

LONDON, UK

8

BEHNISCH & PARTNER

VOCATIONAL SCHOOL COMPLEX

ÖHRINGEN, GERMANY

9

BENTHEM CROUWEL ARCHITECTS

NETHERLANDS DESIGN INSTITUTE

AMSTERDAM, THE NETHERLANDS

10

HELLMUTH, OBATA & KASSABAUM (HOK)

REORGANIZED CHURCH OF JESUS CHRIST

MISSOURI, USA

11

KISHO KUROKAWA ARCHITECT & ASSOCIATES

MUSEUM OF MODERN ART/PREFECTURE MUSEUM

WAKAYAMA, JAPAN

12

MICHAEL HOPKINS & PARTNERS

GLYNDEBOURNE OPERA HOUSE

SUSSEX, UK

13

PEI COBB FREED & PARTNERS

UNITED STATES HOLOCAUST MEMORIAL MUSEUM

WASHINGTON DC, USA

13

14

SANTIAGO CALATRAVA

TGV RAILWAY STATION

LYONS, FRANCE

15

SIR NORMAN FOSTER AND PARTNERS

CARRÉ D'ART

NÎMES, FRANCE

16

JO COENEN & CO. ARCHITECTS

NETHERLANDS ARCHITECTURE INSTITUTE

ROTTERDAM, THE NETHERLANDS

17

EVANS AND SHALEV

TATE GALLERY

ST IVES, CORNWALL, UK

12

4

3

P U B L I C

GROWING CULTURAL AND COMMERCIAL COMPETITION BETWEEN CITIES AND REGIONS IS REFLECTED IN A NEW GENERATION OF OPEN PUBLIC INTERIORS WHICH ARE SYMBOLIZING CIVIC ASPIRATIONS WHILE DISSOLVING THE BOUNDARIES WITH THE STREET.

Public and civic values have made a comeback in the architecture, design and urban planning of the 1990s. Growing competition between cities, regions and prefectures for inward investment, jobs and status has been a catalyst for a myriad of new cultural and public amenity schemes – from libraries, art galleries, railway stations and airport terminals to opera houses, media centres and museums. As this selection demonstrates, the result has been a rich new crop of public interiors: landmark projects often involving costly and complex interventions in both urban and rural fabric alike, and reflecting the aspirations of local, regional and national peoples and governments.

A defining characteristic of the selection is the way that exterior and interior design concerns are seamlessly integrated in so many projects. It is almost as though covered public environments are reaching out to embrace the street. The mood is described most clearly in architect Volker Giencke's term for his Austrian village church – an "öffentliche Gebäude" – literally, an open building. This openness takes many forms. A new library at Münster in Germany designed by Julia Bolles and Peter Wilson is divided into two halves by a narrow public alleyway. In Sir Norman Foster's Carré d'Art cultural centre in Nîmes the boundaries are dissolved through the transparency of the structure. HOK's Missouri Temple of Christ extends the mood of awe-inspiring design to a pedestrian plaza. Even the way architect Shin Takamatsu floats a series of negotiable geometric elements in a giant public atrium at the Kunibiki Messe in Japan creates a dynamic and enigmatic play on interior and exterior space.

Inevitably, many of the projects set out to create visible symbols on the skyline, as a reflection of civic ambition and pride. Giencke's bell tower at Aigen, HOK's spiral-shell steeple in Missouri, Antoine Predock's copper-clad pyramid-shaped heritage centre on the Wyoming prairie, Jean Nouvel's high-tech new opera house at Lyons (literally rising above the façade of the original 1831 building), and a sinuous glass and steel roof on Nicholas Grimshaw's Waterloo rail terminal in London all fall into that category.

The architectural conception of these towering structures also generates some fine interior spaces. Santiago Calatrava's TGV rail station at Lyons, for example, shelters a central hall of quality beneath the spreading wings of a giant steel bird. Some public interiors, however, are conceived on such a dramatic scale and with such depths of imagination that they almost transcend their purpose. Renzo Piano's glider-shaped Kansai air terminal on an artificial island in Osaka Bay has the light touch of tomorrow's technology. Pei Cobb Freed's Holocaust Memorial Museum in Washington DC has the heavy shadow of history casting strange patterns through its dignified halls of witness and remembrance.

7

SHIN TAKAMATSU
ARCHITECT AND
ASSOCIATES

KUNIBIKI MESSE

MATSUE, JAPAN

Throughout the world, the concept of the competitive "city-state" is on the advance, with landmark architecture often used in an overt way to symbolize the cultural and commercial potential of a particular locality or region. The Kunibiki Messe in Matsue, the capital of Japan's Simane prefecture, is a conference and exhibition centre built on a grand scale by architect Shin Takamatsu to promote the prefecture's key industries. The six-storey building with basement level has four main interconnected areas: offices, an exhibition space, a public lobby and two conical conference spaces. It has a conventional steel and reinforced concrete structure which only reveals its unorthodox content on close inspection of a massive public atrium space through its large glass-wall façade.

The design and organization of formal geometric elements seemingly floating within the 24-metre-high atrium – "a garden of abstract forms", according to the architect – provides the core of this ambitious project, which has a total floor area of 15,726 square metres. This public space unites the disparate activities within the building, from large and small-scale meetings and trade shows to the administration of a diverse group of prefecture organizations. It also acts as a compelling area of interchange for visitors who trail through tunnels and encounter light-filled objects in an environment dedicated to promoting industrial futures.

"The condition in which a variety of space factor configurations were allowed to swim freely in a tank filled with water was directly transferred to architecture," says Shin Takamatsu of the resolution of the spatial relationships between different atrium elements which create such a dynamic play between interior and exterior space. The use of light tubes to illuminate the simple configuration of cones, spheres and cylindrical walkways has the artful manner of a science-fiction stage set. The largest cone, clad in aluminium panels, houses a tea-ceremony room. Others house light fixtures. Yet it is all done with such clarity and conviction that the lasting image is of the dynamic durability of the region's industries, not the slick manipulation of space and material by the architect. There is a poetry to the technology forms, as if industry can achieve myth-like qualities. But then the name "Kunibiki" – which means literally "pulling land" – derives from the Japanese birth-of-the-nation myth in which the gods of Izumo are said to have joined many islands together to form the country.

AN EXPRESSIVE CONFERENCE AND EXHIBITION CENTRE IN JAPAN SETS OUT TO SELL THE INDUSTRIES OF SIMANE PREFECTURE WITH A SCIENCE-FICTION APPEAL TO THE SENSES.

Opposite: Exterior façade
revealing the unorthodox
public atrium within.
This page: The sci-fi world of the
atrium within the Kunibiki Messe
is based on clever use of light
tubes to create conical and
spherical forms. Visitors trail
through tunnels and encounter
light-filled objects in "a garden of
abstract forms" which promotes
industrial futures.

"THE CONCEPT IS SUMMARIZED BY THE
ELEMENTS IN THE ATRIUM. SO OUR BIGGEST
CHALLENGE WAS HOW TO ORGANIZE THESE
ELEMENTS SO THAT THEY WOULD BE CLOSE
TO EACH OTHER WITH AN INTENSE
RELATIONSHIP. OUR PURPOSE HAS BEEN
TO CREATE AN ARCHITECTURE WHICH
SYMBOLIZES THE SPIRITUAL CLIMATE
OF THE REGION."

SHIN TAKAMATSU

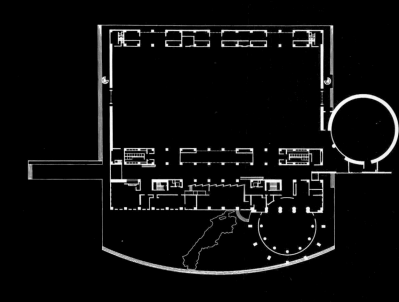

Above: Plan shows a basic
rectangle given an unusual twist
in Shin Takamatsu's interior
scheme.

Left: At night the Kunibiki conference and exhibition centre is
a glowing advertisement for the
industries of Simane prefecture,
the atrium elements creating
an intriguing play on interior and
exterior space. The structure is
divided into four main elements,
including office, exhibition,
conference and lobby spaces.

Above: The largest aluminium-clad cone in the atrium houses a tea-ceremony room.

Opposite: Low-voltage lighting, colour and form enliven the lobby area.

VOLKER GIENCKE & COMPANY

CHURCH OF AIGEN IM ENNSTAL

AIGEN, AUSTRIA

Architect Volker Giencke's expressive modern church in the Austrian village of Aigen was designed not just to act as a place of worship but also to provide a local community centre right in the heart of this small rural enclave. A key objective was therefore to create an open environment, with local people playing a collaborative role in the development of the project.

The scheme has three main elements: the church itself, with giant spreading roof making a welcoming gesture; a bell tower, and a pastoral house, both of which are satellite structures, separate yet essentially related to the mother building. The laminated timber roofline of the church, which projects its profile on steel legs, provides the visual link between all three elements. Its enveloping form suggests shelter and protection, also the idea of the Ark upon the waters. Its underside is carefully detailed with white steel ribbing; its upper side is a green section of soil-bearing grasses and wildflowers which replaces the meadow taken up by the footprint of the building.

The church interior has raked timber flooring, seating for 120 people, and simple rendered concrete walls on which the roof sits. A cross is simply cut into the concrete wall, so creating a sacred cross of light. The space is faced by translucent, steel-framed double-glazing units to weatherproof the building. On the outside of the glazing, a series of coloured glass panels designed by the architect and handmade by a local glassblower creates a pleasing decorative pattern of light and colour. The ecclesiastical tradition of the stained-glass window is reinterpreted here in a fresh and contemporary way, and at night spotlit from the roof edge for dramatic effect.

Within the dynamic and irregular plan of the whole scheme, the adjacent bell tower and pastoral house both suggest movement in their visible steel-frame structures. The bell tower is an overt, beckoning visual symbol in the landscape, crowned with a steel cross clad with translucent glass panels, and containing its bells within steel louvres. There is a small reading room for parishioners in its base. The pastoral house contains the priest's office on two main floors, with plant in the basement and a small dwelling at the top.

THIS AUSTRIAN VILLAGE CHURCH COMBINES A PLACE OF WORSHIP WITH THE ROLE OF LOCAL COMMUNITY CENTRE BY TAKING A DYNAMIC AND CONTEMPORARY APPROACH TO PLAN, DETAILS AND MATERIALS.

Volker Giencke's achievement with the Aigen church has been to project a strongly contemporary approach to plan, details and materials on to the sacred traditions of the religious building, without in any way compromising or trivializing the act of worship. The interior spaces are warm, welcoming and even womb-like in places, as befits a complex which has a secondary role as a local community centre.

"A CHURCH MUST BE
AN *ÖFFENTLICHE GEBÄUDE*,
THE GERMAN PHRASE FOR
A PUBLIC BUILDING,
BUT LITERALLY
AN OPEN BUILDING."
VOLKER GIENCKE

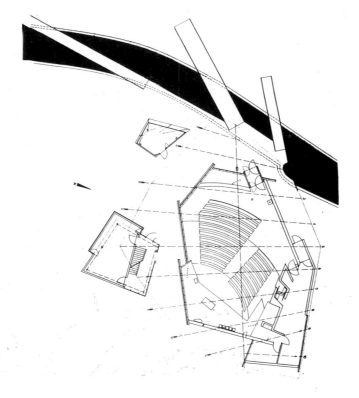

Above: The ecclesiastic
tradition of stained glass is
given a fresh contemporary
treatment. The church has
a raked timber floor and
a sacred cross of light is cut into
the rendered concrete wall.
Left: Plan showing the
dynamism and irregularity
of the scheme.
Opposite: Exterior view
showing the relationship
between the projecting
timber roofline of the church
and the translucent glass-
clad bell tower which rises
above it.

43

JEAN NOUVEL
ET ASSOCIÉS

OPERA HOUSE

LYONS, FRANCE

**A BLEND OF RICHNESS AND SPARSENESS,
TRADITION AND INNOVATION,
MARKS FRENCH ARCHITECT JEAN NOUVEL'S
GILT-AND-GLAZE REWORKING OF THE
HISTORIC LYONS OPERA HOUSE.**

Jean Nouvel's extension to Lyons' old opera house signals its arrival on the cityscape of France's second largest city in startling fashion. A large new glass vault rises above the colonnade that forms the original building's façade, simultaneously echoing existing proportions and making a bold new statement of its own. This tension between old and new offers a foretaste of what is to be found inside.

Structurally, the extension consists of 12 light-grey enamel arches supporting a glass roof made up of an inner glazed skin and an outer protective layer of 8,000 screen-printed glass sunshades. The opacity of the screen-printing varies progressively, responding to the varying strength of the city's sun light as it hits different aspects of the building. The scheme marks the latest chapter in the history of the Lyons Opera House which has been rebuilt several times over the past three centuries on different sites around the city. Nouvel's work extends Chenavard and Pollett's Opera House, constructed in 1831.

Visitors entering from the Place de la Comédie through the old peristyle see the theatre itself darkly suspended in the 30-metre-high vault of the entry hall. The hall manages to suggest, through layout and scale, some degree of continuity between exterior streetscape and interior confines. This slightly ambiguous effect is enhanced at night by means of lighting which makes the interior both visible and inviting from the street – a familiar Nouvel approach. The transparency of the building not only makes it more open but adds a depth and dimensionality as it is constantly reinterpreted by light at different times of day and night.

Once inside, the visitor is presented with an array of escalators, passageways and suspended platforms leading to the entry levels of the main auditorium. On the way up there is a ticket office, cloakrooms and the opera bookshop. Only then does Nouvel create self-consciously transitional spaces between "outside" and "inside". Entry to the auditorium is through sound-proofed corridors suffused with red light, creating a theatrical effect that anticipates the more traditionally sumptuous Italianate interior of the auditorium. That same red light is used to create rich illumination for the drum of the arch, making the Lyons Opéra as striking a landmark by night as it is by day. The auditorium interior (seating 1,300 people as opposed to just 800 in the old Opera House) uses contrasting textures: black enamelled wood, leather, rubber, perforated metal, and gold in gilt ceiling panels. Six levels of balconies above the stalls afford excellent views. The distance between the farthest spectator and the orchestra conductor is only 22 metres. Here the reason for suspending the theatre also becomes clear: it is immune to the vibrations to which ground-based auditoria are susceptible.

The general building design also affords other internal benefits. Metal evacuation stairways are unobtrusively slipped in between the two façades, whilst on two upper levels dance rehearsal studios use the full width of the vault to excellent advantage. A wealth of other interior facilities includes a public restaurant and terrace, meeting rooms, administrative offices and a subterranean amphitheatre with seating capacity for 200 people. There are also two public foyers for interval drinks: one, mirror-floored, retains a nineteenth-century gilded spirit; the other offers panoramic city views at the top of the building.

The latest electronic technology is deployed in everything from computer-controlled acoustic testing to remote-controlled fibre-optic indicators in the audience's seats and a completely reconfigurable orchestra pit. The scheme's internal richness is easily the equal of the building's external impact. As a result, Lyons' Opéra has already been widely recognized not just as an architectural *tour de force* but also as an imaginative and technological reinvention of the classical European opera house.

Left: Jean Nouvel's striking new glass vault rises above the colonnades that form Chenavard and Pollett's original Lyons Opera House. The drum of the arch is lit with red light as a contemporary expression of the plush red-velvet traditions of the ornate European opera house. Above: The same red lighting bathes the soundproofed transitional spaces between the lobby areas and the main auditorium.

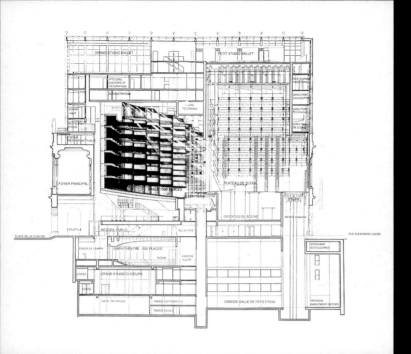

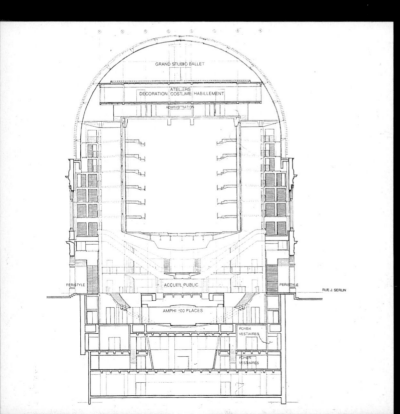

Opposite: Inside the auditorium of the Lyons Opera House, which is suspended in the 30-metre-high vault of the entry hall to improve acoustics and minimize vibrations. Six levels of balconies above the stalls provide excellent views. Above and left: Plan and cross-section through the glass vault showing the arrangement of facilities and Nouvel's skilful integration of old and new. Spacious ballet rehearsal studios were created in the vault.

Above: The ground-floor public reception area is constantly redefined by changing light. It has an emptiness and transparency which unites interior and exterior concerns. Its glass curtain walling with aluminium girders was designed to echo the vertical rhythm of the Lyons Opera House's original pillars. Opposite: Escalators leading up to the main auditorium in an atmosphere of dark material invention.

44

SMITH-MILLER & HAWKINSON

ROTUNDA GALLERY

NEW YORK, USA

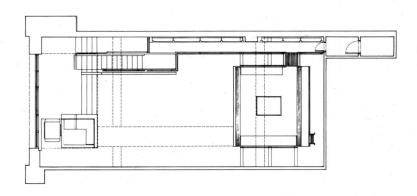

The Rotunda Gallery is an exhibition space that owes its existence to the migration of artists from Manhattan to Brooklyn in the 1970s. At the time they were searching for cheaper housing and studio space. But while the artists moved, the critics, curators and dealers continued to resist Brooklyn until a small gallery was eventually established in the rotunda of Borough Hall in 1981. It was then nearly a decade before work could begin on a new Rotunda Gallery. Occupying a Brooklyn Heights storefront, this has now been designed by New York architects Smith-Miller & Hawkinson. The Rotunda Gallery's design treatment is based upon the idea of it being primarily a 2,500 square-foot exhibition space on ground floor and mezzanine. As Henry Smith-Miller observes, "Artefacts are important, not architecture."

A BROOKLYN ART GALLERY BECOMES A MOVABLE FEAST OF EXHIBITION POSSIBILITIES AS ITS DYNAMIC TWO-STOREY PIVOTING PARTITION SIGNIFICANTLY ALTERS SPATIAL RELATIONSHIPS.

The key to adapting this otherwise rather unremarkable rectangular space into a dynamic and engaging place of exhibition lay in the installation of a large two-storey pivoting partition that runs on a steel arc set into the concrete floor. Apart from the obvious flexibility for display that this device presented, its positioning was carefully calculated to modulate entry and access to all gallery spaces. In its fully open position, the partition does little to change the loft-like space. Partially open, it significantly alters adjacent spaces, changing access and perspective and opening up variable triangular wedges of space. Closed, it blanks off any view of the gallery from outside and prohibits direct access from the street altogether. Visitors are then presented with two options: to enter via an oblique corridor or to use a bridge suspended above. The closed position also creates a natural auditorium space in the gallery and provides a screen for presentations.

If this partition is the high-profile element in an unusually flexible interior solution, Smith-Miller & Hawkinson have introduced a number of less obvious details that add distinction to the Rotunda Gallery. The architects have clearly relished introducing translucent Plexiglass panels into the rough concrete of the stair balustrades and making a plastic strip double as a foot guard and display shelf. They achieve further spatial flexibility by means of a small secondary gallery suitable for small exhibits or video presentations. This space too can be screened off, this time with sliding wall panels suspended from the underside of the bridge. The panels are constructed of white maple frames stretched with canvas – a painterly touch that also introduces a soft translucent quality to the raw concrete finish of the gallery. Another flexible element is presented by the insertion of a maple strip in the concrete of the stair wall. Positioned at 165 centimetres above the floor marks, it provides for the attachment of displays at the exact height specified by the Modernist curator Alfred H. Barr, founding director of New York's Museum of Modern Art.

Dynamic space and thoughtful detail combine in the Rotunda to create a gallery that interacts with its visitors. Whatever it is showing, the Rotunda Gallery retains the potential never to look the same way twice.

Opposite: First-floor plan.
Above and left: The two-
storey pivoting wall running
in a steel arc on the floor
creates a flexible, multi-use
exhibition space.

RENZO PIANO BUILDING WORKSHOP

KANSAI INTERNATIONAL AIR TERMINAL

OSAKA BAY, JAPAN

The new Kansai International Airport terminal building has been heralded as one of the most important architecture and construction projects this century. Designed by Italian architect Renzo Piano in the form of a sweeping glider and built on a man-made island three miles out in Osaka Bay, it not only spectacularly ups the ante in airport terminal design but also rewrites the way that technology and nature have traditionally related to each other in airport interiors. Everything about the project is larger than life – and stranger than fiction. Only a city like Osaka, with its urban density, rocketing land prices and strict restrictions on overhead flying, could consider building a new airport out into the bay. Only the Japanese could have the technological self-confidence to realize such a proposal.

Initially, the creation of an artificial island made of crushed stone resting on soft clay as the site for the new airport induced a sinking feeling. Buffeted by typhoons and scandals, the project appeared inherently unstable. However, despite a series of setbacks, the scheme has been magnificently realized with Renzo Piano's inspiring curvilinear steel and glass terminal building – a striking 1.7 kilometres in length and able to accommodate 41 planes – at its heart. Piano won an international competition to design the terminal, beating a strong field including Sir Norman Foster to the project. He says of his aerofoil-shaped terminal: "The movement of people is intended to be always direct, simple and based on their intuition." This echoes Foster's efforts at Stansted Airport in the UK to create a transparent, self-explanatory structure for passengers.

Certainly there is a great spatial achievement in the long vistas through the Kansai terminal, which in places give views of a great wing tailing away and put the Renaissance idea of playing with perspective in a late twentieth-century context. UK engineers Ove Arup & Partners with Peter Rice, Japanese architects Nikken Sekkei Ltd, Aéroports de Paris and Japan Airport Consultants played key roles alongside Piano in creating different elements of the total scheme. Computers were central to the realization of every aspect of the terminal, from truss arches and skin to interior configurations.

The most eye-catching and controversial aspect of the interior is a vast 300-foot-high stone-floored "canyon", filled with trees, vegetation and internal spanning bridges. This cathedral-like space sits within the organic form of a building which sandwiches the domestic floor between the international departure and arrival floors. In creating a high-tech structure on a totally artificial island, Piano was concerned to bring nature right into the heart of the interior spaces. Airports built on green-field sites have traditionally been unrepentantly all about science and technology in form and materials. However, the softer terracotta colours and use of natural light and vegetation in the Kansai "canyon" suggests a less mechanistic approach.

Piano describes a search for polarities in his design between weight and lightness, simplicity and complexity, the static and the dynamic. Across a total floor area of more than 290,000 square metres, the scheme succeeds on every level in its flowing geometries and panoramic sense of scale. Technology not only coexists with nature in construction, but also combines with craft: every single tile on the 90,000-square metre roof was put in place by hand. As at least five other new airports are currently in development around the Pacific Rim, including Hong Kong, Bangkok and Singapore, it will be interesting to see the interior lessons learnt from Piano's masterful orchestration out in the bay.

A TERRACOTTA INTERIOR CANYON FILLED WITH TREES AND LIGHT REDEFINES THE RELATIONSHIP BETWEEN TECHNOLOGY AND NATURE IN RENZO PIANO'S KANSAI AIRPORT TERMINAL ON AN ARTIFICIAL ISLAND IN OSAKA BAY.

Above and overleaf: Inside the main terminal building, flowing ceiling shells made of rock wool acoustic board act as open-air ducts, so providing natural climate control for the environment while enhancing the organic contours of an exceptional scheme.

Left: Curvilinear interior forms soften the high technology of this man-made intervention in Osaka Bay.

Opposite: The audaciously constructed island which is the platform for the new Kansai airport.

Above: A perspective view through the wing-like interior reveals the organic scale of the scheme.

Above right: Well-lit passenger facilities en route to the "canyon" at the heart of the scheme. Opposite: Inside the stone-floored Kansai "canyon", softer colours and the use of natural light, bridges and vegetation seek to humanize technology and harmonize with nature.

Opposite, below: Section through the main terminal building showing the domestic floor sandwiched between the international departures and arrivals floors.

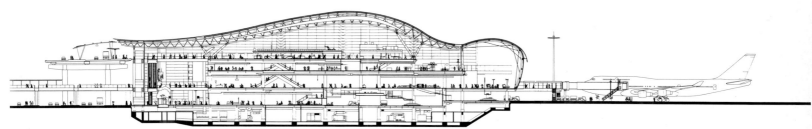

ANTOINE PREDOCK'S ICONIC COPPER-
CLAD PYRAMID ON THE WYOMING PRAIRIE
HOUSES AN ACADEMIC RESOURCE IN
A CALM, SECLUDED SANCTUARY OF
EXCEPTIONAL SPATIAL QUALITY.

46

ANTOINE PREDOCK

AMERICAN HERITAGE CENTER AND ART MUSEUM

WYOMING, USA

Most architects accustomed to tackling the problems of urban fabric would probably be daunted by the prospect of building in the wide open spaces of Laramie, Wyoming. However, architect Antoine Predock, of Albuquerque proved more than equal to the challenge. Working with consulting architects Pouppirt of Cheyenne and university architect Roger Baalman, Predock has given the University of Wyoming a complex containing a landmark building that acts simultaneously as an expressive and mysterious monument and a rational integration of university archive and offices.

There are two discrete elements: a conical structure housing the archive and offices, and connecting rectangular buildings housing a museum. The 130,000 square-foot complex also contains dedicated rooms, visitor research areas, a lobby, and oak-floor galleries for both permanent and travelling exhibitions. But it is the archive building that immediately commands attention, not only from vantage points elsewhere on the university, but also from the interstate highway. Initially Predock's asymmetric copper-clad pyramid appears to be a clear reference to native American tepee encampments and, by association, the culture that predated Wyoming's more recent cowboy ethos. Other university buildings – a basketball arena and a law school – are relatively low-rise, and Predock's focal Heritage Center building stands out primarily as a bold object that soon comes to suggest not only a tepee but also a volcano or, at night, a glowing lamp.

The interiors of such object-sculpture buildings are rarely as satisfactorily realized as in this instance. Here the bold geometric spirit continues inside as the building centres on a five-storey atrium with a timber-framed hearth sitting on top of a crypt-like area. A stovepipe chimney travels up through timber scaffolding at the atrium's centre, finally to penetrate a small plateau at the tip of the pyramid.

From the outside, the Heritage building appears to offer no natural point of access. In fact Predock simply pierces its shell at a dramatic angle to create a two-level entrance leading to a reception area that incorporates a balcony overlook and fanning skylights. The central concern of the Heritage Center seems to be one of protection and enclosure. Standing almost alone in an epic landscape, the building offers only "edited" views of its surroundings through relatively small and highly selective windows that penetrate the shell apparently at random. Despite natural light coming in from above, the internal atmosphere is predominantly one of seclusion and sanctuary. The complementary museum block can be reached via a rotunda which acts both as a gallery in its own right and a pivotal point of connection with the archive building. The entire scheme took seven years to build at a cost of $13.8 million.

Despite its iconic strength, so apparent from the outside, Predock's Heritage Center creates a unique series of calm and secluded interior spaces that successfully reinvent the idea of academic sanctuary for a landscape dominated by panoramic skies, prairies and mountain ranges.

Above: View of the timber scaffolding which supports the progress of a stovepipe up through the centre of the building. Interior spaces are defined by a sense of seclusion and sanctuary. Above right: The light-filled observation gallery at the top of the Heritage Center, where the stovepipe chimney emerges from the timber scaffolding and disappears into a top-lit cone. Opposite: At night Predock's asymmetric copper-clad pyramid glows like a lamp across the open Wyoming landscape.

"AKIN TO THE BUILDINGS OF THE OLD WEST TOWNS
WHICH ADOPTED CLASSICAL PEDIMENTS TO ASSERT THEIR
PRESENCE, THE AMERICAN HERITAGE CENTER AND ART
MUSEUM IS A CONSCIOUSLY MONUMENTAL LANDSCAPE
ABSTRACTION."
ANTOINE PREDOCK

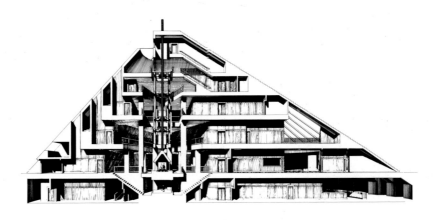

Above West-east section through the building.

Below: Upper floor plans.

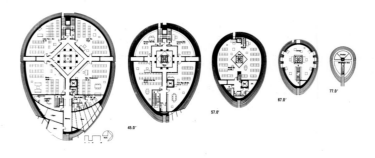

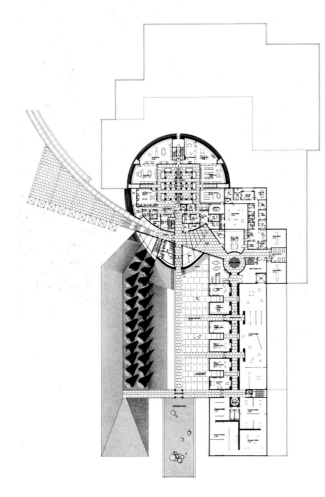

Left: Main floor plan.

Above: A timber-framed hearth provides the centrepoint for the American Heritage Center.

47

NICHOLAS GRIMSHAW & PARTNERS

WATERLOO INTERNATIONAL RAIL TERMINAL

LONDON, UK

London's Waterloo International Rail Terminal by architect Nicholas Grimshaw & Partners is perhaps the most impressive expression of the largest single civil engineering project in Europe this century – the Channel Tunnel, connecting England and France. Much attention has been paid to Grimshaw's excellent glass and steel roof structure, a sinuous carapace composed of articulated rectangular panes and steel ribs. But although the roof is the high-profile public face of the project, it still accounts for only 10 per cent of the total cost – and it is only part of the Waterloo story. The rest of the project falls into three parts: a basement car park which spans the Underground railway lines immediately underneath and forms a foundation for the terminal; a two-storey viaduct that sits upon this base, supports the platforms and forms an enclosure for two floors of passenger accommodation; and repaired and refurbished vaults beneath the existing station.

However, in addition to addressing the complex structural and logistical problems involved in building on the doorstep of a busy existing rail terminal, the architects also had to realize an exceptionally high-quality interior. Waterloo Terminal must compete with equivalent services offered by air terminals. So while confident architectural gestures on the London skyline are important, so too is the quality of the interior treatment and detailing within the facility. Significantly, the architects and the engineers (YRM Anthony Hunt Associates) have also designed many of the environmental details. The quality of light in the terminal was perceived to be of great importance: there should be no gloomy areas. The same metal halide luminaires have been installed throughout, with the luminaire housing designed by Grimshaw in consultation with Lighting Design Partnership. Other purpose-designed elements include a pressed aluminium ceiling for the departure hall which uses wide joints to accommodate curves in the plan, and a cantilevered rail that also acts as a crash barrier.

The lavatories have walls of polished black granite, pale granite floors and basins set individually into pear-shaped slabs of granite. Each hand basin is supported by a stainless steel bracket and is equipped with its own individual hand drier and mirror softly illuminated from behind with a low-voltage spotlight. Such details are complemented by an impressive range of fixtures and fittings, again frequently designed by Grimshaw in tandem with a series of partners. A circular steel customer care desk with a solid 35-millimetre granite surface forms the focal point of the departure lounge. Designed by Grimshaw, this was developed and installed by Tecno. The same team was responsible for the air-conditioned ticket check booths, which proved to be some of the most complicated installations at the terminal due to the variety of materials used and the tight radii required of the glass and steel panels. Vitra's classic Charles Eames wire chairs and Tandem seating in red, providing a rare splash of colour in a predominantly grey and white interior, were specified for waiting room and public areas. Area seating and tables, designed by Antonio Citterio and also made by Vitra, were used for the executive offices.

It is perhaps ironic that a project chronically bedevilled with postponement and confusion should finally spawn a terminal so lucid and elegant. Its success is all the greater for having matched external vision with interior quality.

NICHOLAS GRIMSHAW'S WATERLOO RAIL TERMINAL SUCCEEDS NOT ONLY IN THE GRAND SCALE OF ITS CONCEPTION BUT ALSO ON THE MORE INTIMATE LEVEL OF ITS INTERIOR QUALITY AND DETAILING.

Opposite, top: Air-conditioned ticket booths designed by the architect in glass and steel to maximize throughput of passengers.
Opposite, below: The lavatories feature stainless steel basins set against granite walls and floors. The quality of interior detailing matches the grand architectural gesture of the scheme.

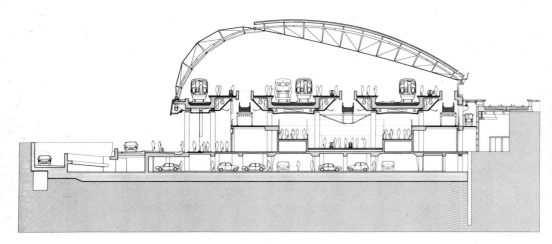

Above: Cross-section through the circulation area.
Right: Beneath the sinuous carapace of a glass and steel roof, the terminal's articulation of space marks the celebration of a new era in rail travel.

BEHNISCH &
PARTNER

VOCATIONAL
SCHOOL COMPLEX

ÖHRINGEN,
GERMANY

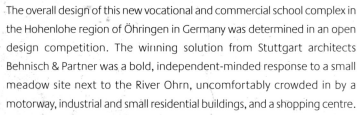

The overall design of this new vocational and commercial school complex in the Hohenlohe region of Öhringen in Germany was determined in an open design competition. The winning solution from Stuttgart architects Behnisch & Partner was a bold, independent-minded response to a small meadow site next to the River Ohrn, uncomfortably crowded in by a motorway, industrial and small residential buildings, and a shopping centre.

ARCHITECT AND ARTIST COMBINE TO CREATE A POWERFUL CIRCULAR DESIGN STATEMENT IN A GERMAN VOCATIONAL SCHOOL BUILT ON A CLUTTERED AND UNINSPIRING SITE.

The architects decided to make no attempt to integrate the school into its motley setting, electing instead to create a building with a strong presence of its own. This takes the form of an elevated two-storey glazed building in the shape of an interrupted circle. A high water table necessitated the use of columns and precluded any basement level – ancillary facilities are located on the entrance-hall level. A 1,826 square-metre gymnasium building was sited between the school and the motorway, leaving the main 4,620 square-metre school building to create its own self-contained world of glass structural ties and expressionistic features like the dramatic eccentric wedge of a glazed staircase. Classrooms within the outer layer of the circle look beyond the site, whilst stairs line the hallways, ancillary rooms and a large hall on the inner layer that forms the heart of the school.

The internal effects are strong and sweeping, although, as the architects admit, the rigid nature of their circular design did present some problems, notably the appearance of the fully glazed inner façade which closes in on itself. The solution was to invite the Berlin artist Erich Wiesner to paint the corridor-side of the corridor and classroom partition walls in strong colours to visually break up the glass membrane. Wiesner moved into the building for several weeks, setting up ateliers in the classrooms. The result is a series of brightly painted panels that animate both interior and exterior aspects of the complex. This is a business school that challenges rather than adds to the urban clutter that surrounds it: in demotivating circumstances that might have led to a dull design, the architects have achieved a powerful coherence that lifts a most uninspiring site and brings a sense of conviction to a building dedicated to vocational learning.

Above: The inner hall which forms
the heart of the circular scheme.
Opposite, top: Exterior view
showing the eccentric wedge
of glazed staircase juxtaposed
against the building ring.

"WITH THIS BUILDING, AS WITH OTHERS
IN THE PAST, WE FOUND THAT OUTSIDE
CREATIVE INFLUENCE IN THE END ENRICHED
OUR WORK... THE ARTIST ERICH WIESNER'S
WORK SUPPORTED AND EVEN ENHANCED THE
MOOD OF THE BUILDING AS WE ENVISIONED IT."
BEHNISCH & PARTNER

Above: Plan showing how the school
makes the best of an uncomfortably
crowded site.
Above left and opposite: The rigidity
of the circular approach is enlivened
by the tensioned expressionism of the
central staircase and by coloured
panels created by collaborating
artist Erich Wiesner.

THE FAMOUS FODOR ART GALLERY IN AMSTERDAM'S CANAL DISTRICT HAS BEEN SKILFULLY CONVERTED INTO THE PROGRESSIVE HIGH-TECH HOME OF THE NETHERLANDS DESIGN INSTITUTE.

BENTHEM CROUWEL ARCHITECTS

NETHERLANDS DESIGN INSTITUTE

AMSTERDAM,
THE NETHERLANDS

The Netherlands Design Institute is a new organization funded by the Dutch Ministry of Culture with a brief to identify ways in which design can contribute to the economic and cultural vitality of the community. Its programme of collaborative projects with designers, artists, technologists and industrialists is being directed from headquarters in the Fodor Gallery on the Keizergracht in Amsterdam. This famous canal-side art museum was designed in 1861 by Cornelis Oudshoorn and later bequeathed to the city of Amsterdam by the coal trader and art collector Carl Fodor, who tragically hung himself on the premises. The building has now been expertly and imaginatively converted by architects Benthem Crouwel to meet the needs of the progressive new Design Institute which, in the words of its director John Thackara, is a "think-and-do-tank". To express this dynamic idea the architects have introduced bold new metallic elements within the interior while conserving much of its original detailing.

So bad was the condition of the four-storey building that the process of renovation entailed replacing all foundations and wall, door and roof frames. The architects additionally chose to make two significant structural interventions. The stairs at the entrance of the Fodor, designed by Mart Stam in 1954, have been demolished and replaced with a galvanized steel staircase and bridges of blue glass, suspended from a steel structural beam inserted as part of the roof construction within the existing skylights.

The second intervention entailed joining basement and first level at the back of the building, and removing a portion of the floor on every level. Into this tall, narrow space running up the spine of the building next to the lightwell has been inserted "The Collector". This is a 10-metre-high steel scaffolding structure designed to hold the "memory" of the Institute, a giant storage unit into which all possessions can be stored – books, records, computers and communication systems. "The Collector" makes all cupboards and storage units within the white-walled interior spaces redundant, so enhancing the feeling of expansiveness. These multi-purpose spaces are treated soberly with large wooden tables sitting on original parquet flooring. The Institute provides a cool, neutral but relaxed backdrop which immediately draws attention to any design object, whether fashion garment or magazine rack or ceramic pot, placed in the environment. As befits an institute which believes that interactive computers pose the greatest challenge to design since industrialization, the building incorporates state-of-the-art multimedia equipment. Gardens at the rear of the Fodor have been landscaped to provide a welcome outdoor extension to the meeting rooms in summer.

The Netherlands Design Institute owes its existence to a decision by the Dutch Ministry of Culture to devolve its activities to a new series of smaller, more focused organizations. The Design Institute takes its place alongside institutes of theatre, film, photography and architecture (see Jo Coenen's scheme, page 230). Director John Thackara's widely quoted mission is to redefine the way in which governments promote design within industry and society. It is to Benthem Crouwel's credit that they have managed to create a landmark public building which is a functional showcase for facilitating industrial change, not a transiently fashionable design statement. Carl Fodor may have hung himself in the Fodor Gallery, but given plenty of creative rope, the architects have not done the same.

Opposite, top left: A galvanized steel staircase and bridges of blue glass bricks bring a contemporary design flavour to Amsterdam's former Fodor Art Gallery, originally designed in 1861 by Cornelis Oudshoorn.
Opposite, top right: A generously proportioned meeting room in a "think-and-do-tank".
Opposite, below: The high-tech gantry signifies an Institute where art meets technology.

"THE MAIN CHALLENGE WAS TO MAKE TWO MAJOR STRUCTURAL INSERTIONS AND TAKE DAY-LIGHT INTO THE HEART OF THE BUILDING WHILE CONSERVING MOST OF THE ORIGINAL HISTORIC DETAILING."

BENTHEM CROUWEL ARCHITECTS

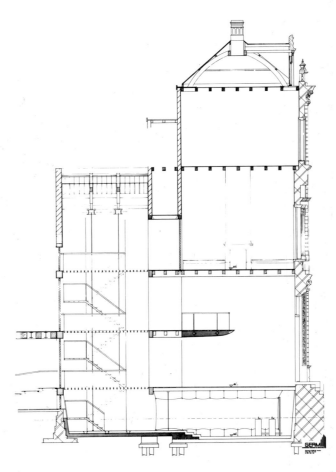

Above left: Wooden furniture, parquet flooring and ornate ceiling cornices temper the intervention of glass and steel in this finely judged interior scheme.
Above: Cross-section through the building – a portion of every floor has been removed to install "The Collector", a 10-metre-high steel storage scaffold.
Opposite: Fashion design showcased on the steps of the new steel staircase at the rear of the building.

HELLMUTH, OBATA & KASSABAUM

REORGANIZED CHURCH OF JESUS CHRIST

MISSOURI, USA

The act of architecture has provided dramatic and symbolic settings for the act of faith through the ages. This American scheme by architects Hellmuth, Obata & Kassabaum (HOK) for the Reorganized Church of Jesus Christ of Latterday Saints Temple in Missouri sets a 300-foot-high steeple in the spiral form of a nautilus shell on a circular base to draw the Missouri faithful.

A RELIGIOUS TEMPLE IN THE CITY OF INDEPENDENCE, MISSOURI, CREATES AN INTIMATE SANCTUARY BENEATH A SPIRAL-SHELL STEEPLE WHICH TAPERS SKYWARDS AS AN APPROPRIATE SYMBOL OF WORSHIP.

Beneath the stainless steel-clad spiral – an image drawn from nature as an inspirational physical expression of growth, dynamism, unity and worldwide presence – the church's interior spaces are bathed in light as a strip of clerestory glass panels follows the spiral form heavenwards to seeming infinity. This tapering form recurs throughout the church; the "uncoiling" of elevations, ribbon windows, spiralling catwalks and interior surfaces was undertaken, say the architects, "to help express the complexity of the design in discernible images".

Given the mathematical form of the spiral with its geometrically precise whirls, the three-dimensional surface of the church's form was achieved using 3D computer modelling techniques. This process has achieved optimum acoustic and sight lines inside the sanctuary, the focal place of worship, which seats 1,800 people in conditions of surprising intimacy. The main spiral-topped Temple building actually abuts school and offices in an L-shaped wing that wraps around the southern edge of the complex. Both are clad in grey granite. A two-storey reception hall topped by a skylight occupies the transitional place between these two elements. In front of the Temple is a pedestrian plaza featuring a map of the world to denote the international following this church sect inspires. In all, the scheme's total size is 130,000 square feet on a 13-acre site.

There is much detail to admire around the site, but the eye is inevitably drawn back to the unified space beneath the complex compound curves of the spiralling ceiling. This is a decorative holy swirl of a place, with bone-coloured marble flooring, walls of bleached maple and granite, and neo-Deco lighting all adding to a rhythmically uplifting environment.

Above: The temple's spiral-shell steeple is clad in stainless steel and reaches a height of 300 feet on the Missouri skyline.
Opposite: A geometrically-precise interior achieves a sense of unity, intimacy and dynamism by developing the helical form in a strip of clerestory glass panels which spiral heavenwards.

"THE NAUTILUS SHELL'S SPIRAL, MATHEMATICAL FORM WAS SELECT-
ED FOR THE STEEPLE, PROVIDING THE CHURCH WITH A SYMBOL OF
NATURE FOUND ALL OVER THE WORLD IN MANY DIFFERENT CULTURES.
AS A LOGARITHMIC SPIRAL, THE WHIRLS BECOME BROADER IN A
GEOMETRIC PROGRESSION WITH EACH REVOLUTION OF THE SPIRAL,
PROVIDING AN UPWARDLY FOCUSING IMAGE UNIQUELY SUITABLE FOR
A PLACE OF WORSHIP."

HELLMUTH, OBATA & KASSABAUM

Above: An inspirational glass window in the double-height transitional space between the spiral-form
church and a rectangular office building which abuts it.

Opposite: The entrance to the main temple interior reflects a concern by the architects to repeat a
tapering form throughout the scheme, with the "uncoiling" of walkways, elevations and surfaces.

KISHO KUROKAWA
ARCHITECT
& ASSOCIATES

MUSEUM
OF MODERN ART/
PREFECTURE
MUSEUM

WAKAYAMA, JAPAN

One of the characteristics of the better examples of Japan's new wave of civic buildings is a formal sensitivity to the country's ancient cultural traditions. Just as the rooflines of Fumihiko Maki's giant gymnasia in Tokyo take the shape of a traditional Japanese tea kettle, so this large-scale museum complex designed by Kisho Kurakawa in Wakayama takes its inspiration from Japanese castle architecture, which first developed in the fifteenth century.

The reason, as Kurokawa's Tokyo design office explains, is because the scheme has been built on a 23,356 square-metre site which used to be part of the ancient Wakayama Castle grounds. The project includes two museums – the Museum of Modern Art and the Wakayama Prefectural Museum – and was given the go-ahead when the university vacated the site. At present only half of the Wakayama Castle grounds are utilized and a road runs through the middle of the site. Eventually a park will be opened and connected to the museum complex by a pedestrian walkway over the road.

Kurokawa's clearest reflection of traditional Japanese castle architecture can be seen in the abstracted design of the roof and eaves, and in the strong use of black and white for exterior finishes. The Museum of Modern Art is clad in black ceramic tiles; the Prefecture Museum in white ceramic tiles. Both are two-storey buildings with a third basement level. Both are designed using simple geometric forms, their dramatic interrelation counterpointed against a giant, glazed, segment-shaped entrance hall.

The external organization of the museum complex demonstrates clarity and conviction, but even so it does not prepare the visitor for the glorious asymmetry of the interior spaces. The Museum of Modern Art has a total floor area of 11,838 square metres; the Prefecture Museum, the smaller facility of the two, 6,866 square metres. Cool, white concrete surfaces, glass planes and strategically placed sculptural art furniture present a picture of airy and spacious sophistication. Here again Kurokawa appears to be motivated by history, arguing that "natural curved lines express the traditional Japanese culture of asymmetry".

Left: Exterior view of a scheme for two museums set in part of the ancient Wakayama Castle Grounds. The use of black and white abstraction refers to traditional Japanese castle architecture. **Opposite, top:** Clarity and openness in the main central space of the smaller Prefecture Museum. **Opposite, below:** The custom-designed reception desk in the Museum of Modern Art.

THE ABSTRACTED ROOFLINE, BLACK AND WHITE CLADDING AND ASYMMETRIC INTERIORS OF KISHO KUROKAWA'S NEW WAKAYAMA MUSEUM COMPLEX OWE THEIR ORIGIN TO ASPECTS OF ANCIENT JAPANESE CULTURE.

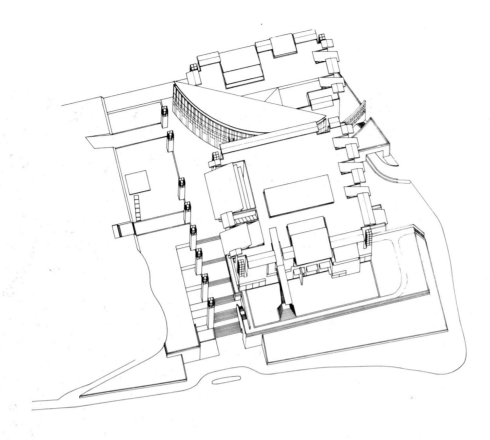

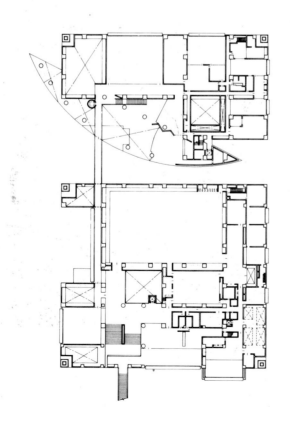

Above: A ground-floor view through the cool, white concrete surfaces of the Museum of Modern
Art, showing the upper-level balcony.
Opposite: Axonometric and plan showing the geometries of the two museums which are joined
by the glazed, curved segment of an entrance hall.

Above and opposite: The sophisticated use of asymmetric forms in the Prefecture Museum, reflecting Kurokawa's interest in Japanese cultural traditions, not simply the white-walled Modernism typical of Western museums.

"THE MUSEUM EXPRESSES A SYMBIOSIS OF THE PAST AND THE PRESENT
BY QUOTING THE TRADITIONAL EAVES OF JAPANESE CASTLE ARCHITECTURE
BUT IN AN ABSTRACT WAY. THE BLACK AND WHITE COLOURS ARE ALSO
QUOTED FROM THE TRADITIONAL CASTLE ARCHITECTURE STYLE."
KISHO KUROKAWA

MICHAEL HOPKINS & PARTNERS

GLYNDEBOURNE OPERA HOUSE

SUSSEX, UK

THE NEW GLYNDEBOURNE OPERA HOUSE
IS A MASTERFUL REINVENTION
OF A QUIRKY ENGLISH INSTITUTION:
PLAIN TIMBER INTERIOR FINISHES CONFORM
TO A RURAL TRADITION WHILE ENHANCING
THE ACOUSTICS.

To many people the Glyndebourne Opera House in southern England must seem an implausible institution. A privately owned, world-class operatic venue nestling in the Sussex countryside, its appeal has always lain in its unlikely blend of English rural quirkiness and international reputation. The original opera house was built in 1934 by John Christie and his wife, the opera singer Audrey Mildmay. That building's village-hall informality, seemingly central to Glyndebourne's appeal, eventually posed a threat to its future, and so an entirely new building was commissioned. The design team comprised architect Michael Hopkins & Partners, acousticians Ove Arup Acoustics and theatre specialists Theatre Projects Consultants.

The £33 million Glyndebourne project was always going to be a daring initiative, running the risk of pleasing neither traditionalists nor modernists. However, the design team took as its priorities three key issues: capacity, intimacy and acoustics. There was a need to increase audience capacity in order to accommodate 1,200 seats, 42 standing places and 12 wheelchair positions. This had implications for the auditorium's volumetric and acoustical properties. In response, a modified horseshoe shape was decided upon – a departure from almost all modern opera house designs of the past 50 years. Hopkins' scheme for the building as a whole was to wrap the auditorium in three tiers of open terraces supported on flat brick arches. The fly-tower, with its exposed crown of structural beams, provides a dramatic contrast of materials, being faced with black lead.

Reclaimed pitch pine, brick and concrete are the materials that Hopkins has chosen to define the character of Glyndebourne's interior and satisfy acoustic demands. The ceilings are finished in pre-cast concrete which has been acid-etched to expose the mica in the mix and give a stone-like finish; the need to exclude aircraft and other external noise was one of the more fundamental acoustic necessities. The auditorium itself is faced in timber throughout – a conscious bid to give Glyndebourne's interior an image of rustic plainness far removed from the traditional urban theatre's trappings of plush red-velvet opulence. Seats are upholstered with timber frames and arms, and cool air is fed from underfloor air plenums up through the seat support pedestals. The ambulatories wrap around the auditorium at all levels, and offices, work rooms and dressing rooms are arranged around the large internal volumes that contain the workings of the theatre.

The new opera house is in fact a highly integrated structure, redefining not only the interior spaces but also the orientation of the entire building and the experience of arriving at Glyndebourne. A foyer acts as a continuation of the garden, a transitional concept borrowed from the old covered way but now reinterpreted using Hopkins' familiar device of a translucent membrane roof. Once inside and seated, the audience can experience an imaginative visual and tactile reworking of one of the world's premier operatic venues, and also enjoy acoustic qualities substantially better than those upon which Glyndebourne originally built its reputation.

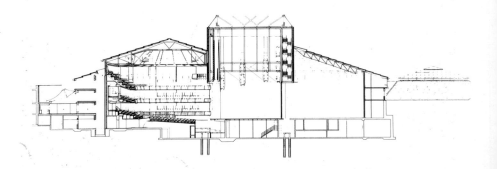

Above: A translucent fabric tent –
a familiar Hopkins device –
provides a foyer-area cover
between the Glyndebourne
gardens and the new auditorium
building.
Left: The Glyndebourne complex
of buildings, united by Hopkins'
new, highly integrated, circular
addition.
Opposite: Section through the
building.

"THE ACOUSTICS IN THE NEW AUDITORIUM PROVIDE FOR GOOD CLARITY TO SUPPORT THE SINGERS. THE VOLUME AND CHOICE OF BUILDING MATERIALS PRODUCE A GOOD REVERBERANCE AND A WARM BASS SOUND. IT IS APPROXIMATELY 50 PER CENT GREATER IN VOLUME PER PERSON OVER THE OLD AND HAS A REVERBERATION TIME OF 1.4 SECONDS. THE OLD HOUSE HAD A REVERBERATION TIME OF 0.8 SECONDS."

MICHAEL HOPKINS & PARTNERS

Above: Part of the rehearsal stage, with stage designer Richard Hudson's set for the opera *Onyegin*.

Opposite: The Glyndebourne auditorium, with three tiers of open terracing, is faced in timber throughout to suggest a rustic plainness in keeping with a country setting far removed from the conventions of metropolitan opera-going.

PEI COBB FREED
& PARTNERS

UNITED STATES
HOLOCAUST
MEMORIAL MUSEUM

WASHINGTON DC,
USA

The completion of the United States Holocaust Memorial Museum on a prominent federal site just off the National Mall in Washington DC represents a significant design achievement by its architects, Pei Cobb Freed & Partners. In both construction and cultural terms, the project, authorized by an Act of Congress in 1980, has taken shape with the eyes of the world on it. Dedicated to the ten million people, Jews and Christians alike, who were killed by the Nazis, the building is actually more than memorial or museum, say its designers: it is a living institution dedicated to research, teaching and the performing arts, as well as to contemplation and commemoration. It also bears the weight of the history of one of the most inhuman episodes in this or any other century, begging the question of its architects: how could the stones be made to speak?

Pei Cobb Freed & Partners have not resorted to rhetorical flourish in any aspect of this highly distinguished scheme. Plan, organization, materials and engineering are instead skilfully subordinated to the evocation of an entire Holocaustal experience which begins in a three-storey Hall of Witness, a giant abstracted space for the arrival, distribution and circulation of visitors, and ends in the hexagonal Hall of Remembrance, a solemn setting for contemplation and private memory. The scheme also includes an education centre, library and archival research centre, a bookshop, cinema and the 414-seat Myerhoff Theatre.

The way the brick and limestone building is put together deliberately invokes the past by using a tectonic vocabulary conspicuously distant from the elaborate steel fabrications of contemporary architecture. The brick is loadbearing, the structure is exposed, suggesting the buildings of 50 years ago. The aim, say the architects, is to suggest the fallibility of technology, the way it can be misapplied for evil purposes – as the Nazis demonstrated.

The seven-level museum (five floors above ground, two below) occupies a total of 258,000 square feet on a 1.7-acre site. The Hall of Witness, covered by a great twisted skylight supported by steel trusses and dropped in at third-floor level between the museum's side brick walls, is the largest interior space, measuring 7,500 square feet. Its grey-painted steel bridges, overhead towers, black granite wall, and glassblock and granite paving suggest the start of a forced march to the concentration camp more forcefully than any overt exhibit or statement. Light, shadow and texture articulate this space, and a gap in the flooring funnels light towards the education centre below.

The museum traces in linear fashion the rise of Nazism, the war years, the Holocaust, its aftermath and subsequent efforts to understand it. The visitor travels up to the fourth floor by lift and then down through the third then second level, negotiating translucent bridges, narrow arches and black-box exhibition spaces across a landscape of memory and discovery. Along the route, structural columns are bifurcated to accommodate beams from an Auschwitz barracks, and a three-storey Tower of Faces is covered with the photographs of more than a thousand villagers from Ejsyszki in Poland, all of whom perished on a single day. At the journey's end, the 6,000 square-foot Hall of Remembrance encircles an eternal flame with inscriptions carved into limestone walls. The space is surrounded by a skylit walkway, with niches for memorial candles.

MORE THAN MEMORIAL OR MUSEUM, AMERICA'S LANDMARK CULTURAL BUILDING DEDICATED TO HOLOCAUST TAKES THE VISITOR ON A SOLEMN AND COMPELLING JOURNEY THROUGH A HEART OF DARKNESS.

The flooring is a deep red granite, splattered and cracked by natural fissures; it is a feature "not so much intended to be walked upon as contemplated from the seating terraces that step up around it," say the architects. Above, a skylight floods the space with soft, diffused light.

The extraordinary nature of the museum's subject matter makes this an interior project that almost transcends judgement by conventional criteria. Its richness as a scheme owes less to individual space and material configurations than to the whole conception of a learning experience framed by architectural decision-making. Faced with so many conflicting demands, from government agencies to holocaust survivors and museum curators, Pei Cobb Freed & Partners deserve immense credit for getting so many of the decisions right.

Below: Glazed steel bridges and watch towers (left) and a Tower of Faces (right) – a three-storey space covered with more than a thousand pictures of people from one village, all of whom perished in a single day – speak calmly and eloquently of the horrors of the Nazi Holocaust.

"THE TECTONIC LANGUAGE IS USED HERE TO EXPLORE THE FATEFUL
MISPERCEPTION THAT TECHNOLOGY IS INHERENTLY GOOD. THE SAME
SCIENTIFIC ADVANCES AND TECHNOLOGICAL DEVELOPMENTS EMBRACE
IN PURSUIT OF A BETTER LIFE WERE ALSO APPROPRIATED IN THE
RELENTLESS EFFORT TO PERFECT THE MACHINERY OF ANNIHILATION."
PEI COBB FREED & PARTNERS

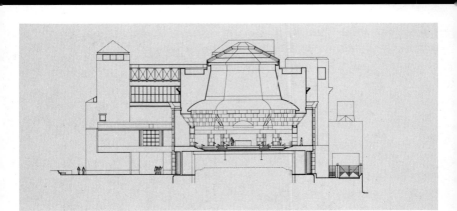

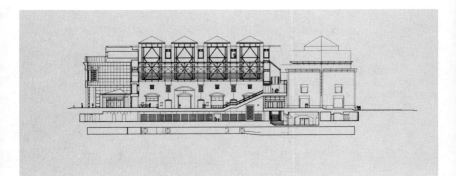

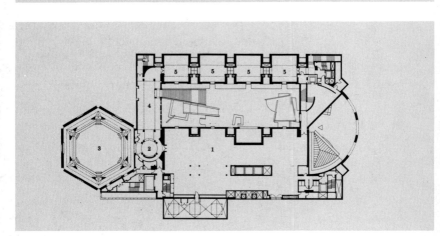

Top and centre: Sections through the museum reveal a conscious mode of construction
from the industrial past.

Above: Second level floor plan.

Opposite: The tectonic language of the interior architecture – in particular the load-bearing
brickwork and girders – sends the message that technology is neither infallible nor benign.

Opposite, top: The Hall of Witness, a pivotal three-storey space of arrival, distribution and circulation, prepares visitors for the disquieting journey which lies ahead. It is crowned by a giant twisting skylight.

Opposite, below: The Hall of Remembrance, a solemn, stepped, 6,000-square-foot space for private contemplation and ceremonies at the end of the museum journey. Inscriptions are carved in the limestone walls. The lighting is soft and diffuse, and an eternal flame burns.

SANTIAGO
CALATRAVA

TGV RAILWAY STATION

LYONS, FRANCE

The soaring international career of architect-engineer Santiago Calatrava is mirrored in the vaulting structural ambition of his finest bridges and transport terminals. Yet, amid all the acclaim, one aspect of the work of this master designer is sometimes neglected: Calatrava's dramatic skeletal forms shelter interior environments of exceptional spatial and aesthetic quality within their expansive and expressive frames.

LIKE A STEEL BIRD ABOUT TO SOAR INTO FLIGHT, SANTIAGO CALATRAVA'S RAIL STATION AT LYONS CREATES MAGNIFICENT INTERIOR SPACES BENEATH SHELTERING WINGS.

Such a case is Calatrava's new TGV rail station, designed at the interchange with Lyons Satolas airport as a symbolic point where train meets plane. Accordingly, the station has been conceived as a delicate steel bird which spreads its protective symmetrical wings over a spectacular central hall, soaring to a height of 38 metres and sheltering the platforms. The entire complex looks set to take flight, its main metaphor powerfully evocative of Saarinen's TWA terminal at JFK Airport in New York. Beneath this curved structure with its protective arched spine and spreading wings resting on two lateral glazed curtain walls, the scheme unites the central hall with a connecting gallery and offices.

The central space has a triangular form interrupted by two cantilevered balconies on the airport side of the terminal. Shops and office space for the SNCF, police and so on occupy the ground floor and mezzanine levels of the hall; an upper level has a bar and restaurant, seating on the balconies, a temporary exhibition space, and access to the airport. The steel-structured connecting gallery to the airport is 180 metres long, and equipped with travelators; it also provides access to the TGV platforms, which are roofed with a lattice concrete and glass vault.

Calatrava's now familiar anthropomorphic language of ribs, spines and trusses is evident throughout the scheme. But he is at pains to point out that his decisions are never the product of architectural whimsy. The 9-metre module used to give a rhythm to the building from north to south was chosen, says Calatrava, "because 9 metres corresponds exactly to the length of a carriage of the TGV – it helps the good working of the station".

Opposite: In Santiago Calatrava's TGV rail station at Lyons Satolas airport, giant trusses span the platforms at nine-metre intervals – a distance which, says Calatrava, corresponds exactly to the length of a TGV carriage.

"IN THE LYONS SATOLAS STATION, AS IN MY OTHER BUILDINGS, I HAVE TRIED TO ESTABLISH A DUALITY – BETWEEN THE GALLERY AND THE PLATFORMS, THE LATERAL WINGS AND THE BUILDING AT ITS CENTRE, THE CONCRETE AND THE STEEL. THE DUALITY CONCEPT IS ALMOST CHILDISH BUT AT THE SAME TIME IT HAS THE GOOD LOOKS AND EFFICACY TO EXPRESS THIS DOUBLE TENSION."

SANTIAGO CALATRAVA

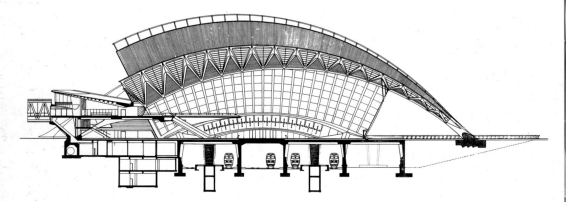

Above: Section through the central hall and tracks.
Right: Symmetrical wings shelter a spectacular central hall, the anthropomorphic language of the roof structure suggesting the idea of a bird about to take flight.

SIR NORMAN FOSTER
AND PARTNERS

CARRÉ D'ART

NÎMES, FRANCE

The Carré d'Art, incorporating a major art gallery and library, was commissioned by the French Mediterranean town of Nîmes to occupy the site of a nineteenth-century opera house destroyed by fire in 1952. It stands directly opposite the impressive Maison Carrée, a Roman temple dating from the first century, on a site of great historical significance. The choice via international competition of the world-renowned British architect Sir Norman Foster to design the delicately sited scheme was regarded with surprise in some quarters, given Foster's track record in designing technologically imaginative and forward-looking buildings. However, it was Foster's respect for the existing historical urban context for the new building that distinguished his practice's entry. The architect noted later that "interestingly our design response was the only one which did not seek to change the nature of that space".

The resulting building is one in which interior and exterior concerns are seamlessly integrated. The exterior envelope uses thermal glass framed by concrete columns designed to match the columns of the adjacent Maison Carrée. Like the Maison Carrée, Foster's building stands upon a limestone plinth and it also incorporates a portico intended to welcome people into the building. To preserve the scale and quality of the location, half of the nine-storey Carré d'Art (occupying 18,000 square metres of space) is built below ground, while the top floor rises well above the apparent cornice. The naturally lit art galleries are located at the top of the building, while the library occupies the floors immediately above and below ground level, for easy access from the street. The basement includes cinema, auditorium and conference facilities, but is largely used for storage.

A five-storey-high internal courtyard introduces light into all of the public levels, and glass is used extensively: there is a glass tread staircase, glazed hydraulic lifts and use of clear, translucent and opaque glass throughout the concrete and steel structure. One significant benefit of the glass staircase is that as the building becomes subterranean, light from above filters down through and between the flights of steps, transforming the lower spaces. The building is characterized by a feeling of transparency. From the sun-control louvres and milky glass walls to the interlocking transparent volumes of the interior spaces, the Carré d'Art constantly manipulates the special light of Nîmes to maximum effect. Topping the building is one of its most successful spaces: an external terrace restaurant almost touched by the uppermost branches of the mature tree outside. This facility provides the most literal expression of Foster's regard for his building's surroundings, offering a perfect view of the Maison Carrée.

In the ten years it took to complete the building, Carré d'Art underwent a number of changes, not all of them improvements. Even so, the strength of the building designer's original vision remains intact, and a decade on, Norman and Sabiha Foster were also able to design the library and minimalist office furniture (made by Tecno) for this civic temple of culture.

A TRANSPARENT TEMPLE OF CIVIC CULTURE IN NÎMES STANDS AS A SUPREMELY CONFIDENT EXAMPLE OF HOW TO INTRODUCE A MODERN BUILDING INTO AN IMPORTANT HISTORICAL SETTING.

Left: On a delicate historical site, Sir Norman Foster's Carré d'Art sits directly opposite the first-century Roman building, Maison Carrée. Its concrete columns, which frame the glass façade, were designed to match the columns of the Roman temple.
Opposite: The main internal courtyard with staircases leading up to naturally lit art galleries at the top of the building.

Above: In the library space, custom furniture designed by Norman and Sabina Foster (made by Italian manufacturer Tecno) is set against the imposing backdrop of a Richard Long painting.

Opposite, top: A view of the Maison Carrée from inside Foster's transparent building, with its sun-control louvres and milky glass walls.

Opposite, below: Section through the building, half of which is underground to preserve the historical scale of the location.

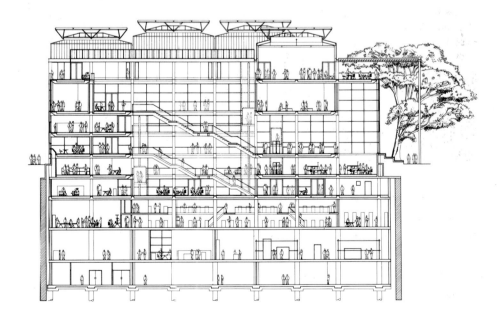

JO COENEN & CO.
ARCHITECTS

**NETHERLANDS
ARCHITECTURE
INSTITUTE**

ROTTERDAM,
THE NETHERLANDS

**THE NETHERLANDS ARCHITECTURE INSTITUTE REFLECTS
THE VIGOUR OF A PLURALISTIC PROFESSION IN THE
WAY ITS MANY DIFFERENT AND CONTRASTING INTERIOR
FRAGMENTS CREATE A COHERENT WHOLE.**

It took 150 years after the idea was first mooted to create an architectural institute for Holland. Debate, discussion, disagreement and delay marked the long road that eventually culminated in architect Jo Coenen's powerful and imaginative building in Rotterdam's Museumpark. As the building at last began to take shape, so did the independent professional body it was to house: the Netherlands Architecture Institute (NAI). Formed from three smaller institutions (the Architecture Museum Foundation, the Stichting Wonen and the Dutch Documentation Centre for Architecture), the NAI was still resolving issues of policy, organization and programme as Coenen began to build its home.

This fraught history might have produced a building whose lines all too clearly reflected the problematic circumstances of its creation. Instead Coenen has managed to create a forceful, theatrical environment in which fragments, transitions and overlaps combine to suggest the vigour of a pluralistic profession rather than the discord of a divided one. Perhaps predictably, the Netherlands Architecture Institute is a three-part drama full of tension. It consists of three main construction elements intended to reflect the three NAI requirements for a treasury, study room and events area. This approach also happily accommodates Coenen's response to the complexity of the site, which approximates a truncated quadrant.

The rectangular archives building facing on to Rochussenstraat clearly identifies the whole Museumpark with a public arcade. A large square exhibition hall and, the third element, a skewed main building are also connected, each looking quite self-consciously different from its neighbour. The contrasts continue inside. A wooden duckboard on steel columns forms the floor of an entrance hall encased in a glass membrane. A bridge leads visitors to the transport house, to coloured ramps or to lifts and stairs. Here they can go down to a waterside terrace, an auditorium or the big exhibition space, or up to halls, galleries and a study room.

There are many contrasts of mood in the 10,000 square-metre scheme. Study areas are spacious and tranquil, while some of the transitional spaces are very tightly managed, offering brief glimpses into neighbouring areas. The library makes clear reference to the great cast-iron structures of nineteenth-century libraries, while the USM-Haller furniture used throughout for offices, reading room and archives study hall has a severe and restrained modernity. These contrasts play against a sober material backdrop: wood, steel, glass and brick supplement a concrete skeleton.

The real building design skill at NAI resides in the way all the project's contrasting elements are disposed: overlapping, each artfully giving way to the next, and all surprisingly well-realized, despite budget cuts which at one point threatened to dilute Coenen's original proposal. The architect describes the building as "complex but uncomplicated". It is certainly an effective response to the NAI's brief calling for a building with a universal and timeless appeal. In approving Coenen's scheme, the NAI concluded that what he had proposed was a timeless repertoire of effects rather than an environment rooted in the ideology of one particular movement.

Above: The exterior view of a building section that contains offices, library, archive study hall, reading room and entrance – one element in a scheme which overlaps and integrates a number of architectural fragments.

Above right: The bridge which runs from the entrance hall to lift, ramp and stairs, providing a link to all other sections of the Netherlands Architecture Institute building.

"THIS GAME OF SETTING SCENES PRODUCES
ALTERNATING ATMOSPHERES IN THE BUILDING.
FROM ONE SECTION, YOU LOOK BACK
AT THE OTHER. THE ROOMS SUCCEED EACH
OTHER AS IN A SERIES."
ARCHITECT JO COENEN

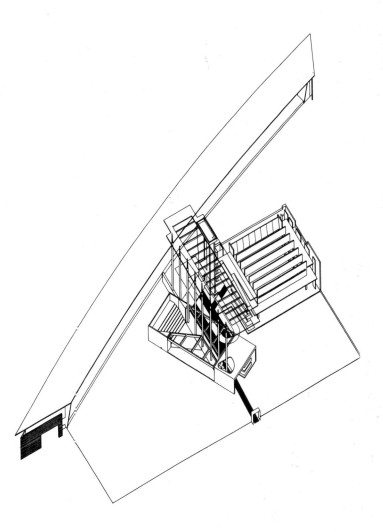

Above: Axonometric showing
the artful overlapping of three
distinct building elements to form
one cohesive scheme.
Left: The suspended gallery of the
reading hall and library, which
provides a view of the Rotterdam
Museumpark.

EVANS AND SHALEV

TATE GALLERY

ST IVES,
CORNWALL, UK

The St Ives school of Modernist painters, ceramicists and sculptors has long commanded international attention. The Cornish town's new £3.3 million Tate Gallery, overlooking Porthmeor Bay on a steeply sloping north-facing site, is a gallery with space, light and proportions which faithfully reflect the lives of the St Ives artists, Ben Nicholson and Barbara Hepworth among them.

ON A STEEP CLIFF OVERLOOKING THE ATLANTIC, THE TATE GALLERY AT ST IVES REFLECTS BOTH THE LIVES OF LOCAL ARTISTS AND LOCAL BUILDING VERNACULAR IN A SERENE SHOWCASE.

Architects Eldred Evans and David Shalev won a competition to design the new art gallery largely on the strength of an earlier commission, the Law Courts at Truro, which is widely regarded as one of the finest new buildings in Cornwall. The new Tate Gallery shares with the Truro project some exterior similarities, notably the white rendered walls and slate roofing which respond to the local building vernacular. The architects acknowledge the powerful context: "St Ives is a town of white walls, grey slate roofs and small windows; so is the building." Indeed one of the successes of the scheme is its relationship with the tourist town it was built to enhance.

The building is perched on top of a sheer wall and has a total floor area of 1,728 square metres on four levels. It is entered from a beach road below via a loggia, a small circular amphitheatrical gallery which looks out on to the Atlantic Ocean. Visitors then progress through a room dominated by a large stained-glass window by the artist Patrick Heron. The art gallery proper runs the length and breadth of the second floor. Five top-lit exhibition rooms of differing scale, form and proportion are arranged in a simple sequence around a secret courtyard which visitors discover at the end of their journey. "The rooms are no larger than those of a St Ives artist," according to the architects. "Sparse in detail with silent floors and softly it, the spaces allow the exhibits to come into their own." The largest room is the second in the sequence: a circular gallery for sculpture and ceramics which has a curved structural glass wall of sand-blasted glass blocks and hugs the loggia. The sculpture gallery and intermediate spaces share rustic slate flooring. The flooring in the painting rooms is a silent rubber. Interior walls are of white-painted medium-density fibreboard.

The Tate Gallery includes a rooftop restaurant with panoramic views of St Ives Bay, a bookshop and a work demonstration area to introduce children to art. Its thought-provoking serenity and the inherent richness of its simple interior forms have led a number of critics to comment on the legibility and grace of the architectural language. But what really elevates the scheme is the way in which the design so directly mirrors the daylight mood and essential spirit of the famous St Ives artists.

Above: A stained-glass window by artist Patrick Heron dominates the route from the entrance rotunda.

Opposite: The museum sits on the St Ives shoreline, its white rendered walls and slate roofing a response to the local building vernacular.

"FROM THE OUTSET, WE INTENDED ART, BUILDING, TOWN AND NATURE TO FORM PART OF ONE EXPERIENCE. THE EXPERIENCE OF VISITING THE GALLERY IS AN EXTENSION OF VISITING ST IVES AND THUS PROVIDES SOME INSIGHT INTO THE ARTISTS' INSPIRATION."

EVANS AND SHALEV

Above: The simply detailed staircase to the upper level.

Opposite, top: The circular gallery for sculpture and ceramics, the second in a sequence of five top-lit galleries.

Opposite, below: Axonometric revealing the rich geometries of the scheme, with the sculpture gallery hugging the loggia.

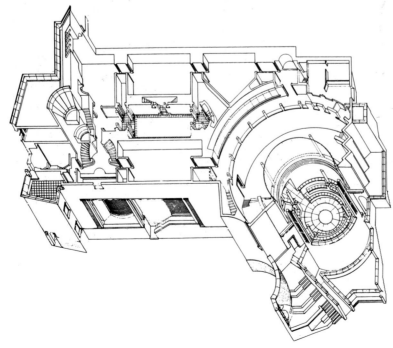

SAMYN & PARTNERS

FACULTY OF MEDICINE
AUDITORIUM BUILDING

BRUSSELS, BELGIUM

Universities throughout Europe today face an increasingly common conundrum. How can they reconcile rising student numbers and the growing demand for better-designed teaching accommodation with static or falling capital investment budgets? The new Faculty of Medicine auditorium building on the Anderlecht campus of the Brussels Free University shows how: it presents a low-cost construction solution in the round, suitable for heavy-duty student use but also highly satisfactory in terms of architectural quality. Brussels-based architects and engineers Samyn & Partners responded to the administrative, exhibition and educational needs of the building by designing a circular steel and concrete structure which incorporates around 2,000 square metres on three levels. The site is a prestigious one within the university; the Faculty of Medicine auditorium was conceived as a new landmark on the campus at the axis of a pedestrian thoroughfare.

The upper level is the core of the project: a circular auditorium which seats 500 students in a configuration which optimizes sightlines and access to the podium. An S-shaped central corridor or aisle between the seats meets strict fire regulations which require rows to have a maximum of 20 seats, and avoids encroaching on central seats. Entrance doors are placed tangentially to the walls in chicane form: this enhances concentration by making access to the hall more discreet and filtering out light and sound. The auditorium is ventilated by placing ventilator blocks in a suspended plasterboard ceiling and air extractors under the seats, in the form of openings placed in the angle of the steps. Auditorium seating, made by Fibrocit, is the architects' own design. The ground-floor level is given over to an inviting, naturally lit, circular lobby area which doubles as an exhibition and performance space. The basement level accommodates the Faculty's administrative offices, meeting rooms and the Dean's office, again exploiting the acoustic and visual advantages which the building's circular plan offers.

The Faculty of Medicine auditorium building achieves a level of design sophistication using utilitarian and functional finishes. Its plain concrete block walls are painted light yellow in the office areas, counterpointing black linoleum flooring, and clad with standard perforated corrugated steel sheet in the cylindrical auditorium. Otherwise simple white and grey industrial finishes predominate.

As a design practice, Samyn & Partners has shown strong interest in the potential of steel construction to create good-quality spaces: it recently completed the new OCAS steel application research centre in Zelzate-Ghent, Belgium, as a demonstration of the material's strength and finesse. The mood of elegant experiment continues on the Brussels Free University campus with this inexpensive and fast-track project designed for very heavy use. It is a model for the type of building which European universities will increasingly demand during the 1990s.

THE FACULTY OF MEDICINE AUDITORIUM BUILDING AT BRUSSELS FREE UNIVERSITY BRINGS LOW-COST LEARNING IN THE ROUND TO A LANDMARK CAMPUS SITE.

Opposite: Views of the exterior, lobby area and auditorium. The scheme's materials and finishes are utilitarian yet achieve a level of design sophistication.

BOLLES-WILSON &
PARTNER ARCHITECTS

CITY LIBRARY

MÜNSTER, GERMANY

The new municipal library at Münster by architects Julia Bolles and Peter Wilson cuts a radical white sweep through the heart of one of the most sober historic districts in this German city. Yet the building is also a profoundly contextual design, responding to a difficult triangular site with a powerfully self-determined sense of form: this has generated a series of memorable public interiors while respecting the many views of the dense exterior setting in which it sits.

The Münster library is actually two buildings in one: a specially created *Gasse* (a narrow pedestrian street) dissects the block. The northern part of this bifurcated five-storey building is devoted to a large reference area and administration; the southern part to the reading areas and open bookstacks of the lending library. The two halves are linked by a bridge at first-floor level, which forms the entrance to the library at the heart of the scheme, and at basement level. There is a further space division in that the main library functions are contained on the lower three levels, and administration and offices on the upper three floors of both parts of the building.

Main circulation staircases in glazed areas flank and animate the *Gasse*, creating a sense of openness and interchange between library users and passers-by. Two triangular bays rounded at their ends project from the block to the north of the *Gasse*, which overlooks quiet back gardens. These bays create special rooms and are used most effectively in the basement children's library which opens on to gardens. The urban context of the southern block is very different, however. Here the architects have chosen to create a curved block in response to the traffic flowing around the site. This drum form has a powerful precedent in Gunnar Asplund's drum-like Stockholm City Library of 1928, and many critics have pointed out that Alvar Aalto later built a series of three roughly semi-circular libraries in Finland and in Oregon in the USA under Asplund's influence.

There is certainly a spirit of Aalto in the play on space and light within the glorious, multi-level interior spaces of the Münster library. Staircases, bridges and giant cranked laminated timber portal frames which carry the sloping walls towards the *Gasse* draw lines on a giant canvas of white plaster and warm birchwood acoustic panelling. Floors are cut back progressively to reveal compelling diagonal vistas between levels. Chair classics by Arne Jacobsen and Harry Bertoia nestle in this landscape of abstracted sculptural grace, as well as the architects' own furniture designs. At the upper levels, tiny windows punch small squares in the façade, allowing unexpected views of the outside world.

Rich in ideas and detailing, this 10,000 square-metre project has brought Julia Bolles, a native of Münster, and Peter Wilson, who hails from Melbourne, to international attention. The couple met at the Architectural Association in London in the 1970s under the guidance of Alvin Boyarsky. When they won an architectural competition to design the library in 1987, they moved into an apartment in Münster, right next to the site in order to shape the building's development. Their dedication has paid off with a scheme which is exciting and radical in interior conception without ever being a frenzied, alien or unwelcome insertion in the fabric of the city.

**MÜNSTER'S NEW LIBRARY IS
AN ARCHITECTURAL GAME OF TWO HALVES,
A PROFOUND CONTEXTUAL RESPONSE
TO THE SITE WHICH YIELDS MULTI-LEVEL
INTERIOR SPACES OF EXCEPTIONAL
LIGHT AND VOLUME.**

Above: Giant cranked timber portal frames carry sloping plaster and birchwood walls in the open reading areas.
Left: A narrow pedestrian street or *Gasse* divides the white sweep of the Münster library into two distinct blocks linked by a bridge at first-floor level. In the background is the Lamberti Church, a reflection of the complex urban context.

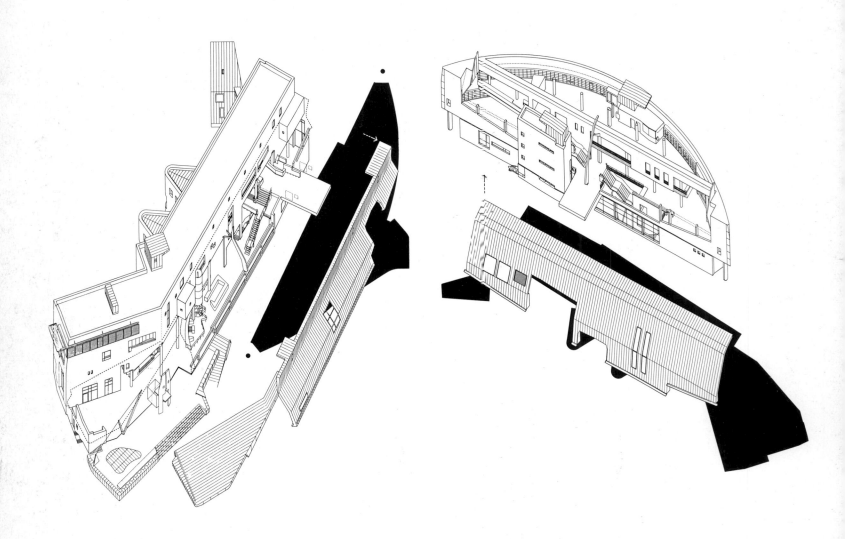

Above: Exploded axonometrics revealing the two parts of the library. The northern wing (left) is devoted to reference and administration; the southern block, with its drum-like form (right), to reading areas and the lending library.

Opposite: A view from the bridge into the lending area up the stairs in the southern block. Compelling vistas are revealed by floors being cut back progressively.

Above and opposite: Spectacular double-height reading-room interiors, suffused with natural light but also skilfully integrating artificial lighting. The scheme is rich in invention and detail, and classic chairs coexist with the architects' own furniture designs.

Apicella Associates

9 Ivebury Court, 325 Latimer Road,
London W10 6RA

Apicella Associates is a London-based practice of architects and designers founded in 1988 by Lorenzo Apicella. Their current projects include everything from interiors and light-weight structures to proposals for a major new arts building in Cambridge. Lorenzo Apicella studied at Nottingham University, Canterbury College of Art and the Royal College of Art in London. He began his career in the USA working for Skidmore Owings and Merrill on the design of the 70-storey Allied Bank Plaza in Houston. Prior to establishing his own practice he led the architecture and design group of the international London consultancy Imagination. He has been a visiting critic at numerous schools of design since 1986 and currently teaches in the graduate school of architecture at Oxford Brookes University.

Arquitectonica International Corp.

2151 Lejeune Road, Suite 300, Coral Gables,
Florida 33134, USA

Arquitectonica was founded in 1977 by Laurinda Spear (FAIA) and Bernardo Fort-Brescia who received Masters degrees from Columbia and Harvard Universities respectively. Today the Florida-based architectural practice is well known worldwide for its inventive use of colour and form, and has offices in Miami, New York, San Francisco and Chicago. As well as extensive work in Miami, recent projects include the Taipei Fine Arts Museum, Taiwan (1990); Centre for Innovative Technology, Virginia (1990); the Gallery MA, Tokyo (1993) and the Banque de Luxembourg (1993). Both partners are in demand by professional, civic and academic groups as lecturers, and the American Institute of Architects has published a book dedicated to their work. The firm has received awards from the AIA and Progressive Architecture. Forthcoming schemes include the United States Embassy in Lima, Peru and a Performing Arts Centre and Urban Complex in Dijon, France.

Alfredo Arribas Arquitectos Asociados,SL

C. Balmes n. 345, 08006 Barcelona, Spain

Alfredo Arribas was born in Barcelona in 1954 and studied architecture at the Superior Technical School of Architecture of Barcelona where from 1978—80 he was Professor of Projects. From 1982—85 he was President of INFAD (the Association of Interior Designers) and in 1990 received a FAD Gold Medal in recognition of his career. Arribas founded his own company in 1986, and recent projects have included the Spanish Contemporary Art Museum, Marugame, Japan (1991—93); Acuarinto Children's Hall, Nagasaki, Japan (1992—93); sceneries and architectural elements – the opening/closing ceremonies at the Olympic Games in Barcelona (1992); the Gran Velvet bar in Badalona (1992—93) and a café/ pavilion annexe at the Schirn Kunsthalle, Frankfurt (1993). Work under construction includes projects in Spain, Japan, Germany and China.

Ove Arup & Partners

Consulting Engineers, 13 Fitzroy Street,
London W10 6BQ

Ove Arup is an international organization which provides consulting civil, building and industrial engineering and related services. It employs 4,000 staff working in 40 countries and has worked with most of the leading architects worldwide. Operational decisions are in the hands of units which vary in size from a dozen to two hundred or more and which represent specific areas of technical or geographic activity.

Shigeru Ban

5-2-4 Matsubara, Setagaya, Tokyo, Japan

Shigeru Ban was born in Tokyo in 1957 and studied at the Southern California Institute of Architecture and the Cooper Union School of Architecture. From 1982—83 he worked with Arata Isozaki. He established his own company in 1985. Since 1993 he has been the Adjunct Professor of Architecture at Tama Art University.

BDG/McColl

24 St John Street, London EC1M 4AY

BDG/McColl (formerly the Business Design Group) was founded in 1962, specializing in office planning and design. They have offices throughout the UK and also in Frankfurt and Budapest. Clients that Business Design Group have worked with include Thomas Cook, American Express, Inland Revenue, Department of Trade and Industry, Department of Transport, British Gas, Ernst and Young, Smith Kline Beecham and BZW.

Behnisch & Partner

Büro Sillenbuch, Gorch-Fock-strasse 30,
70619 Stuttgart, Germany

Günter Behnisch was born in Dresden in 1922. He studied at the Technical University of Stuttgart and set up his own office in 1952. In 1979 he founded Behnisch & Partner along with Winfried Büxel, Manfred Sabatke and Erhard Tränkner. Today the practice concentrates on large-scale public commissions. Recent projects include banks in Frankfurt, Munich and Stuttgart, schools, sports facilities and the German Flight Safety Bureau. Behnisch is a member of the Akademie der Künste, an Honorary Doctor at the University of Stuttgart, a member of the International Academy of Architecture in Sofia and an Honorary member of the Royal Incorporation of Architects in Scotland. In 1992 he was awarded the Gold Medal by the Architectural Academy in Paris.

Benthem Crouwel Architekten BV

Weerdestein 20, 1083 GA Amsterdam,
The Netherlands

Benthem Crouwel Architekten was founded in 1979 by Jan Benthem and Mels Crouwel who both studied at the Technical University of Delft. Their practice is involved mainly with public works in the fields of urban design, utility buildings, offices and museums. Recent projects include the AHOY Exhibition Centre (1993); the West Terminal at Schiphol Airport 1993), and the Museum Nieuw Land at Lelysted (1994). They are currently working extensively at Schiphol Airport on a railway station and World Trade Centre.

Architekturbüro Bolles-Wilson & Partner

Alter Steinweg 17, 48143 Münster, Germany

Architekturbüro Bolles and Wilson was founded in 1987 by Julia B. Bolles-Wilson and Peter Wilson, architects who had previously worked together in their own London-based practice, Wilson Partnership. Peter Wilson was born and studied in Melbourne, Australia. Before starting work with Julia Bolles he had undertaken further training at the Architectural Association where he was Unit Master from 1978—88. Julia Bolles was born in Münster and studied at the University of Karlsruhe. Postgraduate studies were followed by a teaching position at the Chelsea School of Art which came to an end when she started working with Peter Wilson in 1980. Projects include a government office in Münster (1991—95); an exhibition stand at the Osaka Expo' 1990 and a waterfront and restaurant in Rotterdam due for completion in 1995.

Branson Coates Architecture Ltd

23 Old Street, London EC1V 9HL

Branson Coates was founded in 1985 by Nigel Coates and Doug Branson. Nigel Coates was born in 1949 and attended the Architectural Association where he was Unit Master from 1979—89. In 1983 he formed NATO (Narrative Architecture Today) with colleagues from the AA. The group published a magazine and exhibited the architects' work. Doug Branson graduated from the Architectural Association in 1975 after which he worked with DEGW. Before co-founding Branson Coates he worked in the Branson Helsel Partnership. BCA's early projects include the Caffe Bongo at Parco in Tokyo as well as retail outlets for Katherine Hamnett, Jigsaw and Jasper Conran. Their work for these clients continues but recent schemes also include the Silo art gallery building in Tokyo (1993) and the Nautilus and La Fôret restaurants at Schiphol Airport (1993). Currently they are occupied with a new 20th-Century Gallery Building for the Geffrye Museum in London and a restaurant for Liberty, London. Branson Coates have designed exhibitions for Dunhill and the Pompidou Centre, Paris, and Nigel Coates is also involved in furniture design (clients include SCP, Poltronova, Arredaesse and Bigelli).

Santiago Calatrava

Höschgasse 5, Zürich CH 8008, Switzerland

Santiago Calatrava Valls was born in Benimamet, Spain, in 1951. He studied at the Art School in Valencia and later graduated in Urban Studies from the Escuela Technica Superior de Arquitectura. Before founding his own architectural and civil engineering practice in Zürich in 1981, he gained a doctorate in Technical Science at the Swiss Federal Institute of Technology and was Assistant in the Institute for Building Statics and Construction and for

Aerodynamics and Light Weight Constructions, also at the ETH, Zürich. Since 1981 he has opened offices in Paris and Valencia and has exhibited his work worldwide, notably at the Suomen Rakennustaiteen Museo, Helsinki, the Royal Institute of British Architects in London, the Museum of Modern Art in New York and the Museum of Applied and Folk Art, Moscow. He is a member of the International Academy of Architecture, an Honorary Member of the Institute of British Architects and a Doctor Honoris Causa at the University of Seville. Calatrava's work includes furniture design: his 1986—87 leather and metal chaise longue was manufactured by de Sede, and the Montjuic floor lamp (1990) was produced by Artemide. He is best known as an architect of bridges, factory sheds and railway stations.

Capella, Larrea i Castellví Associats
Princesa 56, pral. 2a, 08003 Barcelona, Spain

Juli Capella was born in Barcelona in 1960 and Quim Larrea in Cordoba in 1957. Capella studied industrial design and Larrea architecture. Partners since 1982, they were members of the editorial board of *El Croquis* magazine from 1983 to 1987, and they were the founders of the Spanish design magazine *De Diseño*. At present they are editors of the architecture and design magazine *ARDI*. They have been consultants for the Sevilla '92 International Exhibition and for the cultural Olympics of the Barcelona '92 Olympic Committee; they are also active in exhibition organization in Spain. The two have received various awards and have taught at ELISAVE and EINA, as well as at the Universidad Internacional Menendez Pelayo. In 1990 they were joined by Jaume Castellví.

CD Partnership
22 Shad Thames, London SE1 2YU

The architecture, interior and graphic design practice, CD Partnership, was founded by Terence Conran and today employs over 20 designers and architects. Current projects include the design of the Longman Publishing Group's new headquarters in Harlow, Essex; the Conran restaurant Mezzo; a café and lido on two levels of Celebrity Cruises' new super liner due for launch in 1995; the interior design of a luxury hotel in Vienna and the design of Selfridges' restaurant. Graphic projects include the full design and implementation of the new corporate identity for Cabouchon, the UK's leading fashion jeweller, and a development programme for Providence Capitol's product literature.

Jo Coenen & Co. Architekten
Bouillonstraat 14, 6211 LH Maastricht, The Netherlands

Jo Coenen & Co. was founded in 1979. Major projects include offices and residences in Delft (1986); a lecture hall for the University of Limberg, Maastricht (1991) and Chamber of Commerce and Housing Association offices, Maastricht (1991). Born in Heerlen in 1949,

Jo Coenen graduated from the University of Technology, Eindhoven in 1975 and worked for Aldo Van Eyck before forming his own company. He has lectured widely, most notably at the Delft School of Architecture, Tilburg, for six years and at the University of Technology, Karlsruhe, in 1937. He has recently undertaken master planning in The Hague, Maastricht and Amsterdam and has completed the library for the Technical University, Delft.

Edward Cullinan Architects Ltd
Baldwin Terrace, London N1 7RU

Edward Cullinan C.B.E., R.A. founded his own practice in 1959. He was educated at Cambridge and later at the Architectural Association School of Architecture. In 1955—57 he undertook further studies at the University of California, Berkeley, and in 1978 was awarded the George VI Memorial Fellowship. He is a visiting critic and external examiner at Cambridge University where he formerly taught as Second Year Master. During the mid-80s he held various educational positions: he was external examiner at the Royal College of Art and at the University of Edinburgh, amongst others, and he was Visiting Professor at the Massachusetts Institute of Technology, Boston (1985). Cullinan is a Fellow of the Royal Society of Arts and a Trustee of the Sir John Soane Museum. The practice designs a wide range of buildings from conference centres to visitor centres, from schools to hospitals. Projects include the Fountains Abbey Visitors' Centre (1987—92); Purcell School of Music (1987—91); Winchester College Theatre and Arts College, and the Masterplan and Academy for Reez-Rostock, Germany (1993). They are currently working on a Visitors' Centre at Stonehenge and a new International Manufacturing Centre at Warwick University; they are developing master plans for the University of North Carolina at Charlotte in the US, and for the De Montfort University Campus at Milton Keynes; and they are working on an office and retail space on the last undeveloped bomb site in the City of London.

Denton Corker Marshall Pty Ltd
PO Box 1648N, Melbourne, Victoria 3001, Australia

John Denton, Bill Corker and Barrie Marshall studied together at the University of Melbourne in the mid-60s where they now all hold educational positions. After graduation they worked separately before joining to form DCM in 1972 where today they are senior directors of a practice which employs over 120 people and has offices in Hong Kong, Singapore, Jakarta, Tokyo and London. The firm has completed projects on every scale from residential work to major planning and construction schemes. Built projects are many and varied including the Power House Museum of Applied Arts and Sciences (1988); the Australian Embassy, Tokyo (1990); and the Adelphi Hotel (1993); as well as numerous office buildings and commercial and retail outlets. Recent projects include the Governor Phillip Tower Sydney, part of the First Government House Site project which will

include the Museum of Sydney and the 45-storey Governor Macquarie Tower (now under construction). Future schemes will include Melbourne's Exhibition Centre, due for completion in 1996. Bill Corker is the current president of the Victoria RAIA.

Din Associates
32 St Oswalds Place, Vauxhall, London SE11 5UE

Rasshied Din was born in London in 1956 and gained a BA Hons. in interior design from Birmingham Polytechnic. In 1979 he joined Fitch and Co. where he was responsible for design to on-site supervision. After a short period spent in Rome he worked variously as a freelance designer, as senior designer for Peter Glynn Smith Associates, as assistant creative director for Allied International Designers and as a freelance designer for David Davies Associates before forming his own practice in 1986. Since then he has completed various retail outlets for such clients as French Connection, Nicole Farhi and Next. He is a Fellow of the Royal Society of Arts and the Chartered Society of Designers, and he lectures in the UK.

Ecart
111 rue Saint-Antoine, 75004 Paris, France

The Ecart Group was founded in 1978 by Andrée Putman. The practice is divided into three specific disciplines. Ecart SA is the design office, specializing in interior and product design varying from hotels to boutiques, corporate offices to private houses, and museums to governmental offices. Notable designs include the Office of the Minister of Culture (1984); Ebel Headquarters (1985); Morgans Hotel (1985) and the Im Wasserturm Hotel (1990). Ecart International re-edits furniture and objects by such designers as Eileen Grey and Mariano Fortuny and edits designs by Ecart SA (designers regularly used include Patrick Naggar, Paul Mathieu and Michael Ray). Andrée Putman licensing division designs objects distributed throughout the world and includes rugs, upholstery fabrics, tableware and bathroom accessories. Recent projects by Ecart SA number the Cartier Foundation exhibition areas (1993); the Sheraton Hotel, Paris-Roissy (1994); the Bally Boutiques concept (1993—94) and the Brand images of Baccarat and Swarovski.

Evans and Shalev
2 Belsize Crescent, London NW3 5QU

Eldred Evans and David Shalev have been in private practice since 1965 when they won a limited competition for the design of cluster houses in Exeter. The practice's experience to date consists of buildings for education (Newport High School; the Jesus College Library, Cambridge University), welfare (a Home for the disabled and a Children's Reception Centre, London), work places (Dana Industrial Estate in Kent and The Centrum, London), residential (Levy House and Ellis House, London), public buildings (Taoiseach's Residence and State Guest House, Dublin; Truro Courts of Justice; Tate Gallery, St Ives) and urban design. Recent projects include

the Loggie Baird Museum, Glasgow (1993) and the Museum for Contemporary Arts, Newcastle upon Tyne (1994). Eldred Evans studied at the Architectural Association and at Yale University; David Shalev trained at the Technion School of Architecture, Israel. Both partners have taught at the Architectural Association and other schools of architecture in the UK and have been RIBA external examiners.

Fitch & Co.
Porters South, 4 Crinian Street, London N1 9UE

Fitch & Co. is the London-based branch of Fitch-RS which also has offices in the United States and affiliates in Europe and the Far East. The practice is concerned with interior design, graphic communication, product design and architecture. Major clients include Coca Cola, Reebock, Midland Bank, Hamleys, Woolworths, Virgin Atlantic, Disney Development Corporation, and the Science and Victoria and Albert Museums. Recent projects number the Virgin Atlantic Conservatory (Heathrow Terminal 3); Dillons Bookstore (Birmingham); offices for the London-based newspaper *Loot* and the identity of London Buses.

Sir Norman Foster and Partners
Riverside Three, 22 Hester Road. London SW11 4AN

Sir Norman Foster was born in Manchester, England, in 1935 and studied architecture and city planning at the University of Manchester and at Yale University. He established Team 4 in 1963 – with his late wife, Wendy, and Su and Richard Rogers – and founded Foster Associates in 1967. Today he is internationally famous for his high-tech designs, many of which have resulted directly from competitions, such as the Hong Kong and Shanghai Bank (1979—86), and Stansted Airport (1981—89). Recent projects include the Sackler Galleries at the Royal Academy of Arts, London, which was named the RIBA building of the year in 1993; the Centre D'Art/cultural centre, Nîmes, and the Reichstag remodelling, Berlin. Master plans include the Kings Cross development, London. His most recent projects are a new headquarters for Commerzbank in Frankfurt, and a new airport at Chek Lap Kok for Hong Kong – covering an area of 1.248 hectares, it is the largest project in the world. Norman Foster received a Knighthood in the Queen's Birthday Honours in 1991, and his work has won over 60 awards and citations. He is a well-known figure on the international lecturing circuit. Although primarily concerned with large-scale architectural projects, Sir Norman Foster is also active in furniture design.

Kristian Gavoille Architecte
6 rue de Tocqueville, 75017 Paris, France

Kristian Gavoille was born in 1956 in Brazzaville, Africa, and studied architecture in Toulouse. He has lived and worked in Paris since 1984. He collaborated with several architectural offices in Paris and Toulouse from 1984 to 1986. He then worked with Philippe Starck on a number of projects including the Royalton Hotel, New York, and the Teatriz Restaurant in Madrid. In 1987 he received a grant from VIA which allowed him to produce a range of prototypes. He then began a collaboration with Disform and Néotù, and a range of his products was presented by these companies at the Milan Fair in 1988. He has worked on stage, exhibition and television set design, and since 1990 has become increasingly involved in interior design projects. Gavoille has exhibited his work widely within Europe.

Gensler & Associates/Architects
One Rockerfeller Plaza, Suite 500.
New York, New York 10020, USA

The San Francisco-based company of Gensler & Associates was founded in 1965 by Arthur Gensler, Jr (FAIA). They have offices throughout the USA and in Hong Kong and Tokyo, and have received more than 250 local and national design awards. The practice provides a broad range of services, including architectural design, interior architectural design, building and site evaluation, space planning, graphic design, signage design, product design and master planning. Clients include Apple Computer, Bank of America, Sony Pictures Entertainment Inc., The Walt Disney Company, General Motors and the Pepsi-Cola company.

Geyer Design Pty Ltd
259 Collins Street, Melbourne, Victoria 3000.
Australia

Geyer Design was founded in 1977 by Peter and Sandra Geyer after extensive experience as senior interior designers with major architectural practices. Michael Greer and Stephen Fitts joined Geyer Design in 1985 and 1989 respectively and have since become directors of the practice. Today Geyer Design is the largest specialist interior design practice in Australia, specializing in corporate and retail interior fitouts. Clients include Bankers Trust, Australia, IBM, John Fairfax Group, National Australia Bank, Telecom Australia, Coles Myer Group, Fiorucci, Just Jeans, Kmart and Mobil, Australia. Recently Geyer have been working on a national training centre for Arthur Anderson & Co. in Melbourne; head offices for BHP; offices for IBM Australia and a network management centre for Australia's telecommunications giant, Telecom.

Volker Giencke & Company
Mozartgasse 6, A-8010 Graz, Austria

Volker Giencke believes architecture to be a "complex interaction of construction, material, content and space", a concept which is expressed clearly in his work to date. Born in 1947 in Wolfsberg, Carinthia, he studied architecture and philosophy in Graz. He collaborated in various architectural offices in Geneva, Munich, Cologne, Vienna and Graz before founding his own practice in 1981. Major projects include housing schemes and exhibition design; the Porsche administration building in Salzberg; the Odörfer showroom and warehouse, Klagenfurt; the Congress Hall and Hotel in Klagenfurt (1992); the Cultural Institute of Austria in New York (1992); the Austrian Expo

Pavilion, Seville (1992); the adaptation of the Sechau monastery and gym, Graz (1987—), and the Museum of Modern Art, Helsinki. He is currently Professor at the University of Innsbruck, a lecturer at the Summer Academy for Architecture in Graz and visiting Professor at the Universidad de Buenos Aires, the Arkitekthogskolen, Oslo, and Yale School of Architecture. He has exhibited his work widely.

Nicholas Grimshaw & Partners Ltd
1 Conway Street, Fitzroy Square.
London W1P 5HA

Nicholas Grimshaw founded his own practice in 1980, having already won acclaim for his industrial architecture with buildings for Citroën, Zanussi, Herman Miller and BMW. Today the firm handles a wider scope of projects including sports and leisure complexes, commercial and retail buildings and schemes in the field of television and radio. Notable buildings include the Oxford Ice Rink; the Financial Times Printing Works; a large urban development in London; completion of a new research facility for Xerox Research, and the International Passenger Terminal for the Channel Tunnel at Waterloo. Currently under construction is the Berlin Stock Exchange and Communication Centre. Nicholas Grimshaw believes that architectural form should reflect the function of a building, and his ergonomically controlled designs have been the subject of many awards and commendations including a number from the Civic Trust, the Department of the Environment, the Royal Institute of British Architects and the Royal Fine Art Commission.

Hellmuth, Obata & Kassabaum Inc.
211 North Broadway, One Metropolitan Square, Suite 600, St Louis, Missouri 63102-2231, USA

Hellmuth, Obata & Kassabaum was founded in 1955 and today employs over 1,300 people. Their area of expertise covers work for major corporations, developers, state and local agencies, sports facilities, hospital colleges and universities, the US government and governments in Canada, the Caribbean, Central and South America, the Middle East and Asia. The firm offers services in architecture, engineering, interior design, graphic design, planning, landscape architecture, facility programming/management and consulting. Gyo Obata FAIA, is co-chairman of the firm. He received a Bachelor's degree in architecture in 1945 from Washington University and a Master's in architecture and urban design from the Cranbrook Academy of Art. He has Honorary PhDs from Washington and the University of Missouri. George Hellmuth (now retired) received a Bachelor's and Master's degree from Washington University and also studied at the Ecole des Beaux Arts at Fountainebleau, France. He was given the Gold Medal Award by the St Louis Chapter of the AIA. George Kassabaum FAIA (died 1982) also studied at Washington University. He served as a national president of the AIA in 1968—69 and as chancellor of the College of Fellows of the AIA in 1977—78.

Michael Hopkins & Partners
27 Broadley Terrace, London NW1 6LG

Michael Hopkins & Partners was formed in 1976 and today has five partners: Michael Hopkins, Patricia Hopkins, John Pringle, Ian Sharratt and Bill Taylor. The practice is well known for its advance building techniques which utilize such modern materials as lightweight fabric structures, steel and glass, and its reinterpretation of traditional materials. It is also noted for its work with listed buildings such as Sir Albert Richardson's Bracken House, the Victoria and Albert Museum and Glyndebourne Opera House. Principal projects include the Hopkins' family house in Hampstead, London (1976); the Schlumberger Research Laboratories, Cambridge (1985); and Bedfont Lakes for MEPC (1992). Currently at the design stage are new parliamentary offices for the House of Commons. Michael Hopkins has been awarded a CBE for Services to Architecture. He is a Royal Academician, a commissioner with the Royal Institute of British Architects and Architectural Association Councils and a Trustee of the Thomas Cubitt Trust.

Jestico & Whiles Architects
14 Stephenson Way, London NW1 2HD

The architectural practice of Jestico & Whiles was founded in 1977 by principals Tom Jestico, John Whiles, Robert Collingwood and Tony Ingram and today has offices in London Glasgow, Prague and Munich. Preoccupation with lightweight structures and components can be seen in early industrial projects at Epsom (1979) and Waltham Cross (1982), whilst later schemes for Friends of the Earth, Policy Studies Institute and research for the UK Department of Energy represent the development of Jestico & Whiles' approach to the concept of low-energy work spaces. Further projects include a science and technology park in Scotland and several inner-city industrial/office buildings, including Gallery Court, Stukeley Street and Jockey's Fields. Current work numbers embassies and ambassador's residences in Latvia, Bulgaria and Bratislava; a major CrossRail station interchange, and their largest project to date – Burrell's Wharf, a £28 million residential and leisure development on a Grade II listed site in London's docklands.

King-Miranda Associati
Via Forcella 3, 20144 Milan, Italy

King-Miranda Associati was founded in 1976 by Perry King and Santiago Miranda and today operates in the fields of industrial, interior, interface and graphic design. They have clients both in Italy and abroad and have realized projects in Europe, the United States and Japan. In addition to working with some of the main office furniture and lighting companies in Italy, they have designed for manufacturers in the electromechanical and office equipment industries and were responsible for the design of the exterior public lighting system at Expo '92. King and Miranda are also involved in teaching and research and in 1989 were awarded the Spanish National Design Award.

Yasuo Kondo
T-3 2F Bond Street, 2-2-43 Higashishinagawa, Shinagawa-ku, Tokyo, Japan

Yasuo Kondo was born in 1950 in Tokyo and graduated from the Interior Architecture Department of Tokyo University of Art and Design in 1973. Before founding his own design office in 1981 he worked both for Masahiro Miwa Environmental Design Office and Shiro Kuramata. To date projects have included restaurants, showrooms and domestic schemes in Japan, various national retail outlets and, in 1988, a boutique for Comme des Garçons Shirt (Paris and New York). He has won acclaim for his designs in Japan and the United States, being awarded the American Institute of Architects Design Prize in 1989. In the same year he published a book on his design philosophy entitled *Interior Space Designing*.

Kisho Kurokawa Architect & Associates
Aoyama Bldg 11F, 1-2-3 Kita-Aoyama, Minato-ku, Tokyo, Japan

Kisho Kurokawa was born in Nagoya in 1934 and studied architecture at Kyoto University. In 1960, while studying for a doctorate at Tokyo University, he formed the Metabolist Group, whose philosophy – closely linked with Buddhism – viewed urban architectural forms as organisms capable of growth and change, a belief which is echoed in his designs to date. Major projects include the National Bunraku Theatre, Osaka; the Roppongi Prince Hotel, Tokyo; the Japanese-German Culture Centre in Berlin and the national museums of modern art in Nagoya, Hiroshima and Wakayama. As well as his architectural works, he has designed distinctive furniture for Tendo and Kosuga and has exhibited in New York, Paris, London, Dublin, Moscow, Milan, Florence, Rome, Budapest and Sofia.

MacCormac Jamieson Prichard
9 Heneage Street, London E1 5LJ

MacCormac Jamieson and Prichard was founded in 1972 by Richard MacCormac (born 1938), Peter Jamieson (born 1939) and David Prichard (born 1948). Both MacCormac and Jamieson studied at the University of Cambridge and at University College, whilst Prichard trained at the Bartlett School of Architecture where he is now RIBA External Examiner. MacCormac was president of the Royal Institute of British Architects until 1993 and has taught and lectured widely. Jamieson teaches at the University of Cambridge. The practice encompasses a broad range of building types from highly crafted buildings for Oxford and Cambridge Colleges to offices, public buildings, housing for both the public and private sectors, and large commercial projects such as the redevelopment of Spitalfields Market. MJP have prepared master plans and urban designs for sites such as Paternoster Square and Kings Cross, for green field sites in new towns and for reclaimed land in London's docklands. The practice has published a number of articles on architecture, urban regeneration and planning and in particular on the relationship of new architecture to historic settings. They have also carried out research into office design, energy efficiency and land use.

Lawrence Man Architect
47-13 Cogswoll Avenue, Cambridge, Massachusetts 02140, USA

Lawrence Man founded his own architectural company in 1992, before which he worked for Shepley Bulfinch Richardson and Abbott where his responsibility included design, construction documents and project management. His professional career commenced with a five-year contract with E. Verner Johnson and Associates where his expertise was in the planning and designing of various museums within the United States, including the Yale University Art Gallery. Projects since 1992 number the Tai Pan restaurant, a dental surgery, domestic design schemes, and work continues at present on the Public Museum of Grand Rapids.

Soichi Mizutani Design Office Co. Ltd
3FC Box 8, 4-24-10 Minami-Aoyama, Minato-ku, Tokyo 107, Japan

Soichi Mizutani was born in Fukui in 1955 and studied at the Kyoto Junior Art College. After graduation in 1975 he worked for Plastic Studio, establishing his own practice in 1986. Important projects include the Sakura restaurant (1984); Setsu, Getsu, KA (1985); AOI (1986); Tambaya (1989); Setsugekka Restaurant Bar (1993) and the Sakamoto residence, as well as various showrooms for Kansai, Yamamoto, Katherine Hamnett, Hiromichi Nakano y Renaud Pellegrino and Eyes in Tokyo. Mizutani has been presented with numerous awards in his native country and is a member of the Japan Environmental Architecture Association. He is a part-time instructor at Kuwazawa Design Studio and part-time lecturer at Aoyame Environmental Design Institute – Commercial Architectural Design Major.

Morphosis
2041 Colorado Avenue, Santa Monica, California, USA

Morphosis is a Los Angeles-based architectural practice founded by Thom Mayne and Michael Rotundi in 1975. Thom Mayne trained at the University of Southern California School of Architecture and obtained a Master's of Architecture from the Harvard University Graduate School of Design. Rotundi studied at the Southern California Institute of Architecture where he is now director. Recent projects include the Comprehensive Cancer Centre, Florida (1989); Salick Corporate Headquarters, Los Angeles (1990); the Visual and Performing Arts School, Thomas More College, Kentucky; Chiba Golf Club and Higashi Azabu Tower, Japan (1991) and the Las Vegas Homeless Shelter Educational Facility (1993). Many of the practice's projects have been included in exhibitions and have won a number of AIA and Progressive Architecture awards.

Torsten Neeland
Brahsallee 19, 20144 Hamburg, Germany

Torsten Neeland was born in 1963 in Hamburg and graduated from the Hochschule für Bildende Künste, having studied industrial design. Work for his own practice includes such interior design projects as the Uta Raasch fashion store, Düsseldorf (1988), Hamburg (1991—92); a doctor's office in Hamburg (1993) and the Go shoe shop (1993). He is equally well known for his product design, producing a range of items including candlesticks, lamps and bowls for Anta; a coat hanger for Anthologie Quartett; furniture for Reim Interline and a cosmetic counter for Estée Lauder. He has exhibited his work in Europe and has had a joint show at the Düsseldorf Museum of Arts.

Nikken Sekkei Ltd
4-6-2 Koraibashi, Chuo-ku, Osaka, Japan

Nikken Sekkei Ltd is Japan's largest architectural engineering consulting firm. Since its formation in 1950, it has grown steadily to become a major, multi-discipline design organization with nearly 1,500 permanent professionals and support staff. Nikken has handled more than 13,000 projects to date – including overseas operations since 1964 – and has expanded its field of activity to 40 countries, completing more than 300 projects. Nikken has received many national and international awards for design, engineering and planning.

Jean Nouvel et Associés
4 Cité Griset, 75011 Paris, France

Jean Nouvel was born in 1945 in Lot, Garonne. He graduated from the Ecole National Supérieure des Beaux Arts, Paris, in 1977. His practice became internationally known following the design of the Institute du Monde Arabe, Paris, in 1987. Other important projects include the Hotel-Restaurant St James, Bordeaux (1989); the cultural centre at Mélun-Sér art (1986); the renovation of the Opera House in Lyons (1990 competition award); the Cartier Foundation Paris (1994) and the Tour Sans Fin at La Défense, Paris. Jean Nouvel continues to produce successful furniture designs, collaborating with Ligne Roset, Ecart and other manufacturers. His work has received many major design awards internationally.

O'Herlihy & Warner Architects
San Francisco, California, USA

O'Herlihy & Warner Architects was established in 1987 by Lorcan O'Herlihy and Richard Warner and is primarily concerned with small-scale domestic and retail projects. O'Herlihy previously worked with I. M. Pei – on the additions to the Louvre museum – Steven Holl and Kevin Roche and is presently lecturing at the Architectural Association in London. Richard Warner worked with H.O.K. Architects, Peter Calthorpe and as a consultant with Steven Holl. Their work has been published internationally in *Progressive Architecture*, *Architectural Record*, *G Houses*, *Abitare*, *Architectural Digest* and by Rizzoli.

Pei Cobb Freed & Partners
600 Madison Avenue, New York, New York 10022, USA

Ieoh Ming Pei was born in China in 1917. He moved to the USA to study architecture at the Massachusetts Institute of Technology, receiving a Bachelor of Architecture degree in 1940. He then studied at the Harvard Graduate School of Design under Walter Gropius, at the same time teaching in the faculty as Assistant Professor, and gained a Master's degree in 1946. In 1955 Pei formed I. M. Pei & Associates which became I. M. Pei and Partners in 1966 and Pei Cobb Freed and Partners in 1989. The practice has designed over 150 projects in the USA and abroad, more than half of which have won awards and citations. As well as working for corporate and private investment clients, the practice has executed numerous commissions for public authorities and religious, educational and cultural institutions. Its most important buildings include the Bank of China, Hong Kong; the East West Wing of the National Gallery of Washington D.C.; the Grand Louvre in Paris and the United States Holocaust Memorial Museum which recently opened in Washington. Works in progress include the Federal Triangle, Washington, and the San Francisco Main Public Library. Pei is a Fellow of the American Institute of Architects, a Corporate Member of the Royal Institute of Architects, and in 1975 he was made a member of the American Academy. He has honorary degrees from leading universities in the USA, Hong Kong and France.

Perumal Bogatai Kenda & Freeman
105 Glebe Point Road, Glebe NSW 2037, Australia

Perumal Bogatai Kenda & Freeman is an interior design practice which originated as Bogatai and Associates in 1977 and became Perumal Bogatai and Partners in 1986, dealing with all aspects of interior design. Following its merger with Desmond Freeman in 1992, the practice has specialized in the fields of health facility interior design and graphic design and is currently working for the Malaysian health system. The firm acts as consultants in hospitality projects, restoration works, club and recreational facilities, including the interior design, furniture, fittings and equipment for royal palaces in the Middle East and Asia.

Renzo Piano Building Workshop
IB-C 3F Minamikyuhoji-Cho, Chuo-ku Osaka 541, Japan

Renzo Piano was born in Genoa in 1937 and graduated from the School of Architecture at Milan Polytechnic in 1964. He worked with Louis Kahn in Philadelphia and Z. S. Malowski in London before collaborating with Richard Rogers, Peter Rice and Richard Fitzgerald. In 1981 he established the Renzo Piano Building Workshop and today has offices in Genoa, Paris and Osaka. Recent projects include the Kansai International Airport, the Potsdamer Platz Urban Redevelopment, Cité Internationale in Lyons, the Science and Technology Museum in Amsterdam and the Mercedes Benz offices in Stuttgart.

Antoine Predock Architect
300 Twelfth Street NW, Albuquerque, New Mexico 87102, USA

Antoine Predock studied at the University of New Mexico, Albuquerque and at Columbia University, New York and founded his own practice in 1967. He is a Fellow of the American Institute of Architects and his work has received numerous awards and citations. Recent projects include the Institute of American Indian Arts, Santa Fe; the Student Affairs & Administrative Services Building at the University of California, Santa Barbara and the Hispanic Cultural Centre, Albuquerque. He has held educational positions at numerous universities in the United States including Harvard (1987) and UCLA (1989—90 and 1990—91) and is a well-known figure on the lecturing circuit. Predock's work has been published widely and he has exhibited nationally and internationally.

Michele Saee
3215 Glendale Blvd., Los Angeles, California 90039, USA

Michele Saee was born in Tehran in 1956. In 1973, after a brief stay in London, he moved to Florence to attend the University of Florence School of Architecture where he obtained a Master of Arts in Architecture. He later studied Technical Urban Planning at the Institute of Engineering in Milan and worked for two years with the Florence-based design studio Superstudio. In 1983 he left Italy for the United States and worked for Morphosis, finally forming his own design practice in 1985. He currently lives and works in Los Angeles and teaches at the Southern California Institute of Architecture. Recent projects include the Pave Jewellery Store, Brentwood, California; Angeli Restaurant in the Rodeo Collection and Art-Angeli, the Southern California Institute of Architecture Café in Los Angeles. Saee's work has received several AIA and Progressive Architecture Awards and he is a well-known figure on the American lecturing circuit.

Fernando Salas Studio
Pellaires 30-38, 08019 Barcelona, Spain

Fernando Salas commenced his professional career in the offices of Oriol Bohigas, Josep Martorell y David Mackay before founding his own company in 1975. He was born in Sta Cruz de Modela in Spain and today lives and works in Barcelona. He is active in the fields of office, retail and showroom interiors as well as in furniture design. Clients include Roberto Verino, Deni Cler and Daniel Hechter; he also collaborated on projects with Javier Mariscal for whom he designed a studio in 1989. From 1984 to 1985 he taught at the Elisava Design School in Barcelona and has often received ADI FAD awards.

Samyn et Associés
Avenue H. Boulenger 25,B-1180 Brussels, Belgium

Samyn et Associés was founded in 1980 by

Philippe Samyn and reorganized in 1991 to include associates Richard Delaunoit and Denis Melotte. The firm is active in the fields of research and development, planning, landscape design, architecture and interior design, and has undertaken work in The Netherlands, England, Spain, France, Greece and Italy as well as in its native Belgium. Such projects as the National Bank of Belgium, Brussels (1981—84); the Thompson Aircraft Tire Corporation, Frameries (1991); the renovation of the Solboch University Campus, Brussels (1991—) and M & G Richerche SpA Vanafro, Italy (1990—91), as well as numerous town-planning and housing schemes, demonstrate a preoccupation with form and material. Philippe Samyn was born in 1948 and studied at the Massachusetts Institute of Technology and at the Ecole de Commerce Solvay. He has been Principal Lecturer at the Free University of Brussels in the Faculty of Applied Sciences since 1984 and at the National School of Architecture, La Cambre, since 1978. In 1992 Samyn was elected as corresponding member of the Royal Academy of Belgium and member of the board of SECO (National Technical Control Office for Construction).

Sheppard Robson
77 Parkway, Camden Town, London NW1 7PU

Sheppard Robson was formed over fifty years ago, initially being involved with the design of industrial, housing and educational buildings. Today the practice has expanded and work includes schemes for central area redevelopments involving shopping, housing and office headquarters buildings, hospitals, laboratories, leisure facilities and large-scale development plans for universities and medical research facilities both in the UK and abroad. Completed projects include Churchill College, Cambridge; Brunel University; Manchester Polytechnic; Westminster Hospital and Glaxo Group Research. Sheppard Robson has received numerous professional and civic awards for design and has formed collaborations with leading overseas architects.

Smith-Miller & Hawkinson Architects
305 Canal Street, New York,
New York 10013, USA

Smith-Miller & Hawkinson was founded in 1982 by Henry Smith-Miller and Laurie Hawkinson and has received numerous awards for its work in arts-related projects and work involving renovation of existing structures. Laurie Hawkinson studied art at the University of California, Berkeley, and architecture at the Cooper Union, New York, and has been vice-president of the board of directors of the Wooster Group in New York since 1985. Henry Smith-Miller studied at Princeton University, New Jersey, and later at Yale and Pennsylvania. Before co-founding his own practice he spent several years in Rome as Fulbright Professor and worked for a period with Richard Meier. He lectures widely and has held permanent educational positions at Harvard and the Universities of Washington and Virginia. Recent

projects include an amphitheatre and outdoor cinema for the North Carolina Museum of Art (1992—95); the Corning Museum of Glass, Corning, New York (1993—94) and production offices for Global Pursuits/Sweetlands (USA) (1994—95).

Sottsass Associati
Via Borgonuovo 9, 20121 Milan, Italy

Sottsass Associati was founded in 1980 by Ettore Sottsass, together with Aldo Cibic, Marco Marabelli, Matteo Thun and Marco Zanini. Mike Ryan and Johanna Grawunder have been junior partners since 1989 and James Irvine and Mario Milizia since 1992 and 1993, respectively. Sottsass Associati initially concentrated on furniture and industrial and interior design, but it has since expanded and is now active in the fields of graphic design, corporate identity and architecture. Ettore Sottsass was born in Innsbruck in 1917 and graduated from the University of Turin in 1939. Well known for the "radical architecture" of the Memphis Group, his concern with experimentation and research has also distinguished Sottsass Associati's work over the years. Marco Zanini was born in Trento in 1954 and graduated in architecture from Florence University. After a period of travel and work experience in the United States he started work in Milan, first as assistant to Ettore Sottsass and then as one of the founders of Sottsass Associati. Since this time he has designed products for Knoll and Esprit and has worked on various domestic and industrial interior design projects. In 1988 he held a one-man show of drawings and watercolours at the Galleria Antonia Jannone in Milan. Sottsass Associati's clients include Knoll, Cassina, Zanotta, Philips, Olivetti, Apple Computers, Zumtobel and NTT. Several architectural projects have also been completed including the Wolf House in Colorado; the Oshima Residence in Tokyo; Cei House in Empoli and renovations of buildings in Milan, Austria, Germany and France. The practice has been successful in numerous architectural competitions such as "The Peak" in Hong Kong; the Accademia Bridge in Venice; the MK3 building in Düsseldorf; Twin Dome City in Fukuoka and the interior design for the Flower Dome Stadium in Osaka.

STUDIOS Architecture
99 Green Street, San Francisco,
California 94111, USA

STUDIOS Architecture was founded in 1985 by Darryl T. Roberson, Erik Sueberkrop, Gene Rae and Phillip Olson and today has offices in San Francisco, Washington, New York, London and Paris. Sueberkrop, who today heads the company, was born in Hamburg and educated at the University of Cincinnati, Ohio. Recently completed projects include a manufacturing headquarters in Dublin; a university alumni and visitor centre building for the University of California; the interiors of a showroom for Knoll Group in Germany; conference facilities for Société Générale, Paris; interiors for the Asia and Pacific Trade Centre in Osaka and the Petronas headquarters in Kuala Lumpur.

STUDIOS also designs corporate interiors for many prominent law firms, financial concerns and high-tech companies in the USA, Europe and Asia, including Apple Computer, Silicon Graphics, Arnold & Porter, and Morgan Stanley & Company. The practice has been awarded American Institute of Architects Merit Awards on numerous occasions, and its work has been published in many of the leading design magazines in Europe and the USA.

Shin Takamatsu Architect and Associates
36-4 Jyobadaiin-cho, Takeda, Fushimi-ku, Kyoto 612, Japan

Shin Takamatsu was born in 1948 in Shimane Prefecture, Japan. He trained at Kyoto University and in 1977 established the Takumi Design Office. He held educational positions at Fukui Technical University, Osaka College of Art's architectural department and was Assistant Professor of the Kyoto Seika University until 1991. Shin Takamatsu Architect and Associates was founded in 1980, the Takamatsu Planning Office in 1988 and Takamatsu & Layani Architects Associates in Berlin in 1992. His work has received considerable acclaim within Japan and he was given the Kyoto Prefecture Meritorious Cultural Service Award in 1994. He has exhibited in Europe and the United States, having solo shows at the San Francisco Museum of Modern Art and the Aedes Gallery, Germany. Recent projects include the Nima Museum of Bohemian Art, Shimane (1993) and the YKK Okayama II office (1993).

Togashi Design Studio Co. Ltd
6-8-3-402 Minami-Aoyama,
Minato-ku, Tokyo, Japan

Katsuhiko Togashi was born in 1947 in Japan and graduated from the Kuwasawa Design Research Institute. He is an interior designer and president of Togashi Design Studio Co. Ltd, which he formed in 1986. His professional career started in the Uchida Design Office (Studio 80) where he worked as chief designer until 1984 when he started to work for himself (Togashi Design Studio). To date his work mainly involves the design of restaurants, clubs, department stores and shopping centres in Japan, as well as exhibition design. He has shown his work both nationally and internationally and has won critical acclaim for his designs, including an Environmental Merchandising Design Award in 1994.

Virgile & Stone Associates
25 Store Street, South Crescent,
London WC1E 7EL

Virgile & Stone Associates was formed in 1990 by Nigel Stone and Carlos Virgile with Frances Williams as Associate Director. Following graduation Nigel Stone formed the in-house design office of Paperchase, after which he moved to Fitch PLC in 1984 as Associate Director working with Carlos Virgile on the Special Projects Unit. Virgile ran his own design and retail business before joining Fitch and Co. in 1979, where he was Creative Director of the Retail Division and later head of the Special Projects Unit. Since the

foundation of Virgile & Stone Associates as a subsidiary of Imagination, the two managing directors have built up an impressive client portfolio which includes such companies as de Bijenkorf department stores in Holland, Globus department stores in Switzerland, Safeway PKC, Bodyshop PLC, L'Oreal International, Paramount/UCI, Holiday Inn Worldwide and Heal's store, London.

Tod Williams, Billie Tsien and Associates
222 Central Park South, New York,
New York 10019, USA

Tod Williams received a BA (1965) and MFA (1967) from Princeton University. After spending six years as Associate Architect in the office of Richard Meier, he founded his own practice in 1974. His works have won much acclaim and he was a recipient of a Mid-Career Prix de Rome in 1983. Although primarily known for his built works, he is a familiar figure in the lecture halls of America. In 1974 he was appointed Professor Adjunct at the Cooper Union and has also taught at Harvard, Yale and Columbia Universities. He was appointed to the Thomas Jefferson Professorship at the University of Virginia in the Spring of 1990. He shares an interest in the link between fine art and architecture with his partner Billie Tsien and has worked on exhibitions exploring this theme. Billie Tsien is a graduate of Yale University in Fine Arts and received her Masters in Architecture from UCLA. She is on the Board of Governors of the Public Arts Fund, the Architectural League and the Municipal Arts Society and has taught at the Parsons School of Design, Southern California Institute of Architecture, Harvard Graduate School of Design and Yale University. To date work by the practice includes domestic schemes; the Feinberg Hall at Princeton University; the Downtown branch of the Whitney Museum of American Art; New College (a 500-student dormitory and dining facility at the University of Virginia) and the Phoenix Art Museum and Little Theatre.

Andreas Winkler
Hübschstrasse 11, 76135 Karlsruhe,
Germany

Andreas Winkler was born in Essen in 1955 and before studying in Braunschweig, Perugia and Vienna was an officer in the German Navy. He formed his own company in 1986, ArchiMeDes (Architecture and Metropolitan Design), and completed projects include the Braunsche University Bookstore, Karlsruhe (1986); Spurwlen office, Vienna (1987) and the Golden House for Haus Kellner for which he won a design prize in 1991. In 1993 Winkler founded the PHOS Design Agency and currently work is progressing on a theatre in Pirmasens and a Museum for manufacturers FSB Brakel. Product design includes work for FSB, Belux Suisse, Ventura and Vitrashop.

Babcock & Brown Offices
2 Harrison Street, San Francisco, California
94105, USA

Designer: STUDIOS Architecture

Project team: Darryl Roberson (principal); Cathy
Barrett and Peter VanDine (project designers);
Cindy Knapton (project manager); Bob Bradsby
(project architect). Client: Babcock & Brown Inc.
Collaborators: Glumac (M & E); Paoletti
Associates (acoustics and audio visual);
Luminage Souter (general lighting). Main con-
tractor: Ryan Associates. Subcontractors: LPI
(custom workstation); Alexander Manufacturing
Inc. (woodworking); West Edge (steel fabrica-
tion); Neidhardt (low-voltage special lighting).
Lighting: STUDIOS. Custom workstations,
reception desk and conference tables:
STUDIOS. Custom carpets: Pacific Crest Mill.
Glazing and plasterwork: STUDIOS.

Design Studio/Offices for Wickens Tutt
Southgate
10a Frederick Close, London, UK

Architect: Lorenzo Apicella

Project team: Lorenzo Apicella; James Robson;
Hilary Clark. Client: Wickens Tutt Southgate.
Main contractor: Haymills Ltd (flooring/plaster-
work). Subcontractors: Beaver Building Services
Ltd; P & M Electrical Services Ltd. Quantity
surveyor: Boyden and Co. Lighting: Artemide
(supplied by Atrium Ltd); Reggiani; Spectrum.
Furniture and fittings: Moroso (supplied by
Atrium Ltd); Elementer Industrial Design Ltd;
Vitra UK Ltd; Tecta (supplied by Aram Designs
Ltd); Shannon and Co.; Aram Designs. Carpets:
Munster Carpets Ltd; Manningtons Carpets Ltd.
Ironmongery: GGS Ltd.

British Council Offices
Calle General Martinez Campos 31, Madrid,
Spain

Architect: Jestico & Whiles

Project team: Tony Ingram; Tony Ling;
Tim Janes. Client: The British Council.
Collaborators: Reid Fenwick Asociados (associ-
ate architects); Gleeds Iberica SA (quantity
surveyor). Main contractor: Salconsa.
Subcontractor: Ateclime SL (air-conditioning);
Instalaciones Gonzalez Martin (plumbing).
Lighting: Electricidad Tebar. Fittings: Hermanos
Toledo CB. Flooring: Tariflot SL. Upholstery:
Drappo SA. Glass: Cristaleria Iberica SA.

St John's College Library
Cambridge, UK

Architect: Edward Cullinan Architects Ltd

Project team: Mark Beedle; Ted Cullinan; Miriam
Fitzpatrick; Jonathan Hale; Simon Knox; Joe
Navin; Colin Rice; Louise Clayton. Client: St
John's College, Cambridge. Main contractor: R.
G. Carter Cambridge. Quantity surveyor: Davis
Langdon and Everest. Structural engineer:
Hannah Reed and Associates. Services engi-

neer: Max Fordham Associates. Subcontractors:
Brakefields Ltd (M & E); Cromwell Ironmasters
(St Ives) Ltd (architectural metalwork); Baker
Brothers (brickwork). Brick and stone cleaning:
MIAD (stone cleaning) Ltd. Aluminium win-
dows: Drayton Windows. Steel windows: Monk
Metal Windows Ltd. Sliding windows: Allday
Windows Ltd. Glass lantern: Exterior Profiles.
Plasterwork: G. Cook and Sons Ltd. Decorators:
Metric Painters. Doors: Youngs Doors Ltd.
Joinery: Sindall Joinery Ltd. Shelves: Bruynzeel
Storage Systems Ltd. Stonework: F. W. Bull &
Son (Constructions) Ltd. Stone paving: George
Farrar Quarries. Sliding door: Macwood
(London) Ltd. Tiling and leadwork: Eastern
Roofing. Suppliers: Runtalrad (radiators); W. T.
Lamb & Sons (bricks); Finnmade Ltd (loose furni-
ture); Elementer Industrial Design Ltd (ironmon-
gery); Carpet Specifier Services (carpet);
Concorde Lighting Ltd, Marlin Lighting Ltd, Best
and Lloyd Ltd, Basis Lighting – Friedbert
Meinhert (lighting).

MTV Latino
1111 Lincoln Road, Suite 100, Miami Beach,
Florida 33139, USA

Architect: Arquitectonica International Corp.

Project team: Laurinda Spear (principal); Jenifer
Briley (project management); Joseph Biordi;
Diana Farmer; Hadrian Predock; Richard H.
Talbert. Client: MTV – Music Television.
Collaborators: Lagomasino and Associates
(M/E/P); Riva Klein (structural engineer). Main
contractor: M. K. Roark. Customized tables:
Arquitectonica, built by Desk Concepts.
Seating: ICF; Kita & Oscar; Fritz Hansen;
Arne Jacobsen. Tables: Vecta. Vinyl tile:
Azrock. Fabric: Arquitectonica, printed by
Cristina Roberts, Fabric Workshop. Ceramic
mural: Arquitectonica, made by Bisazza
Mosaico.

Marugame Office Building/Spanish
Contemporary Art Museum
538 8 chome, Higashi, Doki-cho, Marugame-shi,
Kagawa, 763 Japan

Architect: Alfredo Arribas Arquitectos
Asociados, SL

Client: The Daily Shikoku Company Ltd;
Nishinipong Broadcasting Company Ltd.
Collaborator: Shimizu Architects & Engineers
(main contractor). Subcontractors: Fuji Kesetsu;
Yondenko; Chudenko; Kinden Corporation.
Lighting: Panasonic (main building and
Pavilion); Yamagiwa (garden). Furniture
and fittings: Mitsukoshi (main building and
Pavilion – permanent fixtures); Plus (office
furniture); Fritz Hansen (7th-floor furniture –
wood tables, chairs, stools and leather sofa);
Mr Paterarroyo, made by Mitsukoshi (7th-floor
counter and stone table); Alfredo Arribas
(Pavilion furniture). Flooring: Wakita, installed
by Dreamstone (granite flooring – Museum and
Pavilion); Toli (tile carpeting –office); Juken
Sangyo (maple flooring – 7th floor). Wood
sheet supplier: Akumekogyo. Paint supplier:
Komany.

Western Morning News
Plymouth, UK

Architect: Nicholas Grimshaw & Partners Ltd

Project team: Nick Grimshaw; David Harriss;
Christopher Nash; Neven Sidor (directors); Mark
Fisher; Rowena Fuller; Paul Grayshon; Andrew
Whalley (associates); Mark Bryden; Matthew
Keeler; Michael Pross (project associates); Susan
Heathcote (financial manager). Client: Western
Morning News Co. Ltd. Main contractor: Bovis
Construction Ltd. Quantity surveyor: Davis
Langdon & Everest. Structural engineer: Ove
Arup & Partners. Civil engineer: Ove Arup &
Partners. Service engineer: Applied Acoustic
Design. Acoustic panels: Ecomax Acoustics Ltd.
WMN Press Manufacturer: Rockwell Graphic
Systems Ltd. Glazing: Briggs Amasco
Curtainwall Ltd. Structural steelwork: Blight &
White Ltd. Architectural metalwork contractor:
R. Glazzard (Dudley) Ltd. Office partitions: Steel
Support Systems plc. Secondary steelwork con-
tractor: Amrob Engineering Ltd. Spiral stair-
ways: Crescent of Cambridge Ltd. Balustrade:
R. Glazzard. Glass panels: Pilkington Glass Ltd.
Insulation: Rockwool Ltd. Windows: Hyatol
Windows. Window control mechanism: BJP
Window Controls Ltd. Galvanized walkway:
Eurogrid Ltd. Roofing works contractor: Albany
Roofing Services Ltd. Roof System: Hoogovens
Aluminium UK Ltd. Suspended ceiling: Gyproc
M/F Suspended Ceiling System. Suspended
ceilings and works contractor: Special Acoustic
Services. Ceramic wall tiles: Pilkington Tiles Ltd.
Raised timber floor: Contract Flooring Sales Ltd.
Floor finishes – work contractor: Al Flooring Ltd.
Carpet: Heuga UK Ltd. Entrance matting:
Jaymart Rubber & Plastics Ltd. Flooring:
Freudenberg LP. Ironmongery: Elementar
Industrial Design Ltd. Signage works contractor:
Pearce Signs. Internal glass graphic signs:
Signbox.

Bankers Trust, Australia
Levels 23 & 24, 367 Collins Street, Melbourne,
Australia

Architect: Geyer Design

Project team: Peter Geyer; Marni Howard;
Elizabeth Earle; Cameron Harvey; Robert
Speilman. Client: Bankers Trust Australia
Limited. Main contractor: Callagan George
(project management). Subcontractors:
Quadric Interiors (partitions); Parkview Joinery
(wave wall); Co. Design & Artes (loose
furniture); Herman Miller (workstations).
Flooring: Tolga Granite. Rug: Geyer Design,
manufactured by The Rug Company. Artwork:
John Davis, John Firth-Smith, Guiseppe Romero.

The Cable and Wireless College
Coventry, UK

Architect: MacCormac Jamieson Prichard (MJP)

Project team: David Prichard (partner); Stephen
Cherry (associate); Dorian Wiszniewski; David
Whitehead; Pal Sandhu; Simon Usher; David
Franklin; Helen Brunskill; Alison Burns (adminis-

tration). Client: Cable and Wireless plc, John Beatson (project director). Collaborators: Ove Arup & Partners (structural and M & E engineers); Museum Designers. Main contractor: Birse Construction Ltd. Subcontractor: ETB Furniture. Quantity surveyors: Northcroft Neighbour & Nicholson. Construction managers: Buro Four Project Services Ltd; Whiterock (kitchen and wash-up room). Plasterwork: Bellworths Ltd. Armouralia render (green, blue and red walls): Armourcoat Ltd. Mosaics (showers, changing rooms and pool): Domus Tiles Ltd. Carpet: Carpetronic Ltd. Metal doors (teaching wing): Fenlock Hansen Ltd. Timber doors: Raab Karcher. Sanitary ware: Armitage Shanks. Squash Court screen: Prospec. Dampa ceiling: Dampa (UK) Ltd. Timber (maple) elements – stairs, doors, bridge: ETB. White screed: Concrete and Stone. Raised floor: System Floors Ltd. Ironmongery: Allgood G & S (Holding) Ltd; Elementer Industrial Design Ltd; Adamsrite. Servery, bar, kitchen and wash-up: Sutcliffe Catering Services. Flooring (Sports Hall/Squash Court): Junkers Ltd; Durabella Ltd. Blinds: Technical Blinds Ltd. Etch-like logos and screening: Jeffreys Building. Balustrades: Rileys (Metalworkers) Ltd. Lighting: Concorde Lighting Ltd; Erco Lighting Ltd; RADA Lighting Ltd; Thorn Lighting Ltd; Marlin Ltd; Oldham Lighting Ltd; Reggiani Lighting Ltd. VIP flat/kitchen: Alternative Plans. Signage: Modulex Systems Ltd. Furniture: Plumb Interiors Contracting Ltd (Museum display, library and reception desks); Solaglas (glass and mirror); The Splinter Group (teaching alcoves, conference table and delegates' refreshment enclosures); HNB Systems Ltd. (library shelving, bar stools); ETB Furniture Ltd (residential rooms); Srdjan Bosnic (glass screen – Artwork); Landrell Fabric Engineering (boardroom linings); Nicholas Dyson Furniture Ltd (table); David Wye (table base). Billiard and pool table and lights: Thurston; Zumtobel Lighting Ltd. Classroom furniture and VIP living room: INE Ltd; Vitra Ltd. Administration furniture: Aram Design; HNB; ETB; Vitra Ltd; Storwall.

Ove Arup & Partners Offices
Los Angeles, California, USA

Architect: Morphosis

Project team: Thom Mayne (principal); Kim Groves (project architect); John Enright, Steve Chen and Steve Sinclair (assistants). Client: Ove Arup & Partners. Collaborating engineers: Ove Arup & Partners. Project team (engineering): Bruce Gibbons and Atila Zekioglu (structural); Rob Bolin and John Gautrey (mechanical); Jacob Chan and Vahik Davoudi (electrical); Richard Bussell (acoustical) Main contractor: Limbrick A/A Construction Co. Suppliers: unavailable.

The British Council Headquarters
Medlock Street, Manchester, UK

Architect: Business Design Group

Project team: Keith Lawson (project director); Phil Hutchinson (project leader); Mark Myers (construction manager); Victor Spouge; Hans Chu; Julia Johnston. Client: The British Council.

Collaborators: Building Design Partnership; DSSR; Dewhurst MacFarlane. Main contractor: Costains. Furniture: Vitra (chairs); Techno (tables). Carpet tiles: Heuga. Carpet: Patrick Caulfield. Partitions: Logika. Doors: Jutlamdia. Ceilings: Armstrong. Clock: Bill Woodrow.

Society National Bank
2025 Ontario Street, Cleveland, Ohio 44115, USA

Designer: Gensler and Associates/Architects

Project team: Antony Harbour; Charles Kifer; Richard Maxwell; Bonny McLoud; Elyse Dobson; Tuan Nguyen; Mary Stehlin; Anne Burton; Tara Weatherill; Sarah Thompson; Kelly Lee. Client: Society National Bank. Main contractor: The Albert M. Higley Co. Lighting: Nessen Lamps. Lighting consultant: Theo Kondos Associates. Furniture and fittings: Valley City Manufacturing (custom furniture) – J. Robert Scott (silk panel covers); Brickel (seating) – Jack Lenor Larsen (fabric); Bright Chair Co. (seating) – Knoll Textiles (cover); Zographos (coffee tables); Brochstein's (millwork); Helikon (desk chairs) – Jack Lenor Larsen (covers); Donghia (lounge seating and sofa) – Sina Pearson (fabric); Horton Draperies (custom pillows) – Manual Canovas/Fortuny/ Groves Bros (fabrics); Oscar Berman (draperies) – Carnegie (fabrics); Zographos (desk/conference chairs) – Brickel (fabric); Marco (lounge chair) – Manual Canovas (fabric); Zographos (conference table base); Cangelosi (conference table top); Nicholas James Ltd (custom console desk and secretarial desks); Cedric Hartman (occasional table); H.B.F. (guest chairs) – Baker (fabric); Randolf and Hein (executive dining chairs) – Groves Bros (fabric); Lewis Mittman (oriental screen); Pindler & Pindler (canopy fabric, cafeteria); Steelworks (custom cafeteria tables); Shelby Williams, Lowenstein (cafeteria chairs) – Robert Allen and Carnegie (fabric). Harbinger (custom carpet). Leather wallcovering: Barksdale Rudd. Wall fabric: Jack Lenor Larsen. Ceramic wall tiles: American Olean. White plastic laminates: Wilson-art. Red plastic laminates: Formica Corp. Carpet: Bentley Mills. Custom rug: Hokanson. Stone floor: Acme Arsena. Ceramic floor tiles: Cal Tile.

Zygo
The Observatory, 220 Queenstown Road, London SW8 4LP, UK

Designer: Din Associates

Project team: John Harvey; Angela Drinkall; Stephen Papps. Client: The Observatory. Main contractor: Newhard Construction. Flooring: Jaymart (Rushtik Seagrass matting); Forbo-Nairn (marmoleum). Merchandising equipment: OSS Origo Ltd. Tables and fixtures: Rasshied Din.

Beverly Hills Cosmetic Dental Center
Beverly Hills, California, USA

Designer: Michele Saee
Project team: Michele Saee; Eric Rosen; Yasi Vafai. Client: Farzad Okhovat and Janet Okhovat Refua. Main contractor: Begel Construction. Electrical consultant: Saul-Goldin. Mechanical

systems: Dehoibi & Associates. Structural engineer: Miguel Castillo. Steel fabrication: John McCoy; Serop Zagarian.

Government Employees Health Fund (Dental and Optical Clinic)
Sydney, Australia

Designer: Perumal Bogatai Kenda & Freeman

Client: Government Employees Health Fund. Main contractor: Zamonall P/L. Subcontractors: Smithelec (lighting); Heuga Interface (carpet). Furniture and fittings: Kavon Exclusive Joinery (reception desk); Andrews Custom Joinery (woodwork); Walkabout (reception and waiting area); Design Partners (chairs upholstered in wool crepe). Flooring: Altro Safety Flooring (vinyl); Glennor Cerabati Vitrifield (ceramic tiles). Partitions: M & R Interiors; Building Co; Zamonall. Ceilings: Gridcon. Paintwork: Dulux Masterpallette. Consultant: Jane Goodes of Graphics Gallery. Signage: Cent Signs.

Silver Sanz SA
C/Juan de la Cierva, No. 15, Sant Just Desvern, Barcelona, Spain

Architect: Fernando Salas Studio

Project team: Fernando Salas Sierra; Ester Balaña; Miriam Izquierdo; Barbara Fernandez. Client: Silver Sanz SA. Main contractor: Construmafe SA. Air-conditioning: Tecnifred. Electricity and plumbing: J. L. Andreu. Masonry: Construmafe. Plasterwork: Yesos Grup Gine. Carpentry: Talleres Urbe SL. Marble and stonework: Betamac SA. Metalwork: Talleres Colmenero SL. Glasswork: Granell Germans SL. Artwork: Aplicaciones Decorativas AR. Lighting: Gaudir Illuminazio SL. Curtain: Sistemas de Cortinas Y Estores SA. Venetian blind: Teycesa. Awnings: Catalana de Toldos. Imaging: Signes. Furniture: Vincon; Santa & Cole; Tecno; Akaba. Floral arrangements: Plantae.

MDS Gallery
Miyake Design Studio, 1—23 Ohayama-cho, Shibuyaku, Tokyo, Japan

Designer: Shigeru Ban

Client: Miyake Design Studio. Collaborators: Gengo Matsui (structural engineer); Shuichi Hoshino (structural engineer). Paper tubes: Showa Marutsutsu Co., Ltd. Construction: Nomura Co., Ltd.

Pacha Leisure Centre
Pineda Beach, Vila-Seca, Tarragon, Spain

Architect: Capella, Larrea and Castellvi Associates
Project team: Juli Capella; Jaume Castellví; Quim Larrea (architects); Alfredo Vidal (collaborating architect); Felix Lora; Mercedes Martin; Enrique Suarez (technical architects); Jordi Sabater (coordinator); Maria Clara Bassin; Guillen Berazaluze; Roz Camp; Carme Guixé; Jose Augusto Maciez; Verónica Edith Moure; Neide Maria Rech; Anna Tarrida; Isabel Torrents. Client:

Krisprolls SA. Suppliers: Taller d'Enginyeries; Cemesa (structure). Acieroid (façade); Tudela SA (fittings). Surveyors: Félix Lora, Enrique Suarez. Construction: García Riera. Show lighting and sound: Tudela.

Deep End Café
University of Westminster, Regent Street, London, UK

Architect: Sheppard Robson

Project team: Sheppard Robson; Graham Francis; Ben Morris; Vicky Thornton; Colin Ridley; Peter Henfield; Amanda Culpin; Cliff Gabb. Client: University of Westminster. Collaborators: Whitby and Bird (structural engineer); Ove Arup & Partners (M & E); Hanscomb (quantity surveyor). Main contractor: John Sisk & Son (flooring, ceilings). Lighting: Concord Lighting Ltd. Aluminium furniture and fittings: Astro Designs. Glass block wall: Pittsburg Corning UK Ltd. Roof: Landrell Fabric. Balustrading: K&H Engineering. Architectural steelwork: M&M Steelwork. Curtain walling: Baldwins. Kitchen fit-out: Berkeleys.

Nautilus Seafood Bar/La Fôret Brasserie, Schiphol Airport
Amsterdam, The Netherlands

Architect: Branson Coates Architecture Ltd

Project team: Nigel Coates; Doug Branson (design direction); Catherine du Toit (project architect); Allan Bell; Dickon Irwin; Anton Jeanes; Geoffrey Makstutis; Gerrard O'Carroll; Peter Thomas; Dominic Tolson. Client: Schiphol 2000, Project Group Terminal. Main contractor: Lems vd Ven BV. Sculptural trees: Poly Products BV. Fibre optic lighting: Absolute Action Ltd. Projector lighting: Lightworks Ltd. Aerofoils: Airwave Gliders Ltd. Fish mobiles and sea crisps: Cellbond Composites Ltd.

Setsugekka Restaurant
310-1-5-4 Inman Sibuyaku, Tokyo, Japan

Architect: Soichi Mizutani Design Office Co. Ltd

Client: Haricot Trading Company. Main contractor: Inter Design. Collaborator: Simus. Lighting: Usio Spex by Masaaki Sato.

Adelphi Hotel
187 Flinders Lane, Melbourne, Victoria 3000, Australia

Architect: Denton Corker Marshall Pty Ltd

Client: Adelphi Pty. Collaborators: Ove Arup & Partners (structural engineers); Lincolne Scott (mechanical & electrical engineers); Emery Vincent & Associates (graphic designers/ signage). Main contractor: Conteco Pty Ltd. Windows: Select Windows. Structural systems: RM Bently Structural Engineering. Glazing: Heritage Glazing. Paintwork: Locom Painting. Joinery: Dalhaus Pty Ltd. Furniture: Sumna Furniture Pty Ltd; Radii; Eymac Catering Equipment; A Grade Cabinets. Floor finishes:

Larosa Tiling Co; Prestige Products Pty Ltd (timber floor). Lights: Wharrington International.

Estandard Barcelona. AM/PM Bar and Club, Primera Planta Café
Travessera de Gràcia n. 39, Barcelona, Spain

Architect: Alfredo Arribas Arquitectos Asociados, SL

Client: Probindos SA. Main contractor: Eduarmar. Air-conditioning: Siclima. Woodwork: Cadesa. Upholstery: Tapiceria Moderna. Carpets: Alterra; Gra. Painting: Abel. Main door: Mansergas. Glasswork: Toch; Cristal Studio. Lighting: Trilux; Mundo Color; Erco. Video: FDG. Furniture: Carlas Jane; Amat.

Mezzanine, Royal National Theatre
South Bank, London, UK

Designers: Virgile & Stone Associates

Project team: Frances Williams (project director/lead designer); Rachel Toomey (senior designer); Toby Johnson (senior designer); Jon Turner (graphics). Client: Royal National Theatre. Main contractor: Barlows Shopfitting. Lighting: Ecart Intl. Furniture and fittings: Dutch Design Centre (chairs); Ease & Co. (banquette seating). Flooring: Victorian Wood Works. Mural: Jon Turner, painted by scenic artist at Royal National Theatre.

Tai Pan Restaurant
Cambridge, Massachusetts, USA

Designer: Lawrence Man Architect

Client: Tai Pan Group Inc. Collaborators: Delta Design Consultant (engineers); MCM Inc. (main contractor/working drawings). Lighting: Lichtolier. Furniture and fittings: Shelby Williams (chairs); Alden (tables and banquette); Millrock (cocktail tables). Flooring: Dal Tiles; Shaw Carpets. Drywall: US Gypsum. Ceiling: Armstrong. Paint: Gliden. Glass block: Pittsburgh Corning. Railings/screens/grill/woodwork/planters: Millrock. Upholstery: Momentum. Lighting design: Lawrence Man.

Café Gavoille
Place Leon Gauthier, BP 0631, 8000 Amiens, France

Designer: Kristian Gavoille

Client: Ville d'Amiens. Main contractor: SOGEPIC. Furniture subcontractor: TCA (armchair, stool, bottle rack). Furniture and fittings: Philips. Flooring: Sommer.

Quaglino's Restaurant
16 Bury Street, London SW1, UK

Designer: CD Partnership

Project team: Terence Conran; Keith Hobbs; Linzi Coppick (project leaders); Simon Simpson (designer); Alan Hole (technical designer). Client: Terence Conran. Main contractor:

Howard & Constable. Subcontractors: Chris Johnson at Logic Design; Mosaic Workshop. Structural engineer: Waterman Partnership. Mechanical engineer: Stewart Harries. Quantity surveyor: Mike Porter. Lighting: Marlin Lighting; J. M. Nash Ltd. Furniture and fittings: Benchmark; P. J. Cooper. Flooring: Geoffrey Pike. Carpets: C. P. Broadloom Carpets. Kitchen floor tiles: Domus. Ceilings: Seobil Interiors. Bas relief: Dhruva Mistry. Mural: Ned Conran. Mosaic: Mosaic Workshop. Columns painted by the following artists: Javaid Alvi, Peter Marsh, Philip Hughes, Michael Daykin, Patrick Kinmouth, Catherine Keraly, Jane Harris, Estelle Thompson.

Go Shoe Shop
Eppendorfer Baum 20, 20249 Hamburg, Germany

Designer: Torsten Neeland

Project team: Torsten Neeland (project director); Chistiane Axer (assistant). Client: Hans Joachim Rebenstorf. Suppliers: Marschner & Krogmann (carpenter); Paul Bolzmann (steelwork); Carl Jenssen (Fritztile). Paintwork: Friedrich Malereibetrieb.

The Asia and Pacific Trade Center
2-1-10 Nanko-kita, Suminoe-ku, Osaka 559 Japan

Architect: Nikken Sekkei Ltd. Interior Design: STUDIOS Architecture

Project team: Erik Sueberkrop (principal); Gail Napell (studio director); Jon Dick; Jim Gota. Client: Asia and Pacific Trade Center Corporation. Main contractors: Takenaka Corporation; Fujita Corporation; Tokyu Construction Co. Ltd; The Zenitaka Corporation; Asanuma Corporation; Overseas Bechtel Inc.; Okamura Corporation; Konoike Construction; Aoki Corporation. Lighting: Matsushita Electric Works Ltd. Flooring: Tori.

La Casa Rossa
Applicazioni srl, Via Guizzetti 73, 31030 Dosson di Casier (Treviso), Italy

Architect: Perry A. King and Santiago Miranda

Project team: Perry A. King; Santiago Miranda. Collaborator: Malcolm S. Inglis. Client: Applicazioni srl, Via Guizzetti, 73 Dosson D Casier (TV). Main contractor: Cenedese. Subcontractor: Falpa srl (specialist items such as curved wall cladding, stair, totem). Carpet: King and Miranda, manufactured by Interface. Coloured wall: Settef SpA. Lighting: Sosia by Castaldi Illuminazione. Furniture: Pianeta Uffocio by Marcatré.

Kashin Store
1-10-1 Azabu-dai, Minato-ku, Tokyo, Japan

Designer: Togashi Design Studio Co. Ltd

Project team: Katsuhiko Togashi (project director); Takashi Yachida (general director); Setsuko Yamada (merchandiser); Masio Fujimura (pro-

ject control); Toshifuki Oyamatsu (graphic designer). Client: Meisei Co. Ltd. Main contractor: Shinei Construction Co. Ltd. Subcontractor: Sogo Design Co. Ltd (interior and furniture). Lighting: National Matsushita Electric Works Ltd. Furniture and fittings: Cassina/Interdecor Group (chairs). Flooring: Juken Co. Ltd. Wall and ceiling (1st floor): Kansai Paint Co. Ltd. Wall (2nd floor): Mitsui Engineering Co. Ltd. Ceiling (2nd floor): Kansai Paint Co. Ltd.

Harriet Dorn Clothing Store
Santa Monica, California, USA

Architect: O'Herlihy & Warner Architects

Project team: Lorcan O'Herlihy (principal); Richard Warner (principal); Mark Hirt (assistant). Cabinetry: Steve Shelley (folded birch wall); Michael Warner (birch shelves). Metalwork: American Metal Company Inc.

Ing Automated Bank
De Amsterdamse Poort, 1102 MG Amsterdam, Zuidoost, Postbus 1800, 1000 BV Amsterdam, The Netherlands

Designer: Fitch

Project team: Neil Whitehead (project director); Nick Butcher; Christian Davies (interior designers); Mike Curtis, Darren Whittingham (graphics). Client: Ing Bank, NMB Postbank Group. Main contractor: Parnashov BV. Subcontractors: Projet Techniek (structural engineer); Ver Kaart (services engineer). Lighting: Phillips. Technological fittings: NCR. Flooring: Interdec (timber floor); F. Guisse (limestone); G. V. Williams (stone floor); Rijnvis (carpet). Special paintwork: Valentine Abbatt. Laminates: Formica.

Imagine Showroom
Akasaka .. House, Akasaka 3-9-9, Chuoku, Fukuoka, Japan

Architect: Soichi Mizutani Design Office Co. Ltd.

Client: Imagine Co. Ltd. Main contractor: NICCo. Ltd. Lighting: Usio SPEX by Masaaki Sato.

Habitat Store
King's Road, London, UK

Designer: Din Associates

Project team: Rasshied Din; Angela Drinkall; Kirstie Moon. Client: Habitat UK, Ltd. Collaborators: Mike Porter Associates (quantity surveyor); Parkman Engineers (M & E); Jim Shephard (consultant M & E engineer). Main contractor: Charles Barret Shopfitters. Lighting: Erco; Targetti; I Guzzani supplied by Russel Lipscombe. Furniture and fittings: Rasshied Din. Flooring: Stoneacte (Flora marble); C. F. S. (timber floor).

Habitat Store
Bromley, Kent, UK

Designer: Din Associates

Project team: Rasshied Din; Angela Drinkall;

Kirstie Moon. Client: Habitat UK, Ltd. Collaborators: Lesley Clark Partners (quantity surveyor); Jim Shephard (consultants M & E). Main contractor: Britannia Construction. Lighting: Erco; Targetti; I. Guzzani supplied by Russel Lipscombe; Toscarini (feature lights over stairs). Flooring: Acero Stone; Stoneage; Stoneacte (Flora marble); C. F. S. (timber floor). Furniture and fittings: Rasshied Din.

Musikhaus Padewet
Kaiserstr 132, 76135 Karlsruhe, Germany

Designer: Andreas Winkler

Project team: Andreas Winkler; Eva Kellner; Verena Stumm. Client: Mr and Mrs Padewet. Carpentry: Karl Geburtig. Tiling: Hermann Pelz. Stonefloor: Schroetter GmbH. Carpet: W. Kapusta. Windows: Heinrich Seipel GmbH. Locksmith: Th. Falsst. Brickwork: gipsbaugesellschaft mbH. Heating: Koch GmbH. Glasswork: Glasarbeiten. Graphics: Karola Stiffel.

Go Silk Showroom
530 Seventh Avenue, New York, USA

Architect: Tod Williams Billie Tsien and Associates

Project team: Billie Tsien; Tod Williams (partners-in-charge); Martin Finio (project architect). Client: L'Zinger International. Collaborators: Ambrosino Depinto and Schneider (hvac engineer). Main contractor: Selby Construction. Cabinetry: William Somerville. Furniture: USE. Silver lead: David Anderson.

Erg, Convenience Store "La Bottega"
Bergamo, Italy

Architect: Sottsass Associati

Project team: Ettore Sottsass; Marco Zanini. Client: ERG Petroli, Italy. Collaborators: Gianluigi Mutti, Tim Power, Massimo Pertosa. Graphics: Douglas Riccardi; Sergio Menichelli. Contractors and suppliers: unavailable.

Toyota Car Showroom, Amlux Osaka
Komatsubar-cho, Kita-ku, Osaka, Japan

Designer: Yasuo Kondo

Client: Toyota Motor Corporation. Collaborators: Daiko Advertising, Inc. (Environmental Design Department); Lighting Planners Associates Inc. Main contractor: Tanseisha. Subcontractors: Build; Tansosha. Fluorescent lamps: Matsushita Electric Works Ltd. Flooring: AICA. Walls: Nippon Sheet Glass (sandblasted glass walls); Hokushin (MDF on silicic acid calcium board with UV coating; Pilot (aluminium).

Flagship Bally Shoe Shop, Cologne
Hohe Strasse 101, 50667 Cologne, Germany

Designer: Ecart

Client: Bally Inc. Main contractor: Dennery.

Furniture supplier: Cassina. Flooring: Hulot. Carpeting: Flipo. Lighting: Megalit.

Kunibiki Messe

3669, Nishi-kawatsu-cho, Matsue-shi, Shimane 690, Japan

Architect: Shin Takamatsu Architect and Associates

Client: Shimane Prefectural Government. Collaborators: Yamamoto-Tachibana Architects & Engineers (structure); Architectural Environmental Laboratory (mechanical engineers). Main contractors: Obayashi Corporation; Morimoto Corporation; Tamaki Construction; Ito Komuten. Lighting: Yamagiwa Corporation. Ceramics: Innax Co. Ltd. Floorings/ceilings: Nitto Boseki Co. Ltd. Glass: Asahi Glass Co. Ltd.

Church of St Florian

Community of Aigen im Ennstal, Austria

Architect: Volker Giencke & Company

Project team: Volker Giencke; Fredl Bramberger; Robert Felber, Eckhart Rhode. Client: Diözese Graz–Seckau. Collaborator: Fritz Panzer (painter). Structural engineer: Alois Winkler. Lighting: Erich Podesser; Fa Landmarket KG. Furniture and fittings: Kompacher GesmbH. Flooring: Franz Keittele GesmbH. Glass façade: D. Meisl Liebenauer. Wooden structure: Stingl GesmbH.

Opera de Lyon

Place de la Comédie, 69001, Lyons, France

Architect: Jean Nouvel et Associés

Project team: Jean Nouvel; E. Blamont; Eric Maria (principal-in-charge); Françoise Raynaud; Marie France Baldran; Léa Thirode; Arnold Lee; Said Farhat; Stéphane Robert, Viviane Morteau. Client: Ville de Lyon. Structural engineer: Société Kephren. Acoustics: Peutz & Associés. Lighting for public spaces: Isometrix. Lighting: Legrand; Mazda; Guzzini; Erci. Quantity surveyor: Sery Bertrand. Glasswork: Durand Structure; Vilquin. Escalators: Koné. Armchairs: Figueras. False ceiling: Gantois. Woodwork: Segransan. Metalwork: Vilquin.

Rotunda Gallery

33 Clinton Street, Brooklyn, New York 100201, USA

Designer: Smith-Miller & Hawkinson Architects

Project team: Henry Smith-Miller; Laurie Hawkinson (principals-in-charge); Starling Keene; Randy Goya; Charles Renfro; Stephanie Tran. Client: The Rotunda Gallery/Fund for the Borough of Brooklyn. General contractor: Kennedy Construction. Contractor: John Millich (metalwork). Collaborators/Lighting consultants: John Wood; Claude Engle. Collaborator/Structural engineers: Severud Szegezdy. Graphic design consultant: Silvia Kolbowski.

Kansai International Airport Passenger Terminal Building

Kansai, Japan

Architect: Renzo Piano Building Workshop Paris/Ove Arup & Partners

Project team for Renzo Piano: Renzo Piano (architect); Noriaki Okabe (associate architect/project leader); Jean-François Blassel; Ariel Chavela; Ivan Corte; Kenneth Fraser; Robert S. Garlipp; Marion Goerdt; Greg Hall; Kohji Hirano; Akira Ikegami; Shunji Ishida; Amanda Johnson; Christopher Kelly; Tetsuya Kimura; Stig Larsen; Jean Lelay; Ken McBryde; Takeshi Miyazaki; Shin'ichi Nakaya; Norio Takata; Taichi Tomuro; Olivier Touraine; Mark Turpin; Masami Yamada; Hiroshi Yamaguchi; Tatsuya Yamaguchi. With the collaboration of: Alexandre Autin; Geoffrey Cohen; Anahita Golzari, Barnaby Gunning; Gunther Hastrich; Masahiro Horie; Ikauko Kubo; Simone Medio; Keisuke Miyake; Sandro Montaldo; Shin'ichiro Mukai; Kamran Afshar Naderi; Koung Nyunt; Stefan Oehler; Tim O'Sullivan; Patrizia Persia; Milly Rossato; Randy Sheilds; Takehiro Takagawa; Takuo Ueno; Kiyomi Uezono; Jean-Marc Weill; Tetsuo Tamakoshi. Project team for Ove Arup & Partners: Peter Rice, Tony Stevens, Philip Dilley and Alistair Guthrie (project leaders); Paula Beever; Rod Buchanan; Mark Chown; Martin Cooper; Rod Davis; Nick Dibben; Giovanni Festa; Jeppe Hundevad; Rory McGowan; Alain Michaells; Paul Murphy; Roberto Muzzetto; Catherine O'Brien; Heraclis Passades; Tony Philiastides; Andrew Sedgwick; William Stevenson; Chris Taylor; Tom Tomaszczyk; Mike Wilford; Raymond Yau. Client: Kansai International Airport Co. Ltd. Design leader: Renzo Piano. Design/Architecture/Engineering: Renzo Piano and Ove Arup & Partners (Roof structure, cladding, exterior curtain wall design, interior design of the PTB, design of building services); Nikken Sekkei Ltd (plan, section, interior design, fire prevention, planning, structural design, mechanical design, electric and telecom design, construction planning). Basic concept/functional aspect and design of moving elements: Aéroports de Paris. Negotiation with Customs/Immigration and Quarantine plus Civil Aviation Bureau, design of the CIQ facilities and airside planning: Japan Airport Consultants, Inc. Acoustic consultant: Peutz et Accociés. Quantity surveyor: Davis Langdon & Everest.

American Heritage Center and Art Museum

University of Wyoming, Laramie, Wyoming, USA

Architect: Antoine Predock Architect

Project team: Antoine Predock (principal-in-charge); Geoff Beebe (associate-in-charge); Derek Payne (project architect); Ron Jacob; Jorge Burbano; Brett Oaks; Paul Gonzales; David Hrabel; Sam Sterling; Chris Romero; Rob Romero; Phyllis Cece; David Somoza; John Flemming; Rebecca Riden; Lorraine Guthrie; Jon Anderson; Pedro Marquez; Linda Christensen; Jeff Wren; Hadrian Predock; Peter Karsten; Eileen Devereux; Chris Purvis.

Client: University of Wyoming. University architect: Roger Baalman. University construction manager: Mark Shively. Main contractor: Kloefkorn-Ballard Construction/Development Inc. Consulting architect: Pouppirt architects. Engineers: Robin Parke Associates Inc. (structural); Bridgers & Paxton Inc. (mechanical); Tierra del Sol Engineering Inc. (electrical); Chavez-Grieves, Inc. (civil). Landscape architect: Antoine Predock. Lighting: Edison Price; Prescolite. Glazing: Fisher Skylight Systems; Don Reynolds. Windows: Winco. Copper roof: A. Zahner Company. Concrete blocks: Powers Building Products.

Waterloo International Terminal

Waterloo, London, UK

Architect: Nicholas Grimshaw & Partners Ltd

Project team: Nick Grimshaw; Rowena Bate; Ingrid Bille; Conal Campbell; Garry Colligan; Geoff Crowe; Florian Eames; Alex Fergusson; Sarah Hare; Eric Jaffres; Ursula Heinemann; Doug Keys; David Kiorkland; Chris Lee; Colin Leisk; Jan Mackie; Julian Maynard; Neven Sidor; Ulriche Seifutz; Will Stevens; George Stowell; Andrew Whaley; Robert Wood; Sara Yabsley; Richard Walker; Dean Wyllie; Paul Fear; Steve McGuckin. Construction manager: Bovis Construction Ltd. Engineers: YRM Anthony Hunt Associates (roofing and glazing); Cass Hayward & Partners with Tony Gee & Partners (terminal viaduct); British Rail Civil Engineer (approaches viaduct); Sir Alexander Gibb & Partners (basement and external works). M.E. engineer: J. Roger Preston & Partners. Consultants: Davis Langdon & Everest (quantity surveyor); Sir Alexander Gibb & Partners (flow planning); Ove Arup & Partners (fire); Sean Billings (cladding); Lighting Design Partnership (lighting); Henrion Ludlow Schmidt (signage); Montagu Evans (planning).

Vocational School, Öhringen, Germany

Anstrasse 21, Öhringen, Germany

Architect: Behnisch & Partner

Project team: Dagmar Schork (project architect); Sandra Seibold; Jürgen Mattmann; Martina Höh (project group); Sigrid Duffner; Armin Gebert; Wolfgang Leukel (site management). Client: Hohenlohekreis. Main contractor: KE Baden-Württemberg GmbH. Structural engineer: Arbeitsgemeinschaft Ing.-Büro Schlaich, Bergermann u. Partner. Heating, ventilation and sanitation engineer: Ing.-Büro Keppler. Electrical engineer: Ing.-Büro Rolf Goegelein. Quantity surveyor: Ing-Büro Doll. Testing engineer: Ing.-Büro Stätter. Ground surveyor: Geologisches Landesamt. Lighting: Elektra Müller GmbH. Furniture and fittings: Fa Schaffetzel GmbH & Co. (specialized fittings); Fa Karl Gutmann KG; VS Spezialmöbelwerke. Flooring: Breüminger GmbH. Colour schemes: Erich Wiesner. Landscape design: Hans Luz & Partners.

Netherlands Design Institute

Keizersgracht 609, 1017 DS Amsterdam, The Netherlands

Architect: Benthem Crouwel Architekten BV bna

Project team: Jan Benthem; Mels Crouwel; Ton Liemburg; Heike Löhmann. Client: Municipality of Amsterdam. Main contractor: Schakel & Schrale. Contractors: GTI Amsterdam BV; Siem Steur (steel constructions). Lighting: Erco Lighting Nederland BV; Lumiance BV. Furniture and fittings: Benthem Crouwel; Ruud Jan Kokke; Ahrend Design. Flooring: Van Besouw; Forbo. Walls, ceilings and partitions: SSI Schäfer BV.

Reorganized Church of Jesus Christ of Latter Day Saints

1001 W. Walnut, Independence, Missouri 64051, USA

Architect: Hellmuth, Obata & Kassabaum Inc.

Project team: Gyo Obata (design principal); Robert Stockdale (project designer); Charles Hook (project manager); Richard Tell (project architect). Client: Reorganized Church of Jesus Christ of Latter Day Saints. Main contractor: J. E. Dunn Construction Company. Structural engineer: HOK. Mechanical engineer: Smith & Boucher. Structural steel: Havens Steel Company. Interior plastering: Schowengerdt Plastering. Sheet metal roof: Zahner Company. Exterior: Cold Spring Granite. Acoustic consultant: Kirkegaard & Associates.

The Museum of Modern Art, Wakayama

Wakayama Prefectural Museum, 1-4-14 Fukiage, Wakayama-shi, Wakayama 640 Japan

Architect: Kisho Kurokawa Architect & Associates

Client: Wakayama Prefectural Museum. General contractors: Takenaka Corporation, Shimizu Corporation; Toda Construction Co. Ltd. Mechanical consultant: Sogo Consultants. Landscape design: Urban Design Consultants. Curtain wall: Sankyo Aluminium Industry Corporation (Art Museum); Tateyama Aluminium Industry Corporation (Prefectural Museum). Lighting: Matsushita Electronic Works Ltd. Furniture: PPM Corporation.

Glyndebourne Opera House

Glyndebourne Festival Opera, Glyndebourne, Lewes, East Sussex, UK

Architect: Michael Hopkins & Partners

Project team: Michael Hopkins; Patty Hopkins; Robin Snell (project architects); Andrew Barnett; Pamela Bate; Arif Mehmood; Peter Cartwright; Andrew Wells; Lucy Lavers; Edward Williams; Nigel Curry. Client: Glyndebourne Festival Opera. Construction managers: Bovis Construction Ltd. Engineers: Ove Arup & Partners. Quantity surveyor: Gardiner & Theobald. Acoustic consultant: Arup Associates. Theatre consultants: Theatre Project Consultants. Mechanical and electrical: Matthew Hall. Steelwork: Littlehampton Welding Ltd; Hollandia BV. General metalwork: Cromwell of Reading; Meech (International) Ltd. Window supply: Allday Windows Ltd.

Lifts: Otis Lifts plc; Glantree Engineering Ltd; Telestage Associates Ltd. Foyer fabric roof: Landrell Fabric Engineering. Glazed screens: T. W. Ide. Acoustic doors: Telestage Associates Ltd. Metal doors: Bostwick Doors Ltd. Timber doors: J. L. Joinery Ltd. Flooring: Derry Treanor. Auditorium seating: Audience Systems. Auditorium fitout: Cheesman Interiors. Foyer and shop fitout: Sherlock Interiors Contracting Ltd. Toilet fitout: Grant Westfield Ltd. Back of house fitout: Wilson Fitting Out. Stage lighting: Strand Lighting Ltd. Auditorium lights: D. A. L. Ltd.

United States Holocaust Memorial Museum

100 Raoul Wallenberg Place NW, Washington DC 20024-2150, USA

Architect: Pei Cobb Freed & Partners Services

Project team: James Ingo Freed (partner-in-charge); Werner Wandelmaier (partner/administration); Michael Flynn (partner/technology); Craig Dumas (associate partner/administration); Beatrice Lehman (associate partner/production); Michael Vissichelli (senior associate/production); Harry Barone (senior associate/site architect); Wendy Evans Joseph (senior associate/design); Marek Zamdmer (senior associate/design); Jean-Pierre Mutin (associate/design); Stephen Ohnemus (associate/administration); Jou Min Lin (building envelope); Alissa Bucher (associate); Abby Suckle (associate/interiors); Deborah Campbell (associate/theatres); Anne Lewison; Jeff Stumacher; Steven Valentine; Jeffrey Rosenberg; Leslie Neblett; Ray Lee; Howard Settles; Fritz Sulzer; Gianni Neri; Christine Mahoney; Jennifer Adler; Paul Albrecht; Marcos Alvarez; Giovanna Brancaccio; Quin Chen; John Coburn; Monica Coe; Karen Cox; Steven Derasmo; Paul Drago; Richard Dunham; Richard Gorman; Rossana Gutierrex; David Harmon; Reginald Hough; Kevin Johns; Jennifer Nadler; Michael Ngu, Camillo Rosales; Amiel Savaldi; Emily Sidorski; Mercedes Stadthagen; Deborah Taylor; Hieu Vuong. Client: United States Holocaust Memorial Council. Associate Architect: Notter Feingold & Alexander. General contractor: Blake Construction Company, Washington DC. Subcontractors: Columbia Architectural Metals (curtain wall); English Architectural Glazing Corporation (skylights); G-A Masonry Corporation (masonry); Roubin and Janiero Inc. (stone setting); Harding and Cogswell Corp. (limestone); Sopromat (stone); Gichner/Coastal Iron Works Inc. (ornamental metals); Rome Iron Group (structural steel). Consultants: Weiskopf & Pickworth (structural); Cosentini Associates (Mechanical/Electrical); Jules Fisher and Paul Marantz (lighting); Jules Fisher Associates (Theatre design); Jaffe Acoustics (acoustics); Hanna/Olin (landscape); Nancy Rosen Inc. (artwork). Artists: Ellsworth Kelly (Memorial, installation); Sol Le Witt (Consequence, installation); Richard Serra (Gravity, sculpture); Joel Shapiro (Loss and Regeneration, bronze cast).

TGV Railway Station

Lyons, France

Architect: Calatrava Valls Euri (Paris)

Project team: Santiago Calatrava (architect); Sébastien Mémet; Alexis Bourrat; Peter Lüthi; Aldo Cerullo; Christopher Bartz. Clients: SNCF-Département Bâtiments; BEIG. Technical control: Socotec; Apave. Main contractor: Global. Contractors: E. I., C. F. C., M. S. (concrete); Mazza (carpentry); Eiffel, CMS (metal framework); Beretta, Ciradet, Instalux (glazing/metalwork); Sitraba, ETM Voisin, Metallerie du Forez, MGR (locksmith); Bergeon (heating); Jacques (plumbing); CNIM (lifts); Cegelec (electricity); Suscillon (woodwork); Chanel (paintwork); SNC (plasterwork); Isolation Dauphinoise (ceilings); Campoy (granite work). Suppliers: Riccard (concrete frame); Pechiney (aluminium); St Gobain (windows); CNIM (lifts and escalators); Reccord (automatic doors). Landscape: Guillot Bourne. Meeting Hall contractors: Baudin, Chateauneuf (Metal framework); Spie-Batignolles (concrete); Desplaces & Rollet (metalwork); Glazing (Targe-Dumaine).

Carré d'Art, Nîmes

Place de la Maison Carrée, 30000 Nîmes, France

Architect: Sir Norman Foster and Partners

Project team: Norman Foster; Ken Shuttleworth; David Nelson; Graham Phillips; Robin Partington; Rodney Uren; Paul Kalkhoven; Alex Reid; Arthur Branthwaite; Chris Eisner; Jim Quick; Max Neal; Chris Abell; Nic Bailey; Serge Belet; Ruth Controy; Arnauld de Bussière; Katherine Delpino; Pascal Desplanques; Shaun Earle; Nicholas Eldridge; Bertrand Feinte; Julie Fischer; Martin Francis; Jean Pierre Genevois; Bruce Graham; Michael Haste; Edward Hutchinson; Michael Jones; Alexander Lamboley; Eddie Lamptey; Huat Lim; John McFarland; Sophie Mer; Jesper Neilson; Irene Pham; Victoria Pike; Etienne Renault; Joel Rutten; Kriti Siderakis; John Small; Ken Wai; Cindy Walters; Louisa Williams. Client: Ville de Nîmes. Collaborating engineers: Ove Arup & Partners (structural); Oth (M & E). Main contractor: Meridional des Travaux; Ste Meridional du Batiment. Lighting consultant: Claude Engle. Steel structure and glazed façade: Sitraba; GMG. Roofing: Le Ny; Y Le Ny, Air-conditioning: Albouy; Marcou. Interior glazed partitions: Ets Dezelus Lafoucriere. Metalwork: GMG. Inserted ceilings: STE Hiross. Hard floor: Guinet-Cerriaz. Atrium stair: Groupement Metalliers. Quantity surveyor: Thorne Wheatley. Acoustic consultants: Commins.

The Netherlands Architecture Institute

Westersingel 10, 3014 GM Rotterdam, The Netherlands

Architect: Jo Coenen & Co. Architekten

Project team: Jo Coenen; Geert Coenen; Maarten van der Hulst; Marc Hermans; Inge de Neef; Frank Rutten, Ady Stketee; Jurgen Kahl; Pieter van Kruysbergen; Ad Roefs; Thomas Kemme; Sjef Lemmens; Sjef van Hoof; Hans van Reenen, Peter van Dinter; Heather Burns; Gilberte Claes. Client: The Netherlands Architectural Institute. Main contractors: Struckton Bouwprojekten BV; Uticon & Dynatherm BV (installations); Van Den Brandhof (timber supply); G. A van Dijk & Zn nv (pond and site contractor). Consultants: Advues-en Ingenieursburo Van de Laar BV (construction); Projektservice Dynatherm Zuid BV (installations); Lichtdesign (lighting); Adviesbureau Peutz & Associes BV (acoustics); Central Laboratorium voor Onderzoek van Voorwerpen van Kunst en Wetenschap (museum conditions). Structural loadbearing glass walls of entrance hall and foyer: Mick Eekhout, Octatube Engineering BV; Octatube Space Structures BV. Entrance hall counters, foyer furnishings and auditorium lectern: Borek Sipek. Interior of Director's Office: Ben van Berkel. Fittings for offices, reading room, archive study hall: USM Haller.

The Tate Gallery

St Ives, Cornwall, UK

Architect: Evans and Shalev Architects and Planning Consultants

Project team: Eldred Evans; David Shalev; Alun Jones. Client: Cornwall County Council. Main contractor: Dudley Coles. Subcontractors: WES Electrical (electrical); Johnson & Baxter (mechanical); Otis Elevators (lifts); Hooper & Sons (plumbing); Forrester Roofing (roof slating); British Patent Glazing (patent glazing); Solaglas (glazing); Lidstone (floor screeding); Penwith Ceramics (floor/wall tiling); R. S. Stokvis (roller shutter doors); Derix Glasgestaltung (stained-glass window). Quantity surveyor: Monk Dunstone Associates. Structural engineers: Jenkins and Potter. Suppliers: Graham Builders Merchants (general building materials); T. Marsh (granite walling); Blanc de Bièrge (slab paving); Dudley Coles (specialist joinery); Solaglas (glass blocks); James Gibbons Format (ironmongery); Ancon Stainless Steel (stainless steel).

Brussels Free University, Faculty of Medicine Auditorium

Avenue Franklin Roosevelt 50, 1050 Brussels, Belgium

Architect: Samyn et Associés

Project team: Philippe Samyn (project leader); F. El Sayed and D. Mélotte (conception); M. Berckmans and JL Capron (supervisors); A. Charon; F. Courtois; P. de Neyer; W. Dorigo; C Embise; Ch Fontaine; I. Iglesias Martin Benito; T. Khayati; H. Kievits; A. Lahloumimi; F. Lammens; B. Legrand; M. Patel; V. Van Dyck; B. Vleurick. Client: Brussels Free University. Engineering consultant: Spetech sprl. Metalwork: Pannecouke Construction. Woodwork: Dam sa. Paintwork: Iris. False ceiling: Janssen. Acoustics: Willich-Reirsma. Heating and ventilation: GTI Belgium. Seats: Fibrosit. Screens: Audio Visual Partners SA.

City Library, Münster

Stadt Bucherei, Münster, Alter Steinweg 11, Münster 48143, Germany

Architect: Architekturbüro Bolles-Wilson & Partner

Project team: Julia B. Bolles-Wilson; Peter L. Wilson; Eberhard E. Kleffner (architects); Friedhelm Haas; Martin Schlüter; Andreas Kimmel (project assistants); Jim Yohe; Manfred Schoeps; Dietmar Berner; Anne Elshof; Glen Wiedemeier; Cornelia Nottelmann; Jens Ludlof; Laura Fogarasi; Mikkel Frost; Toshi Hisatomi; Dirk Paulsen; Stefanie Schmand; Karen Haupt; Katrin Lahusen; Jean Michel Crettaz; Thomas Müller (assistants). Client: Building Department of the City of Münster. Main contractors: Becker & Börge (basic concept); Zimmerei Sieveke (carpentry). Contractors: Fa Luft and Klima GmbH (air-conditioning); Wolfgang Korn Tief and Strassenbau GmbH (plasterwork); W.P.S. Metalbauges MbH & Co. (façade); Faro Treppenbau GmbH; Fa Wallmeyer (steelwork); Fa Niewerth (painting); Uhlenbrock & Treus GmbH (joinery); E.K.Z. GmbH (library fittings); Fa Kriger GmbH (furniture). Building supervision: Bolles-Wilson & Partner; Harms & Partner. Structural engineer: Ing.-Büro Thomas & Bökamp; Ing.-Büro Menke und Köhler. Service engineers: Ing.-Büro Albers; House and Services Department of the City of Münster. Lighting consultants: Lichtdesign. Acoustics: Büro Stemmer und Tonnermann. Tilework: Fa P.u.D Henrichs GmbH. Stone flooring: Fa ESS Eva-Susanne Schieckel. Landscaping: Fa Benning GmbH & Co.

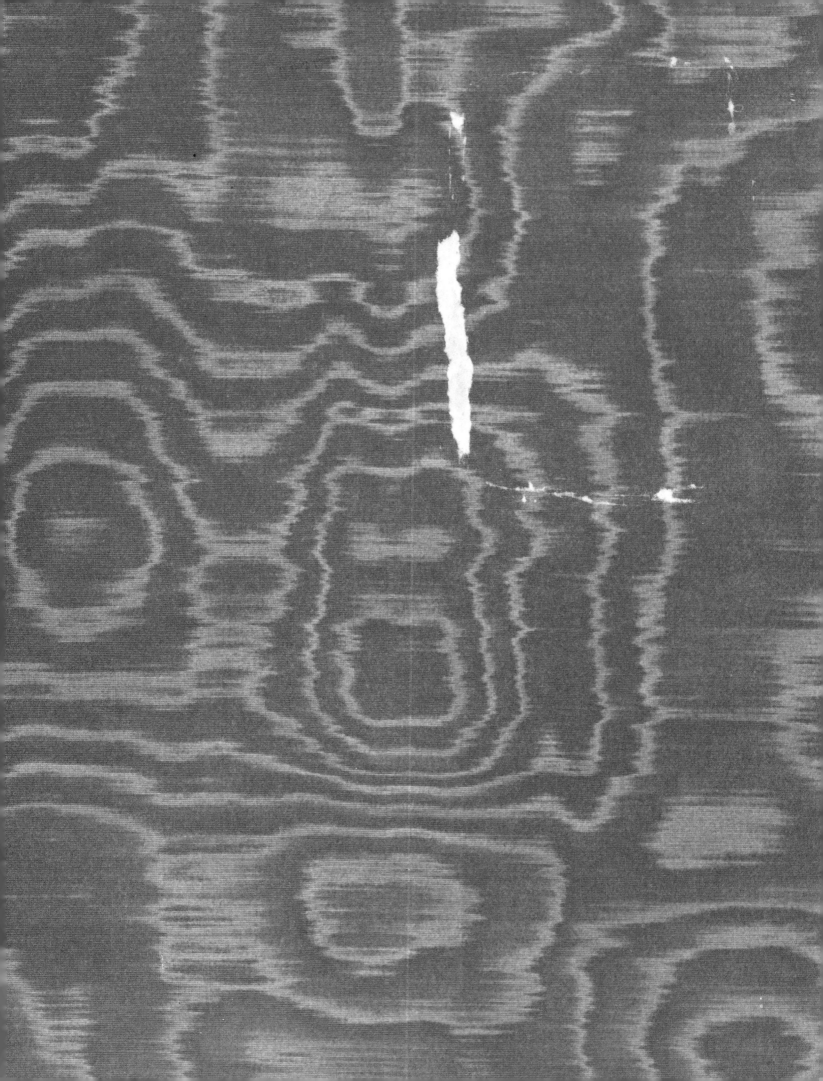